# Financial Aerobics
## *How to Get Your Finances into Shape*

**Richard M. Krawczyk, Ph.D.**
*America's Financial Fitness Trainer*™

Cavalier Publishing, LLC

# Financial Aerobics
## How to Get Your Finances into Shape
### By Richard M. Krawczyk, Ph.D.

Published by:
Cavalier Publishing, LLC
P.O. Box 26479
Las Vegas, NV 89126

**http://www.CavalierPublishing.com**

Unattributed quotations are by Richard M. Krawczyk, Ph.D.

ISBN 0-970-09635-6

Printed in the United States of America.

10 9 8 7 6 5 4 3 2 1

# ACKNOWLEDGEMENTS

I wish I would be able to list every single person who has supported me over the years. To do so would require more space than is available.

Countless hours of research over the past six years to completion were spent by my staff. Some of these individuals went beyond the call of duty in the development of Financial Aerobics such as Timothy Stotenbur, Eric P. Erickson, Michael Neu, Kelly Duffy, Liz Niswonger, Janelle Ruh, Brian Littlefield and Gloria Yanez. Thank you to all of my friends and family.

Thanks to my editor Lindsay Morris who spent countless hours working on this project.

The loyality and support of Helen Montgomery can't be acknowledged enough.

Without the onging support from Becky and David over the years, I don't think I would be where I am today. I can never thank you enough!

Special thanks go to all of the staff at Cavalier Publishing for making this book possible.

The entire staff at Maverick & Accociatess, Ltd were incredible for all of their help in our publicity efforts.

To
Ridge, my son
Mom & Dad
Debbie, my sister
and
Deanna, my wife
My greatest supporters

# CONTENTS

8

# What others are saying about Dr. Richard...

"It's finally here! An easy to read, and comprehendible gem, that cuts through the fat, and gets right down to the nuts and bolts of how anyone can become financially fit. A must have for anyone who's ever wished to receive an MBA of information in the time it takes to read a few hundred pages. Buy this book for yourself, and those you love: it comes with my highest recommendation."

> *- Greg S. Reid*
> #1 Best Selling Author/Speaker
> *The Millionaire Mentor*
> www.AlwaysGood.com

"Just having a clue about getting your finances into shape is a rare thing. So when Dr. Richard gives you a treasury of clues and does so in such a warm and readable manner, I just have to applaud Dr. Richard for doing such a noble thing, you for being the person who will breath vibrant life into Dr. Richard's sgae suggestions, and your banker for being able to handle your soon-to-be impressively substantial deposits."

> *- Jay Conrad Levinson*
> Author *Guerrilla Marketing* series of books
> www.guerrillamarketingassociation.com

"As a former publisher of a monthly financial newsletter, it's been my job to evaluate and critique the books and personalities in the area of personal finance. Even in a long list of money icons, from Sylvia Porter, to Charles J. Givens, to modern-day gurus such as Wade Cook, I have never come across a more comprehensive collection of powerful money tips."

> *- David Patton*
> Former Editor, *Success Insights*

"Dr. Richard is amazing, clever and genuinely for the people. A true professional."

> *- Mike "Bogey" Boguslawski*
> KCBS Consumer Advocate

"In *Financial Aerobics*, Dr. Richard teaches by example, showing us how personal finance needn't be boring. I highly recommend *Financial Aerobics* to anyone who is sick of battling with money and is ready to take hold of their finances."

> *- Katrina Dewey*
> Editor - *Los Angeles Daily Journal*

"Use these techniques taught by Dr. Richard or your retirement years will be anything but golden."
- *Timothy Stotenbur*
Financial Planner

"As the author of 13 books on business excellence and having worked at the highest levels of Hollywood for 20 years, I see Dr. Richard's techniques and strategies are starting a revolution in financial circles. The advice Dr. Richard offers is invaluable and cannot fail to increase an individual's knowledge of finance and investment."
- *Michael Levine*
Prominent Media Expert, Author
Founder of *Levine Communications*
www.levinepr.com

"Holy smokes! This book is turning my head inside out. I never realized all of the ins and outs of insurance, finances, taxes and so much more. Not only is this book clear, easy, and practical, it's also fun. I love it!"
- *Joe Vitale*
#1 Best Selling Author *Spiritual Marketing*
www.MrFire.com

"Dr. Richard has produced something rarely acheive by many - an interesting and itelligent reference guide to finance. Everyone should read Financial Aerobics to gain valuable financial knowledge."
- *Steve Shapiro*
V.P. - *City National Bank*

"Great information and lots of it. I love how you mix finances and fitness. Dr. Richard makes finances no longer a boring subject."
- *Mary Jones*
*The Mary Jones Show*
WDRC AM - *Connecticut's First Radion Station*
www.WDRC.com

"Smart, funny and knowledgeable. Dr. Richard lights up our switchboard with listeners when he's on my show."
- *The Poetess*
100.3 FM - Los Angeles
www.TheBeatLA.com

"Awesome! A how to, practical, inspiring and informational powerhouse book. While other books tout theory, this book gives your the thruths from someone who has actually done it. You won't find better information or advice anywhere. Get this book...it;s FANSTASTIC!"

*- Steven E*
Creator of the #1 Best Selling *Wake Up...Live The Life You Love* series
www.wakeuplive.com

"Dr. Richard is the best of the best."

*- Heather Stevens*
KJSA Radio

"This book will exercise your mind and trim the excess fat off of your financial debt. You work hard for your money and Dr. Richard shows you how to make it work for you.

*- Beatrice Marot*
www.goddesscentral.com

# FOREWORD

You've heard the classic line a thousand times: It's not what you make; it's what you keep. As true as that may be, I'd like to share the same theme from a more realistic viewpoint: It's not so much what you keep, it's what you reap that matters most.

You see, to become a millionaire you don't need to begin with a fortune, or do you have to possess vast amounts of knowledge and experience. What you do need is a foundation of great information so you can maximize what you have and reap the greatest benefits.

In this book, you'll learn firsthand that to become financially independent, all you really need to do is understand the fundamentals that the wealthy already know, and then put those same principles to work for your most precious commodity—you. By applying Dr. Richard's outline for success, you too can create a life for yourself that others only dream about. You'll learn just how easy it is to budget your resources and leverage your capital while consistently and regularly adding to your own customized nest egg. You'll also learn that it's okay to start small, as long as you start today!

Many people say to me, "When I have money, I'll be happy." Well, I'm here to tell you that while money is nice, the *process* of getting to your goal is the most fulfilling part. The skills you learn along the way are much more powerful than the end result.

Have you ever wondered why most lottery winners lose their fortunes in such a short period of time? It's because they're not conditioned to having such wealth, and therefore their minds won't allow them to keep it. In other words, their subconscious mind tells them, "Since this windfall was thrust onto you, and you didn't earn it, you cannot keep it."

On the flip side, by following the guidelines and information so brilliantly laid out in *Financial Aerobics*, you'll begin a journey toward a life of security and abundance few will ever know. Because you'll be doing it for yourself, at your speed, on your level, rather than waiting for luck to shape your destiny, you'll be living the ultimate dream and designing a destiny for yourself.

When I first spoke with Richard, the one thing that really caught my attention was his ability to take the complex and reduce it to simple, layperson's terms. After reading *Financial Aerobics* and its wonderful fitness tips, I finally understood why so many have recognized him as a pioneer all along.

*Financial Aerobics* is a classic in the making. It teaches exactly what the title implies—simple tips for becoming financially fit and getting your finances into great shape. Just as physical aerobics gets your body into shape for a long and healthy future, *Financial Aerobics* gives you the power to take financial matters into your own hands toward a brighter financial tomorrow.

- *Greg S. Reid*
Speaker and #1 Bestselling Author
of *The Millionaire Mentor*
www.AlwaysGood.com

# INTRODUCTION

I got the *business bug* when I was just a kid. At about the age of ten, I ran a lemonade stand in the summertime with my younger brother Rob. My mother would buy the lemonade, and Rob and I would make it and sell it. At the end of each day, we paid Mom back for the lemonade and she set aside the profits for us. In seeing our *newfound wealth* in the lemonade stand business, we opened another lemonade stand in another *strategic* location that went just as well as the first one. At the end of the summer, our mother took us, along with a few neighborhood kids (our *employees*) to Dairy Queen for a major ice cream chow-down. I'll never forget it. This particular experience was one that would help shape my life in years to come.

Being fascinated with business, I was a big fan of Michael J. Fox's character Alex Keaton on the television show *Family Ties*, Fox also starred in the movie *Secrets of My Success,* in which he literally took over a multinational corporation when he was still *wet behind the ears*, fresh out of college (you had to respect that) – all while working as a mail room employee for that very same company. And of course, every young man wanted to be like either Bobby or J.R. Ewing from the TV's *Dallas*.

Like most people, I've always wanted to become wealthy, but I didn't know how. I remember someone telling me once that it was easier to learn something by doing it (with so-called on-the-job experience or street smarts), or just by just reading about it (book smarts). So, I began my quest to learn.

Years ago, I worked at a small investment-banking firm in Chicago. I learned how many of the mega-wealthy people made their money. I was involved in over $700 million in real estate transactions – all before the age of thirty. I needed a new challenge, so I worked in the M&A (Mergers & Acquisitions) Department. It was exciting at first. Then, I received a lesson in business that I would never forget. The greed of one of my first business mentors (who actually ran the investment banking firm) blew a deal from which I was to personally profit $24.5 million. It was just like taking food from my mouth. To say the least, I was extremely ticked off. I left the company with my knowledge and contacts and started off on my own. Shortly after I left, I discovered through the grapevine, that the investment-banking firm went out of business.

With my knowledge and experienced in the field of real estate, I developed an investment course titled *Back to Basics*. In 1996, I was featured in an infomercial titled *Living the American Dream: Today's Success Stories*. I made sure that my old mentor received a copy of my infomercial. Success was my idea of payback.

Since that infomercial aired, I've traveled all over the world and met people from all walks of life – from pizza delivery drivers who earn minimum wage to MBA executives who earn hundreds of thousands of dollars a year. They all expressed the same concerns. Sure they may have used different words, but they were all concerned about money and their retirement.

Did you realize that 90% of all Americans live their lives paycheck-to-paycheck, *regardless* of their level of income?

I understand that dealing with your personal finances may seem as exciting as watching paint dry or a fly crawling up the wall. I was looking for a way to make working on personal finances fun and exciting. That's why I designed the *Financial Fitness Challenge*™(www.FinancialFitnessChallenge.com). This a contest that I started as a way to force people to maintain focus, while applying proper wealth building strategies, rather than just reading about them. If the *Financial Fitness Challenge*™ won't motivate you, I don't know what will!

This is NOT a *get rich quick* type of book. *Financial Aerobics*™ has been written primarily based upon my own life experiences, both personal and professional, as well as the experience and results of my extensive research staff. I have combined much-tested effective strategies, as well as newer cutting-edge wealth-building techniques made available today thanks to our new tax laws.

These strategies and techniques will not only work for everybody, but they work all the time.

The process of *Financial Aerobics*™ is a two-step process. First, you'll learn how to lower your current expenses. As just one example, you will learn how you can lower your auto insurance by as much as 50-60%, thus saving you hundreds of dollars a year. In the second part of the process, you'll learn how to invest safely to increase investment income. One way of accomplishing this would be to set aside money for safe government-backed investments that earn up to 50% a year (which I'll elaborate on later). By lowering your expenses and increasing your investment income, you will significantly increase your monthly cash flow.

Through each chapter, you will be shown how to make small adjustments to your financial habits, so that once you've finished this book, you will see dramatic changes that will lead to personal financial success. All you need to do is follow each step as outlined, and you'll never again find yourself living paycheck-to-paycheck just to make ends meet.

You may discover, as many individuals already have, that other changes will appear in your life. A recent study has shown that money matters are the number one cause of stress in relationships. And as I'm sure you are already aware that 50% of all marriages end in divorce. Once you gain control of your finances, a lot of the stress in your life will disappear. With a reduction in stress, you may end up quitting smoking, losing weight, or maybe even save a failing relationship.

*Applied* knowledge is the only thing that can help you! For every financial question, there is an answer. Don't get in the habit of doing nothing. If you continue to do the same things you have always done in the past, you will only get the same results. **TAKE ACTION NOW!**

Millions of Americans spend **billions** of dollars each year on fitness equipment, nutritional supplements, health club memberships, etc. in order to get, and maintain, their bodies in great shape. Everyday at the gym, I see plenty of people working out their bodies in order to look good.

How often do you work out your financial muscles? Do you think Arnold Schwarzenegger went to the gym only once in his life to become the greatest bodybuilder of all time? Of course not. Getting your financial muscles in shape will be a process. For some, that process will be quicker than others. It is all up to you and your true desire to get you financial muscles into shape.

Peak Performance Coach and Motivational Speaker Anthony Robbins states that people are motivated by either inspiration or desperation in order to make a change in their lives. Regardless of your motivation, this book can become a tremendous tool for you.

After everything is said and done at retirement time (or even tax time), it's your finances that need to be in shape. Neither your creditors nor your landlord care what you look like - all they care about is if you can pay your bills.

Unfortunately, education about the "real (financial) world" is not taught in schools. Even talking about money can be taboo in some families. Besides, how can your family teach you about acquiring wealth if they don't have any themselves?

This is why I've developed *Financial Aerobics*™.

Keep in mind that I can only supply you with the necessary knowledge for you to attain your financial dreams. It's up to you to apply what I have showed you. As the saying goes, "You can lead the horse to water, but you can't make him drink."

Try everything in these pages. Follow the step-by-step techniques. Even if they seem too simple - or too challenging - give them a chance. By doing so, you give yourself a chance to turn around - and move forward to financial fitness.

All I ask for in return for your success is a simple "thank you" if we should ever meet in person.

To Your Success,

Richard M. Krawczyk, Ph.D.

# Chapter One

## *Establishing A Master Plan*

*Life is a mall, and you can go shopping everyday!*
- Richard M. Krawczyk, Ph.D.

Believe it or not, the first step to becoming wealthy is to revert to your childhood. A child's imagination is endless. Remember when you were a kid?

Some of us had dreams of becoming a police officer, an astronaut, or even the President of the United States. Children have great imaginations. They have no concept of the *real world*.

Then, we all grow up. Have you noticed that as we become older, society brainwashes us to believe that we can never fulfill your dreams? It seems that everyone is out to *pop your bubble*. The sad part is that a majority of us actually start to believe **those people** and then **we** become cynical. We lose that wonderful imagination that we had as children.

The voices - you hear them every day, don't you? Maybe they start chattering while you're driving to work. Or maybe it's when you pull those bills out of the mailbox. Are they especially loud on April 15 of every year? Or maybe it's when you're trying to sleep and can't. I know you hear those voices - if you didn't, you wouldn't be reading this book. I used to hear them too - from skeptical clients, financial planners, well-educated brokers, accountants, lawyers, bankers, and MBAs. If you pay attention, you will notice the echoes of these voices everywhere - in the media, the educational system, the rhetoric of politicians, and the conversation of your family, business publications - even yourself.

19

Unfortunately, these salespeople (i.e. bankers, brokers, and financial planners) can cost you $1,000 or more each and every month because of their *professional* commission based advice. Continuing to follow their "sage" advice will never get you rich. They are the only ones getting rich!

I'm here to tell you that it doesn't have to be that way. You can achieve **anything** you want in life. The only thing that matters is your willingness and desire to succeed. Always remember that life is a mall and you can go shopping everyday! You can make life whatever you want it to be.

I'd like to take this concept a bit further. There is a big difference between a *dream* and a *plan*. A dream is something you **hope** to achieve someday in the future. A plan is something you are **going** to achieve. In what I call a *Master Plan*, you plan all of the steps or procedures needed to achieve your Master Plan. As an example, if your Master Plan is to retire with $1,000,000 in the bank, you will have to achieve certain steps to make this a reality. If you currently make $50,000 a year with no savings and have only five years to retire, your Master Plan will be highly unlikely unless you make some drastic changes.

Unless you inherited it or married into it, you have to work for your money. I had to work for my mine.

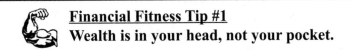

**<u>Financial Fitness Tip #1</u>**
**Wealth is in your head, not your pocket.**

"Money is a thought form. It is a symbol of energy and as such it has no real, intrinsic value," wrote Stuart Wilde in *The Trick To Money Is Having Some.* Did you ever notice that when you are temporarily out of cash, people go out of their way to avoid you? And when you were rolling in it, everyone was attracted to you?

One of my first mentors also taught me this. No one was allowed in the office unless they carried at least $5,000 in cash on them. The purpose of that exercise is a powerful one. When you carry that much money with you, you feel almost invincible. You walk taller. You have an *aura* of confidence about you. People want to come in contact with you just to feed off the energy that you are projecting. If you want to buy something, you buy it. If you want to help a homeless person on the street, you can give them $20 and not miss it.

Now I'm sure that many of you can't afford to carry at least $5,000 with you at all times, at least for now. The concepts that Stuart Wilde describes in his book, is that if you don't have any money, you need to trick your mind in thinking that it already has some. This may take some practice to effectively acquire this skill.

If you had a million dollars in the bank, how would you walk? How would you treat other people? How would you carry yourself? How much confidence would you exude?

The mentality of wealth is a trained response. Do you think children of Donald Trump were trained to think poor when they were young? Of course not. You are a product of your environment. If someone else taught you how to think *poor*, it makes sense that someone else can teach you how to think *wealthy*.

Start programming your brain today to think that you are already a millionaire. Convince yourself that you would like to buy that new Mercedes Benz, but the money hasn't cleared your bank account yet. The money is already in your account (mentally); you just can't access your funds yet. You *choose* to buy it when your funds clear. Remember that the trick to money is having some.

### There's More To Wealth Than Just Money!

Keep in mind that there is more to wealth than just making a lot of money. We all need balance in our lives. As an example, even though you may be doing well financially at your current job, you may feel

under-appreciated by your employer. Maybe you are looking for a
new challenge at work and there is a limit on how far you can advance
in the company. Maybe you would prefer to spend more time with
your family than work 2,000 hours a week at your job.

Many families can't travel as much as they would like due to
financial constraints. I've traveled to many places around the world
myself and found some that are absolutely breathtaking. Whether it
is waking up in the morning to the gently crashing waves along the
coast in Palm Beach, FL to the majesty of the Grand Canyon beneath
an Arizona sunset, there is more to wealth than money. Everyone
should experience the beauty of our country.

A few years ago, I witnessed an incredible sight. It was a
beautiful September evening in Florida with only a few clouds in the
sky. As I looked to the east, I witnessed a bright light coming from
about 90 miles away. It was one of the space shuttles taking off. It
was an amazing sight as the space shuttle lit up the clouds. The very
first thing that came to mind was, "Boy, I am one wealthy guy!" People
travel from all over the world to Florida to see a shuttle launch. And
I was able to see it from my own backyard! Being able to see a
nighttime shuttle launch should be must for everyone to see at least
once in his or her lifetime.

Experiences like this are free. No matter where you live, there
are always beautiful things around you everyday. Learn to enjoy them.
Don't take for granted the simple things in life. Start to live life!

Maybe you may wish to further your education. Whether it
be taking a college course or to learn a new language. A college degree
might be required if you wish to change your career or advance.

---

**<u>Financial Fitness Tip #2</u>**
**The quickest way to becoming wealthy, is to
find a wealthy person who you admire and
do the exact same thing they did.**

---

> *Why re-invent the wheel, when you can just change the tire.*
> - Richard M. Krawczyk, Ph.D.

I'm always amazed - and dismayed - by how many people *talk* about wealth without actually *practicing* it. Talking about money is the great obsession of our culture. Every day I listen to the financial theories of brokers, bankers, politicians, professors, self-help gurus, bosses, benefit advisors, insurance salesmen, TV pundits, tax accountants, psychotherapists and even religious leaders. I hear more and more average folks discuss, in great detail, sophisticated financial products, services, and strategies. I listen to them discuss money - saving it, spending it, budgeting it, earning it, investing it. If words were money, everybody would be filthy rich.

Have you ever wondered why, with all the wealth-building information out there, very few people actually become rich? Here's why: wealth is not dependent on finding the correct theory. It's no more dependent on the advice of so-called experts than it is on winning the lottery. There is only one way to achieve wealth - that's by doing it. **You can't do it by listening to people who have not achieved financial independence themselves.**

Mentally calculate the energy and hard-earned dollars you have invested in the advice, claims, and promises of your financial advisors. Compare that investment advice with the balance in your checking account right now. If you were paying them to make you rich, would you hire them?

According to the U.S. Census Bureau, here are the average annual wages earned in 1999 from a census conducted in 2002:

| | |
|---|---|
| Accountants | $41,488 |
| Lawyers | $82,000 |
| Technical Writers | $46,000 |
| Real Estate Agents | $35,235 |

Are these the types of people you are getting your financial advice from? How can you take advice from some that hasn't become wealthy themselves?

But don't think I didn't *earn* my wealth. I didn't inherit anything. I was raised in modest circumstances - and sometimes our circumstances were a lot less than modest! I started from the bottom - learning from guys in the trenches and making mistakes. There isn't much difference between you and me - like you, everything I've learned about money I've learned the hard way. Like you, I've endured the consequences, first-hand, of all the techniques, schemes, and systems that just don't work.

Perhaps you've tried all the get-rich-quick schemes, the home courses, the motivational tapes, the solid, reputable stuff as well as the complete and utter bilge - I did. Maybe you've been so desperate that you've wasted a weekend sending out a thousand chain letters. (Guess what - they don't work.) Perhaps you dream about winning the lottery. Maybe you even buy ten tickets every week.

Well, I haven't won the lottery and don't plan to. I believe work is more reliable than the lottery. **The only difference between you and me is that every day, systematically, consistently, patiently, joyfully, I work at being wealthy.**

Last year, consumers spent billions on services and goodies that promised to reveal the secrets of abundance, security, and affluence. Twenty percent of that stuff has real substance - good instruction you can put into practice. But most of it is more *sizzle* than *steak*. Maybe you've overdosed on that expensive fluff. I have watched people fill pages and pages with lists of short and long-term goals. I've seen them plot out their financial future. I've observed them writing in wealth journals and diaries, trying to be another John D. Rockefeller.

Sure, as soon as he could write, Rockefeller kept a money diary where he recorded every penny he earned and spent. You too can become Rockefeller by copying his actions. All of the goal setting and planning in the world won't turn into action if your heart's not in the game. I'm not against educating yourself. I'm in the business of teaching because I believe in it. But the finest education money can buy only works if you want it to work. If you are unwilling to consider the theory that you may not yet have the mental discipline to work at being financially fit, no amount of desire, advanced education, creative visualization, or prayer will make you wealthy.

Be honest. Who says you can't be financially fit? Are the most important and influential people around you broke or working towards being wealthy? Do they have what Zig Ziglar calls "stinkin' thinkin'"? If you or most of the people around you keep saying you can't be wealthy, you've got to stop the chatter.

Famous Hollywood Publicist and good friend Michael Levine says people should "Fire their flaky friends." If people that are toxic surround you, stay away from them. Obviously it may be difficult to do that when they are family. Several times a year, I make it a point to *drop the dead weight* from my life. I never surround myself with negativity.

I'm not a spiritual guru - I'm a professional moneymaker - so I'm done preaching. But do yourself a favor. Stop listening to all those voices that say you can't be rich. The simplest way to achieve that is to **do it!**

If you appreciate life, you can appreciate wealth. The two go hand-in-hand - in fact, they are necessary partners. Money is just energy - powerful, necessary, and tricky energy in our crazy world - but that's all it is. You can waste energy - or you can use it to build more. So congratulate yourself for not being completely brainwashed by the well-meaning but empty advice of the non-rich (or, to be politically correct, the "*monetarily challenged*"). You are prepared to consider the fact that, by using whatever money you already have intelligently and mindfully, you can be financially fit *right now*. You're not just intrigued - you're ready to be enlightened!

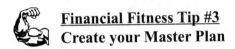

## Financial Fitness Tip #3
## Create your Master Plan

> *If you don't live out your dreams, someone else will.*
> - Richard M. Krawczyk, Ph.D.

Find a quiet, secluded location for about an hour. I know this may be difficult if you always have screaming children running around the house. You may want to choose either the early morning or late evening hours so you can concentrate on this exercise. Fill out your Master Plan. Just let your imagination run wild. Write down all your goals no matter how ridiculous they may seem for right now. If you had no limitations in life - unlimited time, money, talent, ability and support from your family and friends, what would be your Master Plan in life? How would you design your life?

Keep in mind that your spouse doesn't have to have the same plans as you. Do the exercises separately. When you are finished, you should compare your Master Plan your spouse. You might be surprised what you discover.

If you want to build a house, you need to start with blueprints. You cannot haphazardly begin building a house if you don't know certain things (e.g. dimensions, number of rooms, ceiling height).

The same thing is true with your life. In order for your life to be truly magnificent, you'll need to make a blueprint of your life.

**Because if you don't know where you're going, you will <u>never</u> get there.**

Most people spend more time planning their family vacations than they do planning their retirement. Think about it. When you planned your last trip, you needed to plan your itinerary. When was your plane leaving? Did you need to rent a car? What about hotel reservations? Did you have to make dinner reservations at that hot new restaurant? If you can put that amount of effort in creating your Master Plan, you've already won half the battle.

As you are filling out your Master Plan, remove any negative thoughts. What would you like to do? Who would you like to be? How would you like to live? Would you act differently? Would you carry yourself differently? Keep this in mind when you are doing this exercise.

Next, I want you to go to the store and purchase a five-subject notebook. In this notebook, you should tape pictures of some of your Master Plan. As an example, you may want to put in a picture of a Jaguar (if this is the kind of car you wanted to drive), or a photo of a cruise ship (if you and your significant other want to cruise around the world). I think you get the picture – no pun intended. I call this your "Master Plan Workbook." Keep this book in a place where you can see it everyday so you can visualize what you **will** achieve.

This exercise is more important than you think – so don't blow it off. I'll tell you why when we get to Financial Fitness Tip #4. **Your future depends on it!**

## YOUR MASTER PLAN

1. _____

2. _____

3. _____

4. _____

5. _____

6. _____

7. _____

8. _____

9. _____

10. _____

11. _____

12. _____

13. _____

14. _____

15. _____

Make as many copies of this page as you need

## <u>SPOUSE MASTER PLAN</u>

1. _____

2. _____

3. _____

4. _____

5. _____

6. _____

7. _____

8. _____

9. _____

10. _____

11. _____

12. _____

13. _____

14. _____

15. _____

Make as many copies of this page as you need

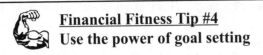

## Financial Fitness Tip #4
## Use the power of goal setting

A 1953 Yale University study revealed that that only three percent of participating graduates had written down their goals <u>with a plan of accomplishing them</u>. Twenty years later, the remaining graduates where again surveyed. Those graduates with written goals were worth more financially than the other 97% surveyed! Also, that same three percent led happier and more fulfilling lives. This is a perfect example of goal setting.

You **must** always commit your goals in writing. By putting you goals in writing, you will have already accomplished more than 95% of Americans. Your subconscious will guide you in achieving your goals. As long as you make a daily effort to achieve your individual goals, you **will** reach them eventually.

In writing your goals, be realistic. If your goal next year is to earn $50,000, chances are that you won't be able to buy the Rolls Royce that you wanted (you may have to wait a little while for that one). If you have ambitious goals and desires, you just need to be more aggressive in your approach. Remember, you can get whatever you want out of life. It's all up to you!

Like many of you, I've heard for years that written goals help you succeed. Unfortunately, it has only been in the past few years that I actually established a written set of goals. My business and personal life then started to take off! I'm kicking myself now, because if I had written my goals years ago when I first heard of this technique, I would have achieved my successes a lot earlier in life.

### <u>What Do You Really Want Anyway?</u>
Nowhere is *fuzzy thinking* more damaging than in building financial fitness. More than half the people I work with are afraid of investing.

Why are they afraid? "The risk." "I don't have enough money to pay my bills, let alone invest!" "It's too much work." "I can't understand this stuff." And so on.

Of course, when you get right down to it, none of these reasons stand up to a clear-cut reality check. I will show you how to reclaim wasted cash. Note that risk is a meaningless concept.

First, it's time to fumigate your brain one more time of all the "stinkin' thinkin'" that might pollute your prosperity. Time for our next Financial Fitness Tip - and it's a big one!

---

 **Financial Fitness Tip #5**
**You can't get what you want, if you don't know what you want.**

---

Sounds obvious? Ask yourself: "Why am I reading this book anyway? Because I want to become financially fit!"

As I mentioned earlier, there's more to wealth than just money. You need to figure out what you want out of life in general. You must be specific on what you want in every area of your life - financially, physically, emotionally, and spiritually.

I am so specific about the direction I'm headed, I've found that people are drawn to me. It's not uncommon for my office to receive a number of calls each week, from people to see if they can work for me for **free**, just to be around me! It kind of boggles my mind. I guess I must be doing something right if others feel the same way I do. As the saying goes, birds of a feather flock together.

---

*Financial security requires a foundation.*
*You can't build a house on a cloud.*
- Richard M. Krawczyk, Ph.D.

---

You've got to have something strong, solid, and concrete, with specific dimensions. You can't build a 5,000 square-foot home on a lot for a 1,200 square-foot bungalow! Dreaming, desiring and even being willing to work hard are all fine activities. But now you are going to add specificity to them - and specificity is what makes or breaks an investment strategy.

### Poverty Is Vague; Wealth Is Specific

Different types of investments achieve different types of results. Again, that may seem obvious. What's not so obvious is that you cannot choose an investment vehicle until you know what results you want to achieve. More investment strategies fail, not because of the investment itself or the return it produced, but because the investor is trying to use a Ford Pinto (remember those?) to win the Indy 500.

For example, if you want a steady income of $50,000 annually when you retire, you have to choose investments that are likely to create that income. You might even have to choose a combination of investments to achieve that goal. Your choices may be entirely different if you want to do is produce a return of 25% over the next 24 months - and keep you cash liquid at the same time!

Financial goal setting is the prerequisite to sound financial planning. In fact, with clearly defined goals you often don't need to work very hard on the plan at all - you just *choose* investments and profit-building techniques which are likely to give you the results you want.

It's also much easier, and much less painful, to explore your dreams, desires, and chosen outcomes on paper before laying down your money. Why learn through real-life failure and disappointment? Why not dream up the retirement, specify the level of prosperity required to achieve it, explore the investment options on paper, and *then* start investing real money? What sounds more sensible - and less likely to "*ouch*?"

I love to go to gym and workout. It makes me feel great, it makes me look great, and it's about attainment. But I don't go to the gym and suddenly add an additional fifty pounds more to the bar than I am used to when I'm bench-pressing. That would not only be stupid, it would *"ouch"* real bad too - the bar just might cave my chest in. Instead, I decide that within a certain period of time, I want to lift "X" pounds. I look at myself, how hard I'm working right now, and how hard I'm willing to work over the next three to six months. I might even consult a specialist - my personal trainer - for advice on how best to achieve my outcome. And then choose the exercises, diet, and lifestyle that will support me in achieving my goal. What I don't do is decide to suddenly lift 50 pounds more than I am used too - or to just keep on lifting the same weight, week after week, month after month, and then sit around saying, "Gee, duh…why ain't I getting any stronger?"

You'll get what you want - financial fitness - faster, easier and more gracefully if you decide what financial freedom means to you. You will get what you want if you know exactly what you want. Why? Because you'll begin to eliminate from your life what doesn't support your goal, and consistently pursue the stuff that does! **You can't expect to become *financial fit* if you continue to eat *"greasy burgers"* everyday**.

So it's time to find out what you really want - and commit to it! Remember, the wonderful thing about financial goal-setting is that you can always revise and refurbish your goals - and in the meantime you have still been working towards a specific outcome and been getting results along the way. Do this goal-setting workout with an open mind. **Do it now!**

No point in lifting weights unless you're getting stronger. No point in doing aerobics if you're not getting fitter. And there's no point in sticking to a plan unless it's working. Evaluate your short-term goals every quarter and your long-term goals every six months or so.

## INCOME GOALS

**Example:**
Year 2004
This year's income   $30,000
What I'm doing to earn this money:  full-time job 40 hrs. /wk

Year 2005
This year's income   $45,000
What I'm doing to earn this money:  full-time job 40 hrs. /wk
                                    Purchase one rental property
                                    and high-yielding tax
                                    certificates

---

Year _____
This year's income  $_____
What I'm doing to earn this money:

Year _____
This year's income  $_____
What I'm doing to earn this money:

Year _____
This year's income  $_____
What I'm doing to earn this money:

# TRAVEL GOALS

List where you would like to travel. Also state the date you wish your travel to begin.

**UNITED STATES**                    **DATE (MONTH/YEAR)**

1. _____

2. _____

3. _____

4. _____

5. _____


**INTERNATIONAL**                    **DATE (MONTH/YEAR)**

1. _____

2. _____

3. _____

4. _____

5. _____

# EDUCATIONAL GOALS

List any courses or programs you wish to participate in to further your intellectual growth. Also list the date you wish to begin by as well as the estimated cost (if any).

**Example:**
> FinancialUniversity.com, learn a new language, night school courses, college degree, speed reading course, acting course.

| COURSE OR PROGRAM | START DATE | COST |
|---|---|---|
| 1. | | |
| 2. | | |
| 3. | | |
| 4. | | |
| 5. | | |
| 6. | | |
| 7. | | |
| 8. | | |
| 9. | | |
| 10. | | |

# CAREER GOALS

Evaluate your current career. List any changes you wish to make, if any. Remember, in this country, you can do whatever you wish for a living. Let your imagination run wild.

1. What kind of work do you do now?

2. Do you enjoy the line of work you are currently doing?

3. Do you want to change careers? If so, what would you like to do?

4. Do you have your own business yet?
    A.  If so, what kind of business? Do you run your business full-time or part-time?

    B.  If not, what kind of business do you wish to start?

5. What are some advances you wish to make in your current career? (Position/Responsibilities/ Salary)
    This Year

    Five Years from Now

    Ten Years from Now

6. Do you wish to change employers?
    A.  If so, why haven't you changed yet?

    B.  Who would you like to work for?

    C.  Salary required for you to change?

# RECREATIONAL ASSET GOALS

List all of the recreational (fun) things you would like to own. Put
pictures of them in your Master Plan Workbook discuss earlier.

| Item | Type | Date to Own | Cost |
|---|---|---|---|
| **Wheeled Sports** | | | |
| 1. Sports Car | _____ | _____ | $ _____ |
| 2. Motorcycle | _____ | _____ | $ _____ |
| 3. Bicycle | _____ | _____ | $ _____ |
| 4. Snowmobile | _____ | _____ | $ _____ |
| 5. Other | _____ | _____ | $ _____ |
| **Water Sports** | | | |
| 1. Sailboat | _____ | _____ | $ _____ |
| 2. Jet Ski | _____ | _____ | $ _____ |
| 3. Fishing Boat | _____ | _____ | $ _____ |
| 4. Houseboat | _____ | _____ | $ _____ |
| 5. Yacht | _____ | _____ | $ _____ |
| **Aerial Sports** | | | |
| 1. Airplane | _____ | _____ | $ _____ |
| 2. Balloon | _____ | _____ | $ _____ |
| 3. Hang Glider | _____ | _____ | $ _____ |
| 4. Other | _____ | _____ | $ _____ |
| **Mobile Sleeping / Camping** | | | |
| 1. Motor Home | _____ | _____ | $ _____ |
| 2. Camper | _____ | _____ | $ _____ |
| 3. Tents | _____ | _____ | $ _____ |
| 4. Camping Equip. | _____ | _____ | $ _____ |
| 5. Other | _____ | _____ | $ _____ |

**Other**

1. _____ _____ _____ $ _____
2. _____ _____ _____ $ _____
3. _____ _____ _____ $ _____
4. _____ _____ _____ $ _____

## ACQUISITION GOALS

List all of the things you would like to own, other than recreational assets. Put pictures of them in your Master Plan Workbook discuss earlier.

**I would like to own:**

| **Item** | **Approx. Cost** | **Target Date (Mo./Yr.)** |
|---|---|---|
| 1. _____ | $ _____ | _____ |
| 2. _____ | $ _____ | _____ |
| 3. _____ | $ _____ | _____ |
| 4. _____ | $ _____ | _____ |
| 5. _____ | $ _____ | _____ |
| 6. _____ | $ _____ | _____ |
| 7. _____ | $ _____ | _____ |
| 8. _____ | $ _____ | _____ |
| 9. _____ | $ _____ | _____ |
| 10. _____ | $ _____ | _____ |

# ACCOMPLISHMENT GOALS

Include positions you would like to hold in clubs, groups, churches, politics, etc. Include sports that you would like to become involved with (or how you can excel in the sport you are already in) and social activities or organizations you want to join. Include awards and other forms of recognition in your career and social life you would like to win.

| Sport, Activity, Organization, etc. | What You Want To Accomplish | Target Date (Mo./Yr.) |
|---|---|---|
| 1. | | |
| 2. | | |
| 3. | | |
| 4. | | |
| 5. | | |
| 6. | | |
| 7. | | |
| 8. | | |
| 9. | | |

# INVESTMENT GOALS

Use the following chart to find out where you are now and where you want to go. This chart will help you measure your progress and your commitment to yourself over the next ten years.

| | This Year | Next Year | Five Years | Ten Years | At Age 65 |
|---|---|---|---|---|---|
| Cash in the Bank | $_____ | $_____ | $_____ | $_____ | $_____ |
| Stocks | $_____ | $_____ | $_____ | $_____ | $_____ |
| Mutual Funds | $_____ | $_____ | $_____ | $_____ | $_____ |
| Retirement Acct | $_____ | $_____ | $_____ | $_____ | $_____ |
| Tax Lien Cert. | $_____ | $_____ | $_____ | $_____ | $_____ |
| Other Investments | $_____ | $_____ | $_____ | $_____ | $_____ |
| Other Assets | $_____ | $_____ | $_____ | $_____ | $_____ |
| **Total Equity, Inv. & Assets** | **$_____** | **$_____** | **$_____** | **$_____** | **$_____** |

# REAL ESTATE GOALS

List all of the real estate that you currently own, if any. Enter your real estate purchase goals in Part 2.

## Part 1: Real Estate Currently Own

| | Date Purchased | Current Value | Mortgage | Equity |
|---|---|---|---|---|
| Your Home | _____ | $_____ | $_____ | $_____ |
| 2nd Home | _____ | $_____ | $_____ | $_____ |
| Investment 1 | _____ | $_____ | $_____ | $_____ |
| Investment 2 | _____ | $_____ | $_____ | $_____ |
| Investment 3 | _____ | $_____ | $_____ | $_____ |
| Investment 4 | _____ | $_____ | $_____ | $_____ |
| **Totals** | | $_____ | $_____ | $_____ |

## Part 2:  Real Estate You Want To Own

| | Target Date | Date Purchased | Purchase Price | Equity |
|---|---|---|---|---|
| Your Home | _____ | _____ | $_____ | $_____ |
| 2nd Home | _____ | _____ | $_____ | $_____ |
| Investment 1 | _____ | _____ | $_____ | $_____ |
| Investment 2 | _____ | _____ | $_____ | $_____ |
| Investment 3 | _____ | _____ | $_____ | $_____ |
| Investment 4 | _____ | _____ | $_____ | $_____ |
| **Totals** | _____ | | $_____ | $_____ |

## <u>Summary of Chapter One</u>

What have you learned so far?
- Started to develop a Master Plan.

- Realized that wealth is in my head – not in my pocket.

- Started a Master Plan Workbook.

- Developed short-term and long-term plans for different areas of my life.

- The Financial Fitness Challenge (www.FinancialFitnessChallenge.com) will help keep me motivated on my quest to financial fitness.

- Signed up for the FREE Newsletter at www.FinancialFitnessTips.com

---

**Need some personal guidance with your finances?**

**Go to: www.FinancialFitnessMonthly.com**

**and talk with one of our Financial Fitness Trainers**

---

# Chapter Two

## *Warming Up Your Financial Muscles*

**WARNING:** *These wealth-building techniques may be harmful to you if you intend on being poor for the rest of your life!*

Now that you've written down your Master Plan, we need to take a quick look at your finances (for some of you it'll be a **very** quick look), to determine your starting point. Fill out the enclosed financial statement **NOW**.

Just think of your financial statement as a snapshot of your finances on any particular day. To calculate your net worth, follow this simple formula:

**ASSETS** (what you *own*)
**- LIABILITIES** (what you *owe*)
**YOUR NET WORTH**

Your Financial Statement will be helpful when you applying for loans and mortgages to increase your wealth.

Don't get depressed. Everyone has to start somewhere.

When I was growing up, I didn't exactly have an imposing stature about me. In fact, in sixth, seven, and the first half of eighth grade I weighed only 59 pounds. I was so skinny I had to run around in the shower to get wet. When I graduated high school, I was 6' tall and I weighed a whopping 135 pounds. I knew where I wanted to be body-wise, I just didn't know how to get there. I was told that when I get married I'd gain weight… NOT! A few years after my divorce, I discovered beer and "ballooned" to 150 pounds. After growing to

45

175 pounds with 25% body fat (a *normal* guy is 13% to 14% body fat), I was a skinny guy with a big belly.

In thinking that being a skinny guy with a belly wouldn't be all that attractive to the women (especially during my single years in Los Angeles), with the help of one of the top personal trainers in the country, Kurt Rexford, I began to start lifting weights and dieting properly. I've personally seen what he has done to some of his clients, which include some of the top male and female bodybuilders and fitness models in the world. It was safe to say I was finally on the right track. I followed his advice and began to see **dramatic** changes in my body. I'm now well over 210 pounds with only 7% body fat.

In your quest for financial fitness, you need a proper *financial* diet and training. You have to start somewhere. It doesn't matter if you're *financially skinny* at this point. This book will **pump-up** your finances.

# Financial Statement

## Assets

**Liabilities**

Current Assets $_____
(Cash and cash equivalents –
any investment that can be
converted to cash within
90 days)

Fixed Assets   $_____
(Market value of houses,
cars, securities, art, etc.)

Mortgage Loans    $_____
(Balances – what you owe)

Car Loans            $_____
(Balances – what you owe)

Credit Cards        $_____
(Balances)

Other Debt          $_____

**Total Assets**   $_____
(Current Assets + Fixed Assets)

**Total Liabilities**   $_____

---

### Net Worth Calculation

| | |
|---|---|
| Total Assets | $_____ |
| minus | |
| Total Liabilities | $_____ |
| **Net Worth** | $_____ |

---

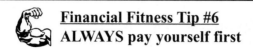

**Financial Fitness Tip #6**
**ALWAYS pay yourself first**

As I stated earlier, ninety percent of all Americans are living paycheck-to-paycheck. The Social Security Administration statistics show that by the age of 65, 95% of Americans are either dead or dead broke? These are some staggering statistics! By using my techniques, you will be virtually guaranteed not to end up in these statistics.

Now is the time to start planning for your retirement. Some of you are starting out after completing high school or college, while others are quickly approaching retirement age. If you're getting close to retirement age now and need to start playing *catch up*, don't worry. Using this simple strategy, you will begin the process for a comfortable retirement.

If you are one of those individuals who are banking on the fact that Social Security will take care of you when you retire, think again. It has been reported that the Social Security fund will run out of money by the year 2042. Today, the government pays out an amazing $750 million per day or $275 billion per year. While politicians fight as they look for a solution to the problem, you should begin learn to live your retirement with the possibility that *Social Insecurity* may not be there. Whether or not the solution is found to the Social Security problem, I'm not planning on being passive and will count on other sources of revenue to support me through my retirement years. I suggest that you *take the bull by the horns* and control your own financial future and not be dependant of others.

The problem with most Americans isn't that they don't earn enough money, because this is simply not the case. You earn plenty. You just need to properly manage what you already have.

## INCOME EARNED IN A LIFETIME

| Monthly Income | 10 Years | 20 Years | 30 Years | 40 Years |
|---|---|---|---|---|
| $1,000 | $ 120,000 | 240,000 | 360,000 | 480,000 |
| 1,500 | 180,000 | 360,000 | 540,000 | 720,000 |
| 2,000 | 240,000 | 480,000 | 720,000 | 960,000 |
| 2,500 | 300,000 | 600,000 | 900,000 | 1,200,000 |
| 3,000 | 360,000 | 720,000 | **1,080,000** | 1,440,000 |
| 3,500 | 420,000 | 840,000 | 1,260,000 | 1,680,000 |
| 4,000 | 480,000 | 960,000 | 1,440,000 | 1,920,000 |
| 4,500 | 540,000 | 1,080,000 | 1,620,000 | 2,160,000 |
| 5,000 | 600,000 | 1,200,000 | 1,800,000 | 2,400,000 |

In general, one earns less when they are younger than when they are older. But if you average $3,000 a month ($36,000 a year) in your entire lifetime, you will earn in excess of $1 million in your lifetime.

**Always** pay yourself first. Begin with your next paycheck. Take 10% right off the top and put it in your mutual fund or investment account. If you need to, create a bill to pay yourself each and every pay period. Take care of that *bill*, before you pay the mortgage, rent, and car payment or even before you buy groceries. Do the same thing with every paycheck for the rest of your life.

"But Richard," you say is a whining voice. "I'm already living paycheck-to-paycheck and I can't afford to take 10% of my earnings and stash it away" you may say. First of all, you're probably mismanaging your money anyway so you won't miss that extra 10%. Secondly, I'll show you how to lower your current expenses by cutting your financial fat throughout this book so the 10% savings won't be an issue. Remember what I said earlier, you need to follow these exercises exactly if you really want to make a change in your situation.

Years ago, I heard of a lady who went to her financial planner for some advice. The story goes that ten years earlier, she had *stashed away* about $100 a month for a few years. She invested it in a mutual fund and didn't touch it for ten years. All she wanted to know was if she had enough money saved up so she could buy her son a new car. She was shocked to find this $100 a month investment had accumulated to over $90,000! Nice car! Nice Mom!

***Later in this book, I will show you how to earn up to 50% guaranteed by the government!*** Let the government finance your retirement. But you need to save at least 10% of every paycheck to make it happen.

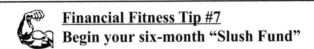

**Financial Fitness Tip #7**
**Begin your six-month "Slush Fund"**

Many of us are only one or two paychecks away from bankruptcy and that's a scary thought. What would happen if your company laid you off or you were the object of corporate downsizing? What if you get "the call" in the middle of the night and found out a relative died on the other side of the country? What would you do?

I instruct people that you should always have a *Slush Fund* equivalent to six months worth of earnings in an account where you have instant access to those funds.

You may have to start out with saving your first fifty dollars. You want your Slush Fund to grow to $1,000 as quickly as possible. By then, you'll already have a savings routine in place and it will quickly grow to $2,000 - until you reach your savings goal of six months of living expenses.

You will learn later on in this book that by having a Slush Fund, you will have another option available to you when you raise your deductible on your insurance coverages thereby drastically lowering your premiums.

 **Financial Fitness Tip #8**
**The quickest and easiest way to become financially fit is to let compound interest do the work for you.**

The easiest way to become a millionaire is to start early. Sounds old-fashioned? If you invest only $30 a month, starting at age 25 - in a 15% investment - and do that every month, and don't touch that money for ANY reason, **you will have $1 million at age 65**. That's not old-fashion - it's just a fact. It's also easy.

If you were to invest 10% of your income every month, an income that is going to increase, as you get older, you will have a lot more than $1 million stashed away for retirement. You must get around a 10% to 15% return on your investments, however. You can't just throw that money in a CD (Certificate of Deposit) at 4% and expect to be rich - at best you'll break even because inflation outstrips your earnings. You must have a plan for maximizing your profits and you must combine that strategy with the intelligent use of the tax system.

## COMPOUND TABLES
### (Based on beginning capital of $10,000)

| Year | 5% | 15% | 25% | 30% | 50% |
|---|---|---|---|---|---|
| 1 | 10,050 | 11,500 | 12,500 | 13,000 | 15,000 |
| 2 | 11,025 | 13,225 | 15,625 | 16,900 | 22,500 |
| 3 | 11,576 | 15,208 | 19,531 | 21,970 | 33,750 |
| 4 | 12,155 | 17,490 | 24,414 | 28,561 | 50,625 |
| 5 | 12,762 | 20,113 | 30,517 | 37,129 | 75,938 |
| 6 | 13,400 | 23,130 | 38,146 | 48,268 | 113,907 |
| 7 | 14,071 | 26,600 | 47,683 | 62,748 | 170,860 |
| 8 | 14,774 | 30,590 | 59,604 | 81,573 | 256,290 |
| 9 | 15,513 | 35,178 | 74,505 | 106,044 | 384,435 |
| 10 | 16,288 | 40,455 | 93,132 | 137,858 | 576,635 |
| 11 | 17,103 | 46,523 | 116,415 | 179,211 | 864,979 |
| 12 | 17,958 | 53,502 | 145,519 | 232,980 | 1,297,468 |
| 13 | 18,856 | 61,527 | 181,898 | 302,875 | 1,946,201 |
| 14 | 19,799 | 70,757 | 227,373 | 393,737 | 2,919,303 |
| 15 | 20,789 | 81,370 | 284,217 | 511,858 | 4,378,954 |
| 16 | 21,828 | 93,576 | 355,271 | 665,416 | 6,568,431 |
| 17 | 22,920 | 107,612 | 444,089 | 865,041 | 9,852,651 |
| 18 | 24,066 | 123,754 | 555,111 | 1,124,554 | 14,778,976 |
| 19 | 25,269 | 142,317 | 693,889 | 1,461,920 | 22,168,464 |
| 20 | 26,532 | 163,665 | 867,361 | 1,900,496 | 33,252,696 |
| 21 | 27,859 | 188,215 | 1,084,202 | 2,470,645 | 49,879,044 |
| 22 | 29,252 | 216,447 | 1,355,252 | 3,211,838 | 74,818,566 |
| 23 | 30,715 | 248,914 | 1,694,065 | 4,174,390 | 112,227,849 |
| 24 | 32,251 | 286,251 | 2,117,582 | 5,428,007 | 168,341,779 |
| 25 | 33,863 | 329,189 | 2,646,977 | 7,056,409 | 252,512,668 |

Keep in mind that this chart is based on a $10,000 investment. If you have more than that to invest? The numbers become obscene!

Use compound interest to make yourself rich. Compound interest works by geometric progression. It starts out slow, but gains momentum as time goes by, like a snowball rolling down a mountain.

Many years ago, I heard a story about a little boy who wanted to deliver newspapers. He was so determined to work as a delivery boy that he insisted on talking to owner of the newspaper himself. When his mom took him to see the publisher, he was immediately sent into the executive office. The savvy youngster negotiated a deal in which he would just work for a penny for the first day, as long as his pay doubled every day. The newspaper owner laughed at this *cute* offer but went along with it and even put it in writing. He thought it was still cute after 10 days. At day 20, it wasn't cute anymore. By Day 30, the savvy youngster with the *cute* offer became the proud new owner of the newspaper.

Turn the page to see how the kid did it.

| | | | | |
|---|---|---|---|---|
| Day 1 | $ 0.01 | | Day 18 | $ 1,310.72 |
| Day 2 | $ 0.02 | | Day 19 | $ 2,621.44 |
| Day 3 | $ 0.04 | | Day 20 | $ 5,242.88 |
| Day 4 | $ 0.08 | | Day 21 | $ 10,485.76 |
| Day 5 | $ 0.16 | | Day 22 | $ 20,971.52 |
| Day 6 | $ 0.32 | | Day 23 | $ 41,943.04 |
| Day 7 | $ 0.64 | | Day 24 | $ 83,886.08 |
| Day 8 | $ 1.28 | | Day 25 | $ 167,772.16 |
| Day 9 | $ 2.56 | | Day 26 | $ 335,544.32 |
| Day 10 | $ 5.12 | | Day 27 | $ 671,088.64 |
| Day 11 | $ 10.24 | | Day 28 | $1,342,177.28 |
| Day 12 | $ 20.48 | | Day 29 | $2,684,354.56 |
| Day 13 | $ 40.96 | | Day 30 | $5,368,709.12 |
| Day 14 | $ 81.92 | | | |
| Day 15 | $163.84 | | Day 38 | just over $1 **billion** |
| Day 16 | $327.68 | | Day 45 | well over $1 **trillion** |
| Day 17 | $655.36 | | | |

Now, think of compounding your money with returns of up to 50% **guaranteed by the government**. You are well on your way to a safe, comfortable retirement.

## What Is Investing?

The key to possessing true financial fitness - for yourself, your family, and your descendants - is to learn to take the money you don't need for immediate expenses and use it to make more money. That's the simple definition of an investment: any asset that generates a profit.

## Savings vs. Investments

Notice how I use the word "investment" and not the word "savings." To become financially fit, you cannot simply save. You must invest.

Millions of Americans make the mistake of assuming that "saving" money - usually by stashing funds at their local bank - will provide them with financial security. Though this attitude is ill informed, it's understandable. Because a successful investment depends on an informed investor, it's easy for unscrupulous "experts" to take advantage of the gullible or ignorant. The investment world is full of half-baked information, phony sales pitches and frauds. The media turns around and publicizes the junk bond pitchman who ends up in jail, or the scam artist who preys on the elderly.

So it's no wonder many people get nervous when they hear the word "investment" - and opt for the safety and security of a savings account. Most investors are motivated by fear - fear of losing what they have. So they trick themselves into believing that their savings accounts are "safe" places to store their hard-earned money.

My father came from *The Old Country*. When he came to America, he was taught a few things: credit is bad, pay off your mortgage as soon as you can, and stuff all of your savings in a bank account.

If your parents were *Depression Babies*, or if they made their money during the fifties, they probably taught you to have a strong moralistic attitude about saving, especially saving accounts. Embedded in your psyche may be all sorts of outdated and completely untested beliefs about what it means to be a stable human being. Lots of foggy assumptions about how to handle money get attached to you in the process. One of those unexamined and essentially false beliefs goes like this: to be a stable reliable citizen, keep lots of money in safe, secure savings accounts. The message is, unless you put you money in the bank, you're not an upstanding member of the community. How did your parents learn this? THE BANKERS OF COURSE! They pay you three percent (if you're lucky) on your hard-earned dollars so they can make 18% to 25% on your money! Why not earn five to ten times the amount you would earn in a passbook account by doing it yourself...safely and guaranteed by the government (just like your banker).

### *"The Passbook To Poverty"*

If you suffer from this type of thinking, prepare yourself to wake up one morning and realize that you're not rich - just broke. Why? In our current economic climate, the half to one percent per year earned on savings accounts is capable of only one result: it makes the banking industry richer and you poorer. The only reliable thing about traditional "saving" is that inflation and taxes are guaranteed, without fail, to erode the value of your money. What is the bottom line? You'll never achieve financial fitness by locking up your money in savings accounts.

The banking industry has known this for a long time. Bankers have developed slick marketing techniques that trick many people into depositing their money in low-return savings instruments, like money market accounts. For example, they try to entice you into believing it's smart to earn a whopping percentage point or two higher in a money market account than you would in your checking account. But if you shop around for other cash receptacles that earn respectable returns, you won't be so impressed by the bank's *deal*. And you'll be further underwhelmed when you read the fine print and discover how the bank finds ways to shave even more from your earnings through complicated fee structures. Or maybe a brand new toaster will entice you into a low-return savings instrument?!

Even worse, banks also do everything they can to discourage you, with the collusion of the tax system and banking laws, from *using* your savings unless you are willing to sacrifice part of your money in penalties and taxes. That means that even those higher-yield instruments, like CDs, have major drawbacks: your money isn't instantly accessible unless you pay a substantial penalty, and your earnings are taxable.

## Security Is A Fantasy

"But investments are risky!" you say. "At least in a savings account my money is safe!" Uh huh. Remember the security provided by the FDIC insurance is no more reliable than most other insurances. Why don't you put you money in a government-guaranteed investment where you can earn 18%, 25%, or even 50%, backed 100% by the government? **WHERE DO YOU THINK THE BANKS INVEST THEIR MONEY?** ...Duh! Besides there are still plenty of mutual funds (ones that are not under a government investigation) that earn well over 20% per year - some over 60%. More about mutual funds in Chapter 10.

If you have a sincere desire to achieve financial fitness, you must grow up - and part of growing up is seeing fairy tales for what they are: fantasies. If you have the maturity to look at recent history, you know banks fail. That's reality. Keeping large sums in a bank or a savings and loan because you're afraid to spend a few minutes a day learning how to profit from your hard-earned cash is just plain childish. I know - I was once a lazy schoolboy, and at times I paid dearly for listening to the hype instead of learning my lessons.

Many people are afraid of investments. These same people afraid of "investments" are more than willing to sign for a thirty-year mortgage. Your home is the best investment you can make. Your perception on investments is your *reality* – whether true or false.

 **Financial Fitness #9**
**Think of yourself as a business.**
**Profit is the bottom line.**

Begin to view yourself as a business and you are the CFO (Chief Financial Officer) of that business. Because money is the primary form of energy exchange in our culture, you will learn that there are basically two ways of conducting your personal finances - in a businesslike manner, or in an emotional and mental fog. All businesses have operating expenses and since you are no different, start exercising fiscal control over your spending instead of frittering away cash flow through unnecessary insurance, taxes, and interest.

> **As an investor, would you buy stock in a company that is in debt up to it's ears, with bad credit and bad management? Of course not!**
>
> **How would your potential creditors view you? Would they buy stock in you?**
>
> **Everytime you apply for credit, you are asking the creditor to buy stock in you.**

No self-respecting business invests its money in conventional savings accounts - and neither should you. Why? The interest rate paid to you on a savings instrument is only a small percentage of what your money actually earns.

Remember, the bank or savings institution can use your money, and the interest it earns, for as long as you keep your money in the account. Ask yourself, could the bank stay in business if it returned most of its profits to you? And if the bank pools the savings, and interest earnings, of thousands of people at one time, month after month, doesn't it earn huge profits? Of course it does.

Don't buy into false logic of "Small Is Not Profitable" - a fallacy many banks push on the financially unsophisticated. For example, the banking industry pretends that if you have only $1,000 in savings, you don't deserve to earn more than 1% interest. The implication is that if you don't have a large sum of money to invest, you can't earn returns of 10%. Sounds logical, right?

Not if you consider how banks *really* earn money on the savings of their customers. Think about it. Banks don't put your $1,000 in one type of investment and someone else's $100,000 in another, higher-yield investment. The bank bundles together everyone's savings and makes money using those combined dollars. The result? The bank makes seven percent on a mortgage funded with your savings, but pays you only 1% interest! Guess who keeps the other six percent (more than quadrupled your rate of return)? Yep, the bank.

What if you are lucky enough to have $100,000 - and your bank wants you to put it into a five-year CD at three and a half percent? Believe me, even at 3.5%, you can't breathe easy. Inflation is waiting to choke your long-term profit - and taxes will finish you off. The bottom line is what actually makes you financially fit. So remember, the point of making investments is making a profit!

Investing is completely different from saving money. It is a strategy designed to create financial fitness through profit. Banks - and for that matter brokerage firms, insurance agents, and financial planners - want to make a profit, too. Bless them, they should - they are businesses, just like you! So start thinking they way they do. Remember that every investment vehicle is basically a profit-generating vehicle, one that you need to drive you down the road to financial fitness.

---

**Financial Fitness Tip #10**
**Pay your bills with an Asset Management**
**Account (AMA)**

---

Think of an AMA like a high-interest bearing checking account. They are not available at your local bank. You can get these through brokerage houses. Some brokerages may also call this a *Cash Management Account*. They are nothing more than a Money Market Mutual Fund that has check writing features. Some even have Debit Cards.

    The interest rates are usually about double that of a bank checking account. Since these are national accounts, as opposed to your local back, there checks may travel thousands of miles to get processed. Why do you care about this? The answer is float. It may take as long as two weeks for these checks to clear. In the meantime, you're racking up a lot of interest on these accounts. And yes, the interest compounds daily!

    If you are worried about risk, most of these brokerage accounts must carry SIPC (Security Investors Protection Corporation) insurance. This is basically the brokerage firm's version of the FDIC, which insures bank accounts. As you can see, there is no risk.

    A few of these AMA's have high initial deposits with lower minimum balances required. Its not uncommon for people (who are starting small) to write a check for the initial deposit and then write a check (from your AMA to yourself) so you still maintain the lower minimum. Using this "Flash Cash" technique, you can get an AMA rather inexpensively.

    There are millions of people across the country that can't open bank accounts. They are listed on a credit bureau called *ChexSystems*. ChexSystems is a credit bureau that only banks and credit unions use if you wish to open up a bank account. If you've bounced any checks in the past, you'll be listed on ChexSystems and can't open another bank account for FIVE years! Even after you made good on the check, you still can't open a bank account. If you're already on ChexSystems, you'll know what I'm talking about.

Since the banks won't allow you to open a bank account for five years, the banks also lose money on the interest they could have made off your deposits. In believing that people need a second chance, Bank of America recently changed its policy and is now allowing you the ability to open a new account if you have been on ChexSystems for at least two years. This savy business move will make Bank of America millions of dollars from interest on deposits it wouldn't have made otherwise. Hopefully, more banks will give the average person a second chance.... soon!

## Asset Management Accounts

| NAME | PHONE | WEBSITE ADDRESS |
|------|-------|-----------------|
| Wachovia | 888.213.1352 | http://www.wachovia.com |
| Peoples Securities, Inc. | 800.392.3009 | http://www.peoples.com |
| Fleet Private Clients | 800.563.0702 | http://www.fleet.com/privateclients |
| Commerce Brokerage Services | 800.453.2265 | http://www.commercebank.com |
| U.S. Clearing (Division of Fleet) | not given | http://www.usclearing.com |

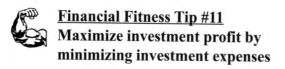

**Financial Fitness Tip #11**
**Maximize investment profit by**
**minimizing investment expenses**

It has been demonstrated, over and over again, that **you can safely earn up to a 50% return on your investments every single year**. It has also been demonstrated that you can accomplish this without dabbling in high stakes, high-risk financial products. In fact, if you practice the art of investing with attention and rigor, you can use the world's safest investments, tax lien certificates (I'll cover these in a later chapter).

Unfortunately, if you start paying other people to make your investment moves for you, your overall profits start to drop. The sanest and safest way to increase profit is to minimize your investment expenses.

Every investment has two potential areas of expense:

- **Commissions (or "load")**:  When you buy or sell your investments, your profit is undercut whenever you have to pay someone a commission or fee. By dealing directly with financial institutions, and avoiding brokers, financial consultants, and salesmen, you get to keep the profit for yourself. As I discuss various investment vehicles in the chapters that follow, I'll remind you to look for low or no-fee ways to buy and sell them.

- **Taxes:**  It is *not* true that the only way to invest without bracing yourself for huge tax hits is to invest in tax-exempt bonds or retirement funds. With sensible tax planning, you can shelter the income from all sorts of investments - *if* you think like a business and remember that taxes are an overall, lifetime expense. If some of your investments generate taxable profits, why not create tax deductions elsewhere in your overall financial strategies to offset the expense. By judiciously using the tax strategies I will teach you, and then consulting a tax expert to make sure your investment plan is sound, you won't need to limit yourself to just a few types of investments in order to minimize your tax burden.

---

**Financial Fitness Tip #12**
**Separate the concept of *investment* from the idea of risk**

---

If the word "investment" makes you nervous, remember that buying a house is the single most common investment strategy. Most people have more equity in their home than they will ever have in a savings account - and that's good! The financial flexibility provided by a $100,000 house is light years ahead of $100,000 in a savings account. You can borrow against the equity in your home, use it as a tax shelter, or sell it and make a profit - not bad for something that's also provides a roof over your head!

The only people who believe that buying a home is a financial risk just don't like to take care of a house. Unless you are completely clueless, or stubborn about selling at the appropriate time, it's hard to lose money on a house in the long run, especially after you consider tax benefits and equity, not to mention the fact that you use it every single day as a source of comfort, rest, and possibly profit if you work out of your house. Owning a home doesn't feel like gambling away your money, does it?

Remember, the best investments are a lot like the investment in your home - they are flexible, offer tax advantages, and can generate profits that will outstrip inflation by at least several percent. And unlike a home, many of them provide instant liquidity without substantial penalty. In this unpredictable world, that should make you feel less - not more - nervous!

Much of the so-called risk in the investment world is caused by the ignorance of the investor - not the particular investment. As a smart businessperson, you can't make decisions based solely on what a salesman or broker claims to be good for you. You wouldn't buy a house in a rundown neighborhood simply because the real estate agent promises the area will get better! You wouldn't buy a car from someone just because the owner says the car runs great - you'd check it out first!

The same is with investments. Buying stock in a company because your parents did, or because the broker predicts the price will go up, or because you just read an article in a business magazine is irresponsible. You must choose wisely, not based on someone else's sales pitch, but on what you hope to achieve through your investments. You wouldn't buy a luxury car to haul construction equipment. Why would you put money you wish to keep liquid in a long-term, tax-sheltered investment?

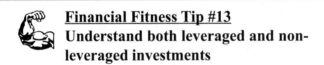

**Financial Fitness Tip #13**
**Understand both leveraged and non-leveraged investments**

Did you know that the most common, everyday investment most American's make is actually a leveraged investment? Buying a home with a mortgage is using leverage - someone else's money - to purchase a major investment. So is borrowing against the equity in your home to invest in a business or some other profit-making venture.

There are only two ways to invest: by using cash on hand, or by using someone else's cash. The first is a non-leveraged investment and the second is leveraged. If you want to become financially fit, you should use each type of investment when it is appropriate.

When you take your own money and buy stocks, bonds, or mutual funds, or when you sink that money into a bank CD, IRA, Treasury Bill, or company retirement plan, you are making a straight forward, non-leveraged investment. The advantage to the non-leveraged investment is that it's direct, it's a no-brainer, and it's usually very easy. The disadvantage is that you are restricted in how much profit you can make because all you have to start with is your own money, often paying taxes on the profits.

When you purchase a house with a mortgage, use a margin account with a brokerage or mutual fund, take an option on real estate, borrow money for your business, or borrow against the equity in your home to re-invest elsewhere, you are making leveraged investments. The advantage of leveraging is that you can create much more profit, and often generate far greater tax benefits than you could if all you had was your own cash to work with. The disadvantage is that leveraged investments require some brainwork and a little more care and attention, especially in choosing the right balance between profit and tax risk.

The point is that one type of investment is not necessarily better than the other - although ideally you want to use both methods if they fit your objectives. To become an empowered investor, you must use this basic leverage/non-leveraged distinction as a first step in training your mind to think profitably. Doesn't it make sense? You can't make an intelligent investment decision without first determining whether you are simply putting your own cash on the line, or whether you are leveraging a responsibility to something or someone (like a bank) against a greater potential profit (a house which becomes a valuable asset and tax benefit).

As you read through the chapters that follow, keep the leverage/non-leverage distinction in mind. I'm always pleased to see how many people - people who have been frightened of investing in the past - suddenly begin to think clearly, logically, and even aggressively once they start analyzing potential investments in these terms. That's because the leverage/non-leverage distinction allows them to gauge risk - risk based on their own comfort level - fairly easily and quickly.

### *Risk* As The Product of Emotion and Knowledge

Before you embark on the rest of the book, it's vital that you understand that *risk* is an almost meaningless concept when it comes to finances. It has about the same meaning as the word *safety* - it's whatever *you* decide it is for *you*. When people start talking to me about an investment being risky or safe, I know they are not talking about the investment - they are talking about themselves, and they are definitely not being rational! Many people would rather carry $250,000 of risk to a bank mortgage than $10,000 of risk in a mutual fund or tax lien certificate - even though the mortgage is actually almost all leverage and the mutual fund and tax lien certificate is zero-leverage! Always remember that risk is an emotional concept, and is basically culturally determined.

Think about your own situation. Let's say you borrow against the equity in your home to pay off credit cards. Does that feel like a terribly risky thing to do? Probably not. Sure, you use a whole lot of someone else's money (the banks) and jeopardize the security of your asset (your house). You do that just to generate a tax benefit (deductible interest) and keep the wolves from your door (the bill collectors). But because the roof is still over your head, your payments are probably smaller, the credit cards paid off, all of your friends have second mortgages, and the tax refund comes in the mail, you don't fret over the fact that you took the bank's money and put your house up for collateral.

Yet, many people do this and then rack up the credit cards again. Talk about a gamble! These are the same people who won't take $10,000 of the home equity loan and put it in a mutual fund account that could earn 20% or more, or even purchase a government guaranteed tax lien certificate that could earn 18%, 25%, or even as high as 50% because that's "speculating." These are often the same people who are terrified to invest $25,000 of that home equity in their home in their own business - yet they complain bitterly about going to a job they hate every single day!

The moral of this story is "risk" is relative. One person's speculation is another person's ho-hum existence. From the perspective of *reality*, it's riskier to blow part of a home equity loan on credit card debt than it is to use it to start your own business or invest in high-yield tax lien certificates. You can always recreate the credit card debt and just end up further in the hole, but if the business fails you can probably sell off the assets and take advantage of some tax breaks. And mutual funds usually just keep going and going - they may not be flashy, but your capital is pretty safe and your earnings just get added in every quarter like clockwork!

Shutting off your brain or modeling your lifestyle on your neighbors is no way to become financially fit!

**Financial Fitness is based on what you do with your extra cash.** The cold hard fact is that if your extra cash doesn't make you richer, you can forget about being financial fit.

*The secret of geting ahead is getting started.*
*The secret of getting started is breaking your*
*complex overwhelming tasks into small managable*
*tasks, and then starting on the first one.*
- Mark Twain

## <u>Summary of Chapter Two</u>

Let's sum up what you've learned in this chapter:
- Started to take control of my finances.

- Began a six-month "Slush Fund."

- Realized the power of compounded interest.

- Opened up an Asset Management Account.

- Minimizing my investment expenses will make me more financially fit.

- Investments don't have to be risky to be profitable.

- Leveraged investments will free up my cash and pump up your financial muscles.

# Chapter 3

## *Flexing Your Financial Muscles 101*

*It is not what comes into a man's hands that enriches him*
*but what he saves from slipping through them.*
H. F. Kletzing

Are you ready to take your first concrete step in the journey toward financial fitness? Begin by memorizing Financial Fitness Tip #14. Half the financial independence strategies available from books, videos, seminars, home courses, and workshops are summarized in these ten simple words:

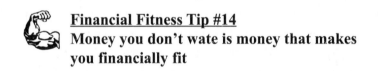

**Financial Fitness Tip #14**
**Money you don't wate is money that makes**
**you financially fit**

As I show you how to use this principle, you will have the power to become financial fit right now - without stress, without pain, without sacrifice.

### Forget The Myths

Most people are convinced that becoming financially fit is complicated. They are intimidated - either by financial *experts*, or by their own negative thoughts. As you learned in the previous chapter, this self-brainwashing is full of false beliefs - plain old lies. One of the worst of these lies is the idea that acquiring wealth is risky, even

71

dangerous. Look inside yourself. Deep down, do you believe that to be financial fit you need the brain of a theoretical physicist, the legal qualifications of a Harvard law professor, the diplomacy of a senior state department official, and the bravery of an Air Force fighter pilot?

No wonder so many hard-working, good intentioned souls don't become financially fit. Ordinary people, trying to make a living, trying to succeed, trying to make it to the next paycheck, don't believe they have the time or brains to become their own experts - and they certainly don't have the money to pay experts. More "stinkin' thinkin'"!

If you have become attached to these false beliefs about wealth, I've got some shocking news for you. **Becoming financially fit is not complicated or risky**. Becoming financially fit is simple, liberating, and fun. It is not a roll of the dice or a turn of the wheel. Nor is it a mental exercise or a psychological obsession. It happens step-by-step, day-by-day, a few minutes at a time, through the repetition of simple actions and disciplined thinking. So if you are someone who says, "I don't want to spend all my time worrying about money," then don't! Don't worry about money - take action.

The actions described in this chapter are almost *too* simple. They don't demand the drama and agony of twenty-four hour a day stress. They don't depend on the mythology of wealth - just the facts. They are all designed to help you develop a healthy attitude toward wealth - the kind that frees you from stress.

You **do** have the time to achieve financial fitness - the twenty minutes it will take you to read the next few sections. And you **do** have the brains - if brains dictated wealth, lots of millionaires would have to turn in their bank accounts to the IQ police. **Wealth is an *experience* as well as a state of mind.**

> *Wealth begins in your head, not in your pocket.*
> Napoleon Hill
> Author of "Think and Grow Rich"

There have been times in my life where I have been *temporarily out of cash*. But I've <u>never</u> at any time did I have the mentality of being poor. To experience wealth immediately, do it a little at a time - starting now.

### *The Three Ways to Get Rich*

1. *Inherit it.* If you are one of these lucky individuals, you don't need to worry. Someone in your family already did all the saving, so you don't have to. Your only concern should be on the ways to keep what you have and watch it grow. You can skip the section on savings and go straight to the section on investments.

2. *Marry into it.* This technique can only work before you get involved with a poor person. You can become what I call a *professional gold-digger*. Believe it or not, women are not the only ones that have the talent to become a gold-digger. Men are equally as proficient as the ladies in this area. A word of warning, many wealthy individuals can smell a gold-digger coming from a mile away. When you have money, it seems like everyone wants to be your friend and/or love interest. I have had plenty of women attempt to attach themselves to me. In other words, I speak from experience!

3. *Spend less than you earn and invest the difference.* If you're not lucky enough to inherit it or crafty enough to marry into it, your only choice would be like the most of us…. Option #3.

## How To Get Financially Fit On Pennies A Day

To become financially fit, there are only two things you need to do:

*1. When you spend, don't waste money (i.e. Save).*
*2. Use the money you have to make more money (i.e. Invest).*

That's it. This chapter, and all the others in the first half of this book, teaches you about that good old-fashioned S-word: **Saving**.

Saving - when you buy necessities, when you pay taxes, when you have fun - is the simplest part of financially fit. It also requires the most discipline. The second half of this book de-mystifies the world of investing. Investing is more challenging than saving, but easy when you know what you want your investments to accomplish.

Saving helps you become financially fit right now, while investing helps keep you financially fit forever. Saving rescues money you would otherwise lose, and makes it available for investment. Saving and investing are two sides of the coin that will make you financially fit. You need to understand both concepts. You must do both to be wealthy.

It's obvious that the sooner that you begin saving, the sooner you will become wealthy.

Begin by not throwing those pennies away on useless expenditures. If your family income before taxes is $45,000 a year, the first half of this book will show you how to rescue, not just pennies, but $5,000 or more a year *without* depriving yourself of security, safety, or pleasure. If you were to invest only one-fourth of that rescued cash in sound investments every year, you'd have to work awfully hard *not* to end up with a million-dollar retirement fund!

No one wants to live like a pauper. This book is committed to showing you how to live better while you are becoming financially fit. I am thirty-eight years old. It makes me sad to watch people live longer without joy, pleasure, and security. Even if you are about to retire - or are already retired - you don't have to live on the edge.

Your first step in becoming financially fit is to increase your discretionary cash - the money left after paying bills - immediately, certainly within the next thirty days. Be like the enterprising little boy who earned a penny a day. Ben Franklin was right - a penny saved *is* a penny earned - and a dollar or two or ten or fifty saved is even better!

## Don't Budget - Save!

Most folks don't get financially fit because they think they will have to suffer to do it. It's a rare individual who wants to be poor while getting financially fit - most normal people want to enjoy themselves, and poverty cramps their style. This is why I want you to eliminate the word **budget** from your vocabulary.

> **Think of it this way...do you know of someone who ever went on a diet? Did they stay on it? Or should I ask, how long they stayed on the diet before they got off of it? EXACTLY! Just as in dieting, budgeting almost never works. With Financial Aerobics, I'm showing you how to <u>spend</u> your way to wealth. Even if you need to create a bill for your savings!**

**Budgeting is a popular concept because it is a lazy, no-brainer technique for "managing" money.** Unfortunately, it doesn't manage your money at all. Instead it locks you into a whole set of false assumptions - i.e. lies. Here are some of them:

### *Lies My Budget Told Me*

- Income after taxes is the only resource you have for paying your bills.
- The month is the unit of time by which financial progress is measured.
- The only way to save money is to treat savings as a monthly "bill."
- "Necessities" are shelter and food. Clothing, dining out, education, travel and entertainment - unless they are used to produce income - are "luxurics".
- "Savings" and "investments" fall into a category called "other."
- If your income only slightly exceeds your expenses, you must use credit to have fun.
- If your expenses exceed your income, suffer by cutting back on luxuries, or use credit to temporarily alleviate your suffering.

Of course, most people who support the concept of budgeting would quarrel with this list of lies. "You're describing *bad* budgeting!" they say. "Nobody should budget that way!"

Sure - nobody should. But the fact is most everybody does. When people sit down to draw up a personal budget, they list all their bills for the month in one column. That list has anywhere from six to twenty or more items on it. In the other column they list their income for the month. That usually means one, two, or three items. It's already starting to look bad, isn't it?

If you are like most Americans, you live from paycheck to paycheck - and you know it. When you write out your monthly budget, this grim fact takes the spotlight, to the exclusion of all other points of view. It also tends to place moral judgments on the way you spend money. For example, $100 a month for "Entertainment" is not a frivolous "luxury" unless you want to live like a hermit. The illuminating process of budgeting does only one thing: it *demoralizes* you. It hasn't shed any light on your financial condition. It probably depresses you. It might frighten you.

To effectively use Financial Fitness Tip #14, *stop budgeting*. Replace budgeting with this simple rule: to start saving, stop wasting.

### Plug The Leaks

What's missing - besides hope - when you make a budget? Remember, you are a business. Multiply your gross pay by the number of years you will work - a quick calculation will do. Now look at that number. It is your lifetime income. Depending on your age, the number may be modest or staggering. But its size is not as important as its potential.

What if you were told you could have that lifetime income, in a lump sum, right now - that's all you would be given, but you could do whatever you wanted with it, right now? What would you do? How would you manage that windfall? Wouldn't you suddenly want to learn more about money - spending it, sharing it, using it creatively? Wouldn't you feel more aggressive about taxes, about waste, about investment? Wouldn't you feel more respectful of this income? Because the potential of this little business is amazing, you would want to make decisions, and take actions, that would get the most "bang" from these bucks.

The last thing you would do is sit down and do a monthly budget! Why? Because a budget doesn't look at the big picture. It is a lopsided way of looking at your financial situation. So much essential information is missing. It doesn't tell you:

- **How much you are overpaying, each and every month, for "necessities."** Remember, in our country, necessities are not just food, shelter, and clothing. This category must include all non-subsidized payments for utilities, transportation, your children's education, health insurance, and two or more different types of additional insurance. (When in doubt about whether it's a necessity, ask yourself

- do I have a choice about whether to spend this money or not? If not, it's a necessity.)

- **How much you are overpaying, each and every month, for "hidden" expenses.** Common examples are banking fees, extended warranties, and unnecessary insurance.

- **How much you are overpaying, every year, for taxes.** (Taxes are a no-choice item - a necessity never exposed to scrutiny in the average budget.)

- **How much you are overpaying, over your lifetime, for big-ticket items** like your mortgage, automobiles, appliances, furniture, computers, and credit (yes that includes home equity loans). Since most people do not pay off unsecured loans - especially credit cards - in twelve months or less, consider all items purchased with them *over*priced.

- **How much you are *under*paying yourself.** This category includes all the money you fail to spend on building your financial independence: the money you *don't* put in an IRA, the money that sits idle in a low-interest savings account, the money you don't invest in improving your home, the money you don't spend on education or services which can save you time, stress, and hardship in the long term. It also includes lost potential income: the money you will never earn from creative investments - in real estate, your own business or businesses, and high-yield mutual funds.

These basic facts represent financial leaks that are never revealed in the typical budget process. Most of us don't even know we are losing this money - and what you don't know can hurt you. Like a slow, steady leak in a hidden pipe, you don't notice the loss for a long time, but when you do, it's too late - the damage has been done. For most of us, these leaks are not just pennies a day, but thousands and thousands of dollars over our lifetimes that could be saved, invested, and enjoyed.

Fortunately, what you do know can help you. You don't have to pay an expensive financial "plumber" to stop these hidden leaks. Consider the next few pages a test of whether you are committed to financial renovation. The following two exercises may seem under whelming - too mundane to make a difference. But true financial fitness begins with respecting the money you have right now - whether that's $1 or $100,000. Do you know where your money is? Do you know where it is going? Do you know what it's buying for you? Is your money powerful, or is it weak?

Your financial independence begins with two essential practices: fact-finding and common sense. Let's get started.

## Exercise One: Get The Facts

You can't stop the leaks unless you find them. That means you've got to grit your teeth, open those drawers, file cabinets, and shoe boxes, and locate all those important pieces of paper! Collect the following items:

- All your credit card statements
- Any credit bureau report less than one year old
- All your loan documents
- All your insurance policies
- Warranties for all big-ticket items
- Bank statements for the last twelve months and old check registers
- Tax documents and any copies of old returns
- Investment documents - all of them, of any kind
- Information on your benefits package from your job, if applicable
- Paycheck stubs - whatever is lying around

- Automobile loan contract, warranty, payment book, maintenance log
- Anything else having to do with money - receipts, expense logs, utility bills, repair bills, etc. *When in doubt, include it.*
- Important stuff that may not have anything to do with money, but would be awful to lose (social security cards, diplomas, awards, certificates, marriage license, that birthday card from your kids, that nice letter from a satisfied client, love letters from your spouse, etc.)

Don't worry right now about categorizing, organizing, or throwing away any of this stuff - we'll worry about that in Chapter Four. In the meantime, just find everything. Disorganized, frantic people rarely know where their money is going. They can't make sound financial decisions because they can't put their fingers on the facts. If you already know where all these important documents are - congratulations! If not, the rainy afternoon you spend rummaging through those piles will pay handsome returns later. Vital information is hidden in these documents. You will need that information to work through chapters 3 through 10.

### Exercise Two: Start Saving Right Now!

**Let's plug a few of the smaller leaks immediately.** The following Ten Instant Saving Strategies are easy, painless, and empowering - if you use them. How's this for an incentive? Look at the cash you have for living expenses over the next thirty days. Would you like to increase that amount by 20 to 25 percent right now? How would you like to reward yourself with 20 to 25 percent of that money?

You can. Choose at least three of the following strategies and implement them consistently for a month. Keep a piece of paper labeled "REWARD MONEY" handy, with a running tally of *the number of dollars you have not wasted* each time you take one of these small steps toward financial fitness. How many rewards can you accumulate? Have fun. Remember that **money you don't waste is money that makes you richer.**

## Instant Saving Strategies

**1. Don't spend more on perishables than you have to.** Join Sam's Club, Costco or another consumer warehouse club. Buy the stuff you use all the time, like baby food, breakfast cereal, videotapes, or computer paper in large quantities at a substantial discount. Starting today, pay for perishables in cash - not with credit cards. If you don't like to carry lots of cash, pay by check, or use a debit or ATM card.

The *only* exception is the quantity perishable expense - prescription drugs, flowers for mom's birthday, contact lenses, office, art, or craft supplies - that you buy direct *over the phone*. While you talk to the sales rep, write a check to your Visa, MasterCard, Discover, or American Express for the exact amount of your order. Mail it. If you don't, any savings you might have realized will be eaten up by interest. And if you mail your order, enclose a check or money order. Your merchandise won't be substantially delayed - and your savings will be *real*, not illusory.

Every time you avoid plastic and pay cash for perishables, deduct 25% from the cost of the item - and consider that savings for your REWARD tally.

**2. Use coupons, especially when a product or service is not on sale**. One of the easiest ways to put ten or more extra dollars in your pocket every week is to use coupons - the ones that come free on the back of your grocery receipts, in the Sunday paper, or from Val-Pak. Don't just focus on supermarket coupons - watch for savings on oil changes, dry cleaning, fast food, cigarettes, pet supplies and grooming, and video rentals.

Especially valuable are coupons for *services*, not just products that you use every day, week, or month. The last Val-Pak I received contained substantial savings on dental services (including orthodontics), laundry, carpet cleaning, car care, copying and shipping, and eyeglasses - all from conveniently located local businesses. Add the face value of these coupons to your REWARDS MONEY.

**You should check out websites such as www.MightyShopper.com for massive savings for your grocery bills.**

3. **Cut transportation and commuting costs.** Car-pool if you can. If you can't, don't waste money on premium gas - with most cars, the improved mileage is in your head, and doesn't offset the additional expense (ask your mechanic). To really improve your per-mile costs, invest the savings in maintaining your car, especially frequent oil changes, tire rotation, and tune-ups. Use discounts and promotions to cut maintenance costs. Be ruthless about your auto club - if it doesn't offer more than towing or jump-starts, shop around. Wash your car yourself or use coupons. Do some quick calculations to see if riding the commuter train is cheaper than driving and parking - sometimes it is, but the price of public transportation is increasing, so do the numbers first. Note all your savings as REWARDS.

4. **Don't buy clothing at status department stores**, especially if you *need* to dress at a certain level of taste and quality for your career. Sure, I love beautiful, quality clothing - but I also *need* to dress well because of what I do. Whatever your income, don't pay more for Hanes or Maidenform, Klein, Beene, or Karan than you have to. Dressing well requires planning as well as taste. If you can't find what you love at a discount store like Target or TJMaxx, *plan* your investment clothing purchases. Some of my worst financial mistakes are hanging in my closet - never buy clothing on impulse. Whether you save money - or resist temptation - that's a REWARD.

5. **Barter, don't pay.** It is easy to make smart financial choices when you realize that money is just a form of energy. Sometimes you can

substitute your own energy - your particular talents, skills and services or sweat equity - for cash. Bartering isn't as old-fashioned or uncommon as you think. Look at computer user groups and shareware networks, or the way local business owners refer customers to each other and save the cost of expensive advertising.

If you have a hobby or skill that generates no income, consider bartering to make it pay. Join a bartering network or start your own. Remember to record REWARDS for these services or products at market rates. If you bake your Decadent Chocolate Mousse Cake for your neighbor's son, make sure the lawn mowing and leaf raking he offers in exchange is of equal market value. Don't sell yourself - or others - short!

6. **Cut childcare costs.** One of the biggest cash drains for the average American family is childcare and maintenance. I am responsible for two young children, and they are my biggest worry. I believe that every financial decision which affects children must take into account their overall well being, happiness, and security. An entire book could (and should) be written about this subject, but until then, here are some creative, win-win ways some parents I know have improved their kids' lives - without going broke.

Enlist the help of good parents who live nearby. Money can't buy the help and support of good friends - but trust and responsibility can! If you trust your friends, and they trust you, you can help each other with childcare - and save not only money but also worry. Build a parents bartering network, and offer your skills or crafts for baby-sitting. Even if your baby-sitter is your mom or aunt, repay her support with non-monetary help. Stop and calculate the dollar value of this type of help. Never *over*estimate the power of money, and never *under*estimate the value of good friendship.

Never buy children's clothing at status stores. Hit garage sales or thrift shops or discount stores, or trade outgrown clothing with friends and family members.

If it's available, investigate day care and preschool programs at local churches, even if you are not a member of the congregation. Their prices are often competitive, and the quality of your child's day will probably be as good as or better than at a commercial day care center. More importantly, you have a better chance of getting to know your child's caregivers through a local church than you do at a for-profit establishment, where the employees are running home at about the time you arrive.

Some parents aggressively pursue jobs at organizations that provide day care and after school programs. You may wish to investigate administrative jobs at local schools, colleges, or universities if they have on-site child care, a laboratory school, or tuition rebates, which can add up to *thousands* in REWARDS for you and your kids. Just remember to *get all the facts* first. Make sure you can realistically make a four to eight-year job commitment so you can continue to receive a tuition discount for your kids

7. **Learn to cook.** Sound trite? One of the most common - and costly - credit card abuses is the restaurant meal. With all the cooking shows, books, magazines, and videos out there, it's never been easier to dine elegantly - without going out. So much restaurant food is priced all out of proportion to its quality, yet many of us use high interest plastic money to spend $50 or more per week on plastic food. Fast food is worse: it may be a necessary evil, but in some areas a greasy burger, fries, and soft drink can drain $5 from your pocket on a daily basis. That's $25 per working week, or $100 per month - pretty expensive for mostly fat and salt.

Remember, financial fitness is about your overall quality of life, about spiritual, emotional, and physical *abundance*. You will feel poor if you eat "poorly." Trying to lose weight? If you never use it, terminate the expensive health club membership and learn spa cooking at home. Unless your employer reimburses you for business meals, consider all restaurant food a perishable item. So brown bag your lunch three times a week, pay cash when you go out, and tally high REWARDS which can buy a *first-class* restaurant meal, a pizza party for your kid's, a food processor, a convection oven, a new gas grill, or some other earthly pleasure.

**8. Never pay full price for an airline ticket, car rental, hotel, motel, or cruise - ever!** Even if you take only one trip a year, get more bang for your travel dollar by taking advantage of advance purchases, stand-by tickets, two-for-one fares, off-season and last-minute discounts. Check with your employer, local consumer club, travel agent, credit union and auto club, even your credit card company for discounts. Travel clubs offer substantial savings for an annual membership fee - some are good values, others aren't. Read the fine print, and ask questions *before* you purchase your membership.

Additionally, there are plenty of travel websites on the Internet that offer substantial discounts. Surf the web and save some money.

Don't waste frequent flyer benefits! Careless travelers forfeit millions of dollars worth of perks because they don't read their frequent flyer statements - don't be one of them. Substantial REWARDS can be realized here!

**9. Ignore TV advertising and aggressively shop for the best value on long-distance calls.** You should know *exactly* what you are paying, per minute, on state-to-state calls. When one of those cute telephone telemarketers calls you with their fancy promotional offers, say this: "I'm not interested in what percent I'll save. Tell me what I will pay per minute." If they can't - or won't - tell you, ask to speak to their manager. If the manager can't or won't tell you, ask them not to call you again unless they can quote you a price.

A minute of daytime, state-to-state telephone time varies wildly: anywhere from four cents a minute to 40 cents a minute or more. If your carrier offers 20% off its "basic" rate, and that rate is 38 cents, you pay 23 cents per minute. If your carrier offers 10% off 20 cents a minute, you pay 18 cents a minute.

In addition to the price-per-minute rate, ask them the following questions:

- Is their plan guaranteed not to go up for at least one year?
- Will they pay to switch your service to their company?
- Will they pay to switch it back if you're not satisfied?
- Is there a monthly fee charge to access the low per minute rate they're quoting you?
- Does their company offer a flat rate plan for unlimited calls?

Notice how they never tell you those basic rates on TV? Now you know why.

Call your long distance company today. Have your latest bill and a calculator handy. Ask for the day, evening, and weekend rates to the area codes you call most frequently. Check the arithmetic as you speak to the customer service representative. Unless you are already paying rock-bottom rates, a straightforward, aggressive call to a couple of competitor carriers should yield an immediate savings of 10-15%. If you spend $100 a month or more, you should be able to do much better than that: 20-30%. Estimate the REWARDS - month after month after month. Just remember, you are not buying a discount. You are buying a "per-minute" rate.

Audit your long distance bills every couple of months to make sure the rates haven't changed. If they have, shop around. The carrier will almost always switch you for free - and you will always pay the lowest price.

**10. If you are spending more than $15 per month on checking account fees, consider changing banks.** Look at your last bank statement. Maintaining a minimum balance in your checking account in return for "free" checking? Look again - "free" checking often means the bank is pretending not to charge you for the privilege of holding and using your minimum balance.

Yet you may be paying a dollar or more for each ATM transaction, a dollar or more for automatic debits to pay a car loan or mortgage (sometimes within the same bank!), three dollars or more if you request a detailed printout of recent transactions (whether from an ATM or the customer service representative at the bank), a dollar or more for inquiries made through automated telephone account access, several dollars to move money from savings into checking, or 50 cents per check after your first 10 checks that month - not the first 10 checks *written*, the first 10 *processed* by the bank.

It's even more surprising to find large, full-service banks charging more of these cryptic fees than smaller, local banks. Banks are out to make a profit, just like the long distance companies. The marketing and the fine print often don't agree. Even a bank that offers good value can change the rules; meaning most of these fees can be raised or added without your knowledge. You may be wasting $180 or more per year on these incidentals - that equals lost REWARDS.

If you have been a regular customer for many years, call your banker, the head of new accounts, or your loan officer. Ask to have these fees waived. If you get the cold shoulder (and you shouldn't, if your bank wants to continue to deserve your business), call three local banks and ask about their personal checking account fees. Find a friendly account representative and look for a better deal. That phone call, a ten-minute visit to the new bank, and signing a few forms could add $180 or more to your wallet each year.

Is it time to replenish your supply of checks? Never buy checks from the bank. Order them directly from the check printers who advertise in Val-Pak or the Sunday supplements. That's where your bank gets them - and marks them up 100% or more before mailing them to you. If you're skeptical, call your bank and ask a clerk in the bookkeeping department if direct-purchase checks are just as good as your bank's. You'll be reassured, and you'll REWARD yourself with $10 to $30 in savings.

You may laugh at the fact that you can save $25 here or $180 there. Just remember that this can mean a saving up to $1,000-2,000 a year. Over the course of ten years, that number becomes $10,000-20,000. And that's without the compound interest that you would have been earning on your investments. THIS IS RETIREMENT MONEY!

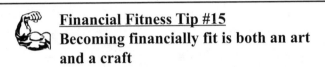

**Financial Fitness Tip #15**
**Becoming financially fit is both an art**
**and a craft**

The art comes when you become an investor - when you take the money you have and create new money. But first you must learn your craft - the essential financial skills that require practice, practice, practice.

I was originally trained as a musician. It's impossible to play competently, let alone beautifully, unless you practice. The two exercises above give you Ben Franklin-style, "a penny saved is a penny earned" practice. The basics of managing money are thinking about it correctly, respecting how much even a little bit of it can do for you, and building on sound financial facts. This craft doesn't have to be complicated or intimidating.  You just have to do it.

Look at your "REWARD MONEY" tally. It doesn't matter if you used the actual savings to buy bulbs for your garden, order Christmas gifts through the mail, tune up your car, or pay your electric bill early. **If someone handed you a check for that amount, would you refuse it?** Not likely. If you could multiply that check by five, wouldn't that intrigue you? Wouldn't you want that check to multiply again, and again? Wouldn't that process be exciting, fun, and rewarding?

The next few chapters will allow you to do just that. If you haven't given the exercises in this chapter a chance to work for you, stop reading and try them. If you have, get ready to watch your "REWARD MONEY" grow in unexpected ways.

*Rule No. 1:*
*Never lose money.*
*Rule No. 2:*
*Never forget Rule No. 1.*
- Warren Buffet

## <u>Summary of Chapter Three</u>

In this chapter, I learned about:
- The lies my budget told me.

- Plugging my financial leaks.

- Ten instant saving strategies.

- How to take advantage of Reward Money.

Have you subscribed to our FREE Newsletter yet?
Go to: www.FinancialFitnessTips.com

**Chapter Four**

# *Getting Your Financial Records Into Shape*

*A businessman's judgment is no better than his information.*
R. P. Lamont

This chapter is the crash course in records management. Like basic training, it may seem mundane. **But you can't skip the basics**. Let's find out why.

### It's A War Out There

Have you ever been harassed by a creditor - even though you paid the bill months ago? Have you ever failed to file an insurance loss because you couldn't prove the value of the stolen item? Have you ever tried to take advantage of a product warranty? Have you ever filled out a loan or credit application? Have you ever wondered whether you could avoid that tax hit by itemizing deductions? Have you ever fought with a hospital or clinic over an insurance claim? Have you ever been audited or sued? Have you ever been embarrassed because your bank made a mistake in recording a deposit? And if you're lucky enough never to have any of these things happen, do you worry about them?

The above situations can make you feel helpless, stressed out, attacked - unless you have some ammunition to back you up. Isn't it nice to know that this ammunition can be yours with a little time, a few dollars -and you can keep it in a two-drawer file cabinet?

**Financial Fitness Tip #16**
**When you're stuck in a financial battle,**
**your financial records are the most**
**powerful weapons in your arsenal**

You can't be caught off guard. It's not just your word against theirs. You have information that protects you from the abuse, sloppiness, and arbitrary harassment of bureaucrats. That's reason enough to become organized.

However, it's even more important to keep good financial records because **the best defense is a good offense.** Wouldn't it be nice to catch that bank error *before* you find yourself shamefaced over a bounced check - and arguing for weeks with the bookkeeping department at your bank? Wouldn't it be better not to discover you've "maxed out" yet another credit card after waiting in line for twenty minutes during the Christmas shopping madness? Wouldn't you feel more comfortable and confident when you mail your tax return if you knew you had all the right documentation at your fingertips? Wouldn't you like to stop paying for (and paying interest on) expensive credit insurance you will never, ever use? In a crunch, wouldn't you like to know which bills you can safely pay a few days late - and which late payments will cost you dearly?

**Financial Fitness Tip #17**
**You can avoid or neutralize financial land**
**mines when you have access to the facts**

"**Applied** knowledge is power" may sound like a cliché. But in an age of information overload, of financial fiction as well as financial fact, you must have access to the truth. The truth begins at home, with all those contracts, receipts, loan agreements, credit statements, tax forms, insurance policies, and warranties languishing around the house.

As you saw in Chapter One, becoming financially fit is a step-by-step process. You learned to respect the money you use on a daily basis. You tested a method for breaking the paralysis of a budget by applying wisdom and discretion to simple spending transactions. You saw that small steps, taken consistently, could begin to take you down the road toward financial fitness. Not only that, you saw that these small steps pay immediate rewards - an instant, measurable rebate you could use to make yourself wealthier.

But it's time to take bigger steps. Although it's important to understand that saving is a daily activity, just recapturing a few pennies or dollars won't make you financially fit. Now that you are free of budgeting, the next logical step is to know how to follow, and catch, the money which escapes your control - often without your knowledge or consent.

You can't navigate the territory without a map - and financial records plot the terrain. Welcome to financial record keeping for fun and profit!

In Chapter Two, you discovered that you could acquire, and spend, lots of money while remaining painfully ignorant of your financial situation - aside from knowing that you need your paycheck to keep you out of trouble. Even though you may have had the best education possible, your financial education is probably woefully inadequate.

When was the last time you received information about an insurance policy, credit agreement, tax service, or investment product from someone who wasn't trying to sell it to you? Even if your parents trained you in basic financial skills, in the last fifteen years the world of money has changed in a very important way. Advertising and marketing have become the primary vehicles for *educating* the public about money, often bombarding us with messages that directly contradict common sense and sanity. Let's see how this happens.

## Financial Facts vs. Financial Fiction

Next time you spend an hour or two in front of the tube, notice the commercials for credit cards, investment funds, automobiles, brokerage firms, banks, financial consultants, money magazines and loan companies. Don't even try to pay attention to all the subtle, tricky marketing techniques - just *count* them. If you listen to your local news radio as you drive to work, just *count* the number of ads which quote interest rates, APRs, zero-down payment/six months cash payment plans, and so on. The sheer repetition of buzzwords creates an illusion that we know what they mean. So we assume that all the marketing out there is somehow based on facts.

Not true - not *completely* true, anyway. Successful marketing depends on giving you just enough information to intrigue you. Enticement is the name of the game - not enlightenment. **All sizzle and no steak**. Throwing out phrases like "2.9 percent financing" while that scrumptious automobile navigates the *autobahn* can make even a hard-boiled cynic like me salivate! Nobody's lying to you in this commercial - well, not exactly. But the rest of the facts - the required down payment, the number of months, the actual cost of the car after all those months - gets buried in that fine print flashed for 10 seconds at the bottom of your TV screen.

If knowledge is power, then a little knowledge can be a very dangerous thing. Incomplete and fuzzy half-truths are the enemy of financial fitness. Don't become a victim of *fuzzy math*. Ask yourself - do you *believe* the half-truths of advertising because they help you lie to yourself? "I really did get a good deal on that new car!" "Look at all the benefits my credit card gives me!" "I need that extended warranty - what if my computer breaks down?"

Making decisions based on inadequate information is living a financial lie. You do have a weapon - knowledge. But you must know how to use it properly or it will backfire on you. You must take action with your newly acquired knowledge. The cumulative effect of this may be costing you thousands of dollars a year - money that reaps no reward. Your financial documents and records contain all the facts - the facts you need to protect yourself.

If you already keep good records, you know what I am talking about. Skim this chapter for some helpful tips, and then skip to Chapter Five.

If you don't keep financial records, it's time to complete the fact-finding mission we started in the previous chapter. Half your work has been done. Follow the instructions in the next section. Within a couple of hours of gathering your supplies you will have an easy, low maintenance record-keeping system. You will also be twice as financially powerful. If you need motivation, remember that what you don't know is hurting you - right now, in your wallet. Ignorance is not bliss. **Get started now!**

## The One-Minute Financial Filing System

I always wonder about people who complain about the piles of paperwork looming over them. Paper shouldn't control you - it's just *paper*, not some ugly behemoth monster from hell waiting to bite you. Of course, most people procrastinate because of *anxiety* - the anxiety of worrying about the stack of paper is preferable to the anxiety of actually sorting through, and understanding, what's in that stack. Most people know instinctively that there are some nasty little surprises lurking in those documents.

Do you use a financial software package like *Quicken or Peach Tree*? Don't assume that you don't need to keep a filing system. Computers are great for speeding up tedious processes like reconciling your bank statements. But remember - garbage in, garbage out. Your computer won't tell you that you are wasting 30% of your monthly income on non-deductible interest payments, useless credit insurance, or overpriced travel. Even if it could, you must feed relevant information into your software - and the only place to get that information is from your financial documents.

Daily record keeping is where small steps, performed consistently, reap massive rewards. The test of a good system is whether it is easy to maintain. This one is. Implement it today.

### *Step One: Acquire the five essential office organization tools.*
You won't maintain your files if you don't make it easy on yourself. Whether you get them new, used, or from the recycling bin at your office, you need the following supplies:

- A two-drawer filing cabinet
- Manila folders (50 to start)
- A calculator (if it prints, get register tape to fit)
- An In/Out box (anything that will hold standard sheets of paper)
- Sticky notes (3" square or larger)

Okay, you will have to buy sticky notes. They may seem like a luxury. They're not. Staples, scotch tape, and paper clips will substitute, but only if you keep them handy. We are trying to eliminate excuses here. Staplers, like scissors and tape, are never around when you need them, and offer a perfect excuse to do something other than your record keeping. Paper clips, and the papers attached to them, have a funny way of getting lost. An economy-sized package of sticky notes, purchased at an office supplies warehouse or Sam's, will provide a dozen or more little pads. Keep them handy - six in the bottom drawer of your file cabinet, the rest scattered in every conceivable place you can reach. No lack of supplies - no excuses. If you purchased your office supplies, save the receipts.

### *Step Two: Spend 15 minutes creating a filing system.*
That's all it takes - 15 minutes. Take out your manila folders. Make one for each of the following categories:

**Automobile** - Contracts, warranties
**Automobile** - Receipts
**Bank** - Accounts, deposit slips, canceled checks
**Bank** - Correspondence
**Bills** - Unpaid
**Credit** - Bureau reports
**Credit** - Unsecured, paid bills and statements
**Dentist** - Receipts, records
**Doctor(s)** - Receipts, records
**Employment** - Contract, handbook, pay stubs, resume
**Home** - Mortgage, receipts, leases
**Insurance** - Auto
**Insurance** - Health
**Insurance** - Home
**Insurance** - Life
**Investments** - Annuity, IRA, miscellaneous
**Investments** - Bonds, mutual funds, stocks
**Investments** - Real estate
**Other Stuff**
**Personal** - Documents
**Personal** - Fun
**Receipts** - Any kind
**Taxes** - documents, returns
**Telephone** - bills
**Travel** - brochures, maps, receipts, tickets
**Utilities** - bills
**Warranties** - guarantees, instructions, receipts
**Will/Estate**

It should take about 15-20 minutes to make these folders. These basic categories will work for the average individual or couple. If you have children, you might want to have separate Dentist and Doctor Files for your kids. You might also want a file called Education, for your children or for you, especially if you attend classes, seminars, or workshops on a regular basis. And if you have been wise enough to make investments, you might wish to have separate folders for each type.

### For the Record Keeping Sophisticate

Perhaps you already keep good records - but you pay dearly for their maintenance. If you are self-employed, own a business, manage real estate, or maintain an office outside your home, record keeping is already part of your wealth-building plan. You probably keep separate personal and business records.

Spend 10-15 minutes right now reviewing your systems. Of course, if it's not broken, don't fix it. But ask yourself a few questions. Am I spending valuable time on routine activities? Do I *need* all this paper? Are my files complete - or are there gaps? Could my files be simplified? What about other systematic tasks? Then ask yourself: How much is my time worth? Should I employ someone to maintain this stuff, so I can spend more time creating wealth?

Wealth is synonymous with quality of life. Stop right now and do a quick calculation of the average number of hours you spend on routine paper pushing. If you had that time for other activities, how would you spend it? Would you use it to generate more business, explore new opportunities, take some classes, play with your kids, exercise, read, write, paint, redecorate, travel and relax?

Promise yourself that you will investigate buying basic services, like accounts payable and receivable, payroll, merchant accounts, even paying your bills, from an outside vendor or an online service. Make a note in your calendar to do it tomorrow - or better yet, do it now! Check the yellow pages, call other business people in your area and contact your local Chamber of Commerce for referrals. *Remember, even though you may have achieved success, to attain financial fitness you must give it the time, discipline, and creativity it deserves.*

Once you've made your file folders, stash them in your file cabinet.

### *Step Three: Complete your first filing assignment.*
Remember the receipts from your office supplies purchases in Step One? Go find them. Look at them. If they are not itemized - if "Post-It Notes" or "Filing Cabinet" is not printed on the receipts - write "Filing System" on the back of each receipt. Throw them in the Receipts folder.

Pat yourself on the back. Go on to Step Four.

### *Step Four: File the rest of your documents.*
Go get that pile of papers you have already collected. Stuff them all in your In Box. Now put on some energetic music. Take a deep breath. Start filing.

Depending on the number of documents, this should take anywhere from 10 to 30 minutes. Use common sense. Got a bunch of unpaid bills? That's easy. Do you have the maintenance log for your car? If you don't have receipts for the work, throw it in Auto - Contracts, warranties. If you have to be psychic to know what a receipt is for, toss it in Receipts - Any kind. Did you find a quarterly report for your employer's retirement plan? Look at it for a moment - is it an annuity? If you can't tell, throw it in Investments - Annuities, IRAs, miscellaneous for now. *The idea is to control the paper so it doesn't control you - not to spend an hour reading a report you've never read before!*

If you think something should go in two different folders, write the name of the file category on a sticky note, stick it on the document, and file it wherever you are most likely to look first.

If you think a document is incomplete, write that on a sticky note, attach, and file. Example: WHERE'S THE EXTENDED WARRANTY?

If you don't know where to file something, throw it in Other Stuff.

Handle each piece of paper only once. Do not throw it back in the In Box.

When you are finished, every piece of paper should be someplace.

### Step Five: One-Minute File Management.

The simplest way to screw up your filing system is not to use it. So make a solemn promise to yourself, right now, that you will spend 60 seconds, every day, six days a week, maintaining your filing system. (Take Sundays and holidays off - there's no mail delivery on those days.)

The "In" and "Out" Boxes, and your sticky notes are your daily maintenance tools. Here are the steps:

**1. Empty your mailbox daily** and put everything in the In Box. (Your kids might like doing this for you.)

**2. Empty your pockets, wallet, briefcase, or purse of all receipts daily.** Put them in the In Box also. (Your kids may want to empty your pockets, too!)

**3.** Each morning, evening, whenever, **spend 60 seconds performing Step Four on the In Box.** Open mail, throw away junk, file unpaid bills, make notes on receipts and toss them in files. If it takes more than 60 seconds - say 120 seconds – and don't worry, it won't hurt you.

**4. Use the Out Box for outgoing mail, bills you need to pay now, magazines you want to take to work, and anything else that's going OUT.** Write instructions, questions, and notes to yourself on the stickups. Every week, do the paperwork in your Out Box.

**5. Once every two weeks, look in your Other Stuff file.** As you use this book, your Other Stuff will get smaller and smaller. You will know what you need to keep, and what you can safely discard.

**6. Once a month reconcile your checking account promptly.** If you own a computer, purchase software like *Quicken*, and learn to use it. (Save the receipt for your file!)

Use the few minutes you spend balancing your checkbook to flag tax deductions, check for bank errors, and note just how much the bank is charging you for transaction fees. If your bank doesn't return your canceled checks, ask for them. You might need them to prove that you paid a bill. You can also circle the check numbers on possible tax deductions.

## Checking Account Basics
It doesn't matter whether you have $100 or $100,000 - if you have never balanced your checking account, learn to do it. It can cost you money - lots of it - if you don't. Banks charge anywhere from $15 to $25 *per item* for non-sufficient funds, and many of them will do so *even if you are 10 cents overdrawn!* Doesn't seem fair? Banks are businesses, out to make a profit - and that's easy money for them. So protect yourself. Use the reconciliation form on the back of your statement. Here's the basic procedure. (It sounds more complicated when you read it than when you do it.)

### *Basic Checking Account Balancing*
1. Make sure deposits are recorded correctly (compare your receipts with the statement).
2. Take out your check register. Make sure checks, ATM/Debit Card transactions, and automatic debits are deducted correctly on the statement.
3. In your check register mark off each check, ATM debit, automatic debit, and all the deposits that the bank shows on its statement.

4. Add any deposits not recorded by the bank to the statement bottom line - and *call your bank to make sure the money was credited!*

5. Subtract any outstanding checks or automatic debits from the statement bottom line.

6. Find all those "bank fees" and subtract them from the balance in your register.

7. Compare the balance on the statement to the balance on your register. They should tally.

Many people now pay for items using their Debit Card or Check Card with the Visa or MasterCard logos on them. Unlike credit cards, any charges made with your Debit Card are immediately deducted from the balance in your checking account. However, they forget to immediately deduct this amount on their check register. These forgotten charges may end up costing you NSF fees on your account so be careful.

*If the bank statement is higher,* check to see if your account is earning any interest - if so, add that to your register balance.

*If the bank statement is lower,* double-check your work, even if it's only a few cents off. If you didn't forget to record a check, ATM, or automatic debit, call your bank. Banks make mistakes, and are often inconsistent in recording automatic debits for insurance, car payments, mortgage payments, or rent on the same day. Those errors and inconsistencies can cost you money, so call.

## Protect Your Papers

If you have a safety deposit box or home safe, these pieces of paper should be stored there: birth certificates, marriage licenses, and diplomas; passports and discharge papers; titles and deeds of all types; a copy of your will and estate plan; property lists and photos for insurance purposes; and shares of stocks, bonds, and mutual funds. It's not just that these documents are difficult or impossible to replace.

<u>If something happened to you or your home your family needs quick access to complete estate and insurance documentation.</u> I wouldn't normally advocate keeping idle cash, but a couple of hundred dollars stored in the box could prove a lifesaver if credit cards, ATM cards, or checkbooks are lost in a disaster.

Remember to make hard copies of all computer-generated financial records, especially tax returns. You know how computers are. Your hard drive can fail. You accidentally delete a file. You back up your documents on disk, and lose the disks. So protect your documents and keep printed copies.

Consider the cost of storing documents. Over the long term, a safe deposit box will cost more because you rent it annually. But if you don't have a permanently installed fireproof (and preferably waterproof) safe, which can run several hundred dollars or more, a safe deposit box, at about $50 per year, is the most secure place for your valuables. Save the receipt or statement showing the cost of your document storage.

### If You Keep Tax Deduction Records - Or If You Don't!

Many people don't bother keeping good financial records because they don't itemize deductions. "I don't own a house yet," they say, "so why should I bother keeping all those receipts and papers? I wouldn't have enough deductions to itemize!"

My response is, *"How do you know?"*

If you don't have the information, how do you know that's true? You don't. This is precisely the type of fuzzy, lazy thinking which prevents many people from achieving financial fitness. *To become financially fit, you must have the facts - especially about taxes.*

Keeping track of possible deductions takes a minute or two a day. That's not much more time than basic records management. If that minute or two could save you $1,000 or more, every year, for the rest of your life, wouldn't that increase your lifetime income substantially? Say you go out and spend $100 on office supplies: a cartridge for your ink-jet printer, a box of paper, manila folders, sticky notes, and a file cabinet. If you can make those purchases deductible, give yourself $30 in REWARDS. That's right - the tax savings yield a return of 30%! If you hit the maximum tax bracket, and include state taxes, you could save much more.

Because of recent changes in tax laws, especially the elimination of the consumer interest deduction and the lowering of business entertainment deductions, many non-home owners assume they can't itemize. Don't make this costly assumption. As an experiment, start to implement tax-saving records management today. Become more aggressive. Give tax savings a chance, especially if you are self-employed, a business owner, a salesperson, a freelancer, or run a part-time, home-based business. By law, it is *your* responsibility to back up your deductions with good records. You should also consider this part of the responsibility you have to yourself - to make yourself richer.

So implement the following five record keeping steps to give yourself a fighting chance at tax time.

### *Tax Step One: Arm Yourself*

- **Buy an expense log at an office supplies store.** (They have pre-printed columns for meals, gasoline, entertainment, lodging, etc.) Save the receipt.
- **Get a debit card, or set aside one credit card, for deductible expenses.** The advantage of a debit card, which works like a check, is that you don't pay interest on the balance - and it can't get you in credit trouble. Either way, these cards generate immediate receipts, a big record-keeping advantage.
- **Call the IRS** and get Publication 17 (General Income Tax). If you are self-employed or own a business, you will also need 334 (Small Business Taxes), 463 (Car

Expenses), 534 (Depreciation), and 535 (Business Expenses). If you sell products or work out of your home, you will probably need 538 (Inventories) or 587 ("Use of Home).

- **Order any and every IRS form you think you might need.** Consider purchasing tax preparation software for your computer, which will automatically generate forms. (The software is deductible - save your receipt). You will learn more about tax strategies in Chapter Nine, but you can make learning easier by having copies of the forms available ahead of time.

*Tax Step Two: Know Your Possible Deductions.*
Memorize this list. These purchases must be documented:
- Office supplies and equipment
- Travel and related expenses
- Automobile expenses (don't forget tolls and parking)
- Food, especially restaurant meals
- Entertainment
- Repairs
- Books, Magazines, Newsletters
- Business/educational video & audio cassettes
- Contributions (don't forget small church offerings paid in cash)
- Salaries you pay to others
- Services (don't forget investment and tax consultants)
- Blank audio and video tapes
- Advertising, including graphic design and printing

*Tax Step Three: Start Keeping Records.*
If an expense is *under* $25, record it in your log when you pay for it.
If an expense is *over* $25, record it in your log when you pay for it and get a receipt. Write what happened on the receipt ("Dinner

with Tom and Eric to discuss marketing their product"). Make sure you save the receipt that night in your files.

Get receipts for all lodging expenses, no matter how much they cost. (This is an IRS rule.)

Every time you balance your checking account, use a colored marker to circle the check number of every possible deductible expense. According to the IRS, you still need receipts - canceled checks, by themselves, are not sufficient documentation. But flagging them helps you match them up with your receipts when tax time rolls around, saving time, saving stress, giving you an incentive to work for the greatest number of deductions.

If you own a PDA, carry it with you at all times and enter your expenses as you pay for them. Get receipts for anything over $25. (Save the receipt if you buy a PDA.)

### *Tax Step Four: Keep 90-Day Logs To Get Deductions On Assets.*
Many assets - VCRs, cameras, camcorders, tools, office furniture, home, laptop, or pocket computers - can yield significant tax deductions. But you must keep track of how often you use them for your small business, financial planning, or investment and tax education, analysis, and record keeping.

An asset usage record is simple - and you only have to maintain it for 90 days. Tape a sheet of paper on each item. As you use each piece of equipment, write down the date, the time you begin using it, the time you stop using it, and what you use it for - deductible or non-deductible activity.

Deductible activities are mentioned above. Non-deductible activities are personal, entertainment, or child usage. After 90 days, sit down with your calculator and get three totals: your deductible usage, your non-deductible usage, and the grand total. Divide the deductible time by the grand total. If you use your asset more than 50% of the time for deductible activity, check out the section on asset expensing in IRS Publication 334. This can generate a substantial, immediate tax saving - up to $50,000 in your first year - and all you did was take a few notes for a few months.

### *Tax Step Five: Keep a Mileage Log In Your Automobile*

If you are self-employed, or if you own even a part-time home business, your car can generate powerful tax deductions. Determining your business use mileage is the key. Here are the record-keeping steps:

- Get an automobile expense and mileage logbook. Keep it in your car.
- Record the date and mileage. It's ideal to start on January 1, but begin whenever you start using your car for business.
- Every time you use your car for business, log the number of miles.
- When the tax year is over, divide the number of business miles by the total mileage. Depending on the percentage, you can either use the Actual Cost Method or the Standard Mileage Rate to compute your deduction.

Don't be frightened off - it's not as complicated as it sounds. IRS Form 2106 is a great worksheet for calculating your automobile deductions both ways - once you've done that, you can choose the biggest deduction. But for now, just promise yourself you will keep good records. Without them, the system can only work against - not for - your financial freedom.

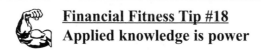

**Financial Fitness Tip #18**
**Applied knowledge is power**

Becoming financially fit is a process. As you experience each stage of the process, you begin to think about money and wealth with more and more discipline, detachment, and insight. You see money for what it is - energy, a force - nothing more, but nothing less either. You begin to notice how you can lose it, not through some catastrophe, but through simple thoughtlessness.

Even though money and wealth are not the same, they are intimately related, the way laughter and happiness are related and the way passion and romantic love are related. It reminds of that line in *Quiz Show*: "You'll forgive me, but anybody who ever thinks money is *just* money couldn't have much of it." The simple experiences of the last two chapters have demonstrated that reality - money isn't everything, but it has a powerful effect on our lives whether we are conscious of it or not.

Do you know where your money is? Do you know what it's doing? Do you know if it's leaking away? Do you know how it's changing your future, for better or worse? All the housekeeping in this chapter was designed to put the answers to those questions right where you can get them. This knowledge will help you as you work through this book, but it will also help you maintain an organized life. Apply some of these management techniques to your hobbies, your education and your personal library, even your messy garage. Teach them to your kids and watch their schoolwork, rooms, toys become more organized. Think that's wishful thinking? How do you know?

## BANKING BONUS SECTION

### *Personal Bankers*

The friendly neighborhood bank is a thing of the past. There have been many local banks, savings and loans, and even credit unions have been swallowed up by big impersonal financial institutions. Up until a few years ago it was still possible to develop a relationship with a loan officer, bookkeeper, or branch manager - someone who knew you by your first name, lived in your neighborhood, shopped at the same stores, served on the PTA. Your business was important to that person - and you knew he or she could give you good advice, and maybe even a lucky break, when you had financial problems.

Try walking into a bank's branch office now. You may be hard pressed to find any *people* in there at all, aside from a security guard or two. ATMs, telephones, and online banking have added lots of convenience to our lives. But the result is that most personal banking has become impersonal banking - and that's unfortunate for consumers.

When it was still possible to get to know a loan officer or manager personally, you could find out their lending limit for automobile, personal, and business loans - and develop a respectful working relationship within those boundaries. You had someone to turn to in emergencies - when you couldn't get to the bank to transfer money, when you made a mistake in your arithmetic and needed some checks covered, or when a flood or fire destroyed your personal property - including wallets and identification - and you needed cash for a motel and food.

Unfortunately, this type of personal banker is an endangered species. No matter how much we hope and pray, the banking industry is phasing out most forms of personal service for all but the rich. If you have a good relationship with a banker, count your blessings, and treat that relationship with the same care and tact that you would give your spouse and children. If you don't know your banker personally, give it your best effort - but don't be disappointed if you find yourself talking to a bureaucrat imported from the parent company. When you shop for a bank, check out the ones with local names and local reputations. Ask your neighbors and friends to introduce you to their banker - especially if they have their own businesses or have lived in your neighborhood all their lives. Even though your chances of success decrease daily, it is still worth it to search for a banker you can know, and work with, for many years.

## *Choosing A Bank*

Finding a personal banker is important. But what if you are just starting out? All you need is checking and an ATM card - so aren't all banks the same?

As you saw in Chapter Two, you can pay dearly for basic banking services, even if all you're paying for is some computer time! Shop around.  Here are some guidelines:

**1.  Find a bank that won't hold your check deposits.** Have you ever deposited your paycheck at the drive-up window, and tried to get some of that money from an ATM two days later without success? Banks can legally "hold" any checks you deposit. The time period is anywhere from two to seven business days, depending on whether it's a local, out-of-town or an out-of-state check. Banks claim that they are protecting themselves from those "bad" checks lurking out there - but your *paycheck?*

It's all smoke and mirrors - your bank gets the money from the Federal Reserve within roughly 24 hours of your deposit, no matter what. The "holding" period allows banks to use your money - lend it, invest it, maintain its own cash flow with it - and not pay you a cent of interest for the privilege. And if you happen to write a check against those "held" deposits, your bank can charge you a $25 NSF fee and bounce that check - even though it has had the money for a couple of days.

The good news is that **banks are not required to hold your checks.** That means some banks only hold a deposit for 24 hours, **and some banks will waive the holding period if you ask them to.** Make a few phone calls to local banks. Ask for someone in new accounts - not just the switchboard operator. You may need to do some other business with the bank - a car loan, a mortgage, a personal loan and a savings account - before the holding period is suspended. When it is, be sure that the branch manager inserts notes, in writing on your account. Confirm it in writing, with a request that you be notified of any change in that policy in advance.

**2.  Find a bank that will give you automatic overdraft protection.** It costs less than a dollar to process an NSF check - but your bank will charge you a $25 fee. I've heard of one bank that charges **up to $120** for an NSF fee! Make sure you get NSF policies in writing. Compare them at different banks. If you keep a high minimum balance some banks will *pay* your NSF checks - but they usually still charge the NSF fees. Don't make the mistake of thinking that your bank will automatically transfer money from savings into checking. You can do that from an ATM or even online these days, but *you* have to do it. See if you can make an arrangement with the bank, in writing, to charge your Visa or MasterCard for any NSF - and that the NSF fees will be waived!

Some banks may offer you a small line of credit (say $1,000) if you keep a high minimum balance (say $5,000). That's rarely a good value, since that $5,000 will only earn a few percent in interest. You'd be better off shopping around, watching your account like a hawk, and balancing your checkbook religiously every month.

**3.  Learn the difference between a *money market mutual fund account* and a *money market account*.** Talk about semantics. These may sound the same, but they are two completely different animals.

A *money market mutual fund account* is an investment account. You don't make deposits at a bank - you make them in the fund. These funds are listed in the newspaper, just like stocks. Whatever you deposit is invested in "shares" in a variety of interest-bearing instruments: jumbo bank CDs, U.S. government securities (like Treasury bills), brokerage repurchase agreements, and so on. Starting deposits are low - around $100 to $500. Some even have no minimum deposit. You earn higher than average interest rates on your balance. And even though these accounts charge you one-half to one percent as a management fee, you can write checks against the account - usually 3 per month. Your interest earnings are automatically reinvested in more shares.

Doesn't this sound like a great place to keep cash that you might need for liquidity? It's better than letting it sit around in conventional checking, or an ordinary savings account, where it's bound to earn the lowest possible rate of interest. In the section on investments, I'll explain some ground rules for deciding whether this is the best place to keep cash. The important thing is not to confuse this with a money market account at your bank.

A *money market account* is a slick name for a checking/savings account that pays a variable rate of interest. While that may be slightly better than your basic checking account, it's never as good as a money market fund account. The difference can be anywhere between one and several percent. Don't be fooled into choosing a money market account at your local bank. It's never a good value.

Remember to look for the word *fund.* If fund is missing, and it's a bank account, then it's just plain old savings or checking that pays minimally higher interest - and usually demands a large minimum balance.

**4. Never keep money in a business checking account if you can help it.** Banks don't pay interest on these accounts.

They will also kill you on transaction fees, not just charging you for every check you write, but every deposit you make. Choose to keep large cash balances, like accounts payable or tax payments, in the money market fund account described above. You'll earn hundreds, maybe thousands in interest if your balances are high, you can write a check to deposit in your business checking account whenever you wish, or you can arrange for wire transfers if you need access to funds immediately. So keep only the minimum balance required in your checking.  The balance of your money should be in a money market mutual fund.

**5. Get rid of your savings account at the bank and put your money in a no-load mutual fund.** While your savings account might earn a *staggering* 1% per year, it's not uncommon for a no-load mutual fund to earn 10-20%+ per year. Some of these mutual funds have very small initial investments. Obviously, as with any investment, a higher rate of return directly correlates with a higher degree of risk. Please investigate any mutual fund before investing.

---

**One of the many great features of mutual funds is that many mutual fund families offer a feature called *Automatic Withdrawal*. With this wonderful tool, you can have a mutual fund family automatically deduct funds from your checking or savings account. You can set the amount you want deducted. This can be as little as $25 per month. What a great way to force you to save for your retirement!**

---

**6. Considering opening an Asset Management Account (AMA) in lieu of a checking account.** Some banks may offer this type of an account in their "Securities" office.

*Nothing in the world can take place of persistence.*
*Talent will not: nothing is more common than*
*unsuccessful people with talent. Genius will not:*
*unrewarded genius is almost a proverb. Education will not:*
*the world is full of educated derelicts. Persistance and*
*dertermination alone are omnipotent.*
- Thomas Watson, founder of IBM

## Summary of Chapter Four

Bodybuilders always use the term, "No pain – no gain." Well in Chapter Four, we've taken an exercise that most people call *painful* and turned it in to an easy task. You learned how to:

- Develop an easy to use 15-minute filing system.

- Determine what is deductible.

- Determine how to choose a bank.

- Learn the difference between a Money Market Account and a Money Market Mutual Fund.

- Open up a mutual fund account instead of a savings account.

# Chapter Five

# *Every Financially Fit Person Should*

# *Workout With Someone Named "IRA"*

*The gratification of wealth is not found in mere possession or lavish expenditure but in its wise application.*
- Miguel DeCervantes

This is only one of the many ways you can invest your 10% savings program. Any contributions you make to your retirement plan are tax deductible (depending on the plan you choose). Your money is compounding tax-free. This double tax-free compounding effect is what will eventually make you wealthy.

### The IRA: One Reason You Can Love The IRS
Okay, I know it's unfashionable to like the IRS - the government agency we all love to hate. But an IRA is still one of the best, certainly one of the easiest investments you can make. They are simple, you can open one quickly, and they are well within the reach of the average American. IRAs, along with Keoghs, are one of the nicest things the IRS has ever done for us - so instead of being ungrateful, let's pause for a moment and say thank you to the Big Bad Internal Revenue Service with our next Financial Fitness Tip:

---

 **Financial Fitness Tip #19**
**Never underestimate the power of an IRA**

---

In case you've just landed from planet Pluto, IRA stands for *Individual Retirement Account*. It's a tax-deferred retirement account - you don't pay any taxes on the investment until you withdraw the money at retirement. The idea is simple - save on taxes while you're stashing money away. Then when you retire and are no longer in the higher wage-earner tax bracket, withdraw your money and pay less in taxes. Great concept - it's simple, it's sane and it's easy to love.

Many people don't realize that an IRA can hold just about any type of an investment, not just cash. You can use a self-directed (who you can direct the investments) IRA to invest in stocks, bonds, CDs, money market fund, stock or bond funds, real estate or even a government guaranteed high-yielding tax lien certificates. Can you imagine how big your fortune could be if your IRA purchased tax lien certificates earning 18% over a period of ten to twenty years. The number would be OBSCENE!

It's also not common knowledge that anyone can set up an IRA - there's no upper age limit, so you can start them for kids - as long as the contribution to the IRA does not exceed their annual income, or $3,000, whichever is less.

How come you don't pay taxes on your investment in an IRA? The money you contribute to an IRA is pre-tax dollars. Pre-tax means you get to deduct the dollar value of the contribution from your Adjusted Gross Income (AGI) on your tax return. Based on your AGI, you're limited to how much of your IRA contribution qualifies for this pre-tax status.

Remember that if you don't qualify for the deduction, you call still open an IRA. Your contribution may not be tax-deductible, but they will still be tax-deferred. *This is the power of compounded interest that I discussed earlier.*

There are two types of retirement plans: one that is created by your employer or one that you create yourself. In order to qualify, you must have "earned income." Earned income is money that you receive from your employer, such as salary, commission or bonus.

Investment income is not considered earned income in this situation. I would strongly urge you use a plan that you create yourself, so you can direct your investment without having to pay any commission or loads on your investments.

If your employer offers a retirement plan - profit sharing, 401(k), 403(b), 457, SEP - find out if they will give you any *matching funds*. If they do, this will only quicken your pace in achieving financial independence.

- **401(k) - Deferred Compensation Plan for Corporate Employees**

    Most 401(k) plans offer mutual funds as investment options. If you are a part of a union, you may have separate pension plan which you have no control over.

- **403(b) - Deferred Compensation Plan (Tax-sheltered Annuity) for Public Schools and Nonprofit Organization Employees**

    Public schools are also covered by a separate pension plan, which you have no control over.

- **457 - Deferred Compensation Plan for State, County and City Employees**

- **408(k) SEP - Simplified Employee Pension Plan for Employees of Small Companies** (less than 25 employees)

- **SIMPLE 401(k) - Deferred Compensation Plan** (for corporations, partnerships, "S" corporations, sole proprietorships, tax-exempt employers and government entities with no more than 100 persons receiving less than $5,000 in compensation during the year).

- **Keogh Plans (HR10)** – Tax advantaged personal retirement program that can be established by a self-employed individual.

- **IRA – Individual Retirement Account (deductible)**

- **IRA – Individual Retirement Account (non-deductible)**

- **Roth IRA – Individual Retirement Account** (contributions are NOT deductible but monies can be withdrawn penalty-free depending on when the taxpayer withdraws the money)
- **Educational IRA – Individual Retirement Account** (a non-deductible contribution of up to $500 per beneficiary. The earnings will be distributed tax-free provided that they are used to pay the beneficiary's postsecondary education expenses.)

*If one advances confidently in the direction of his dreams, and endeavors to live the life which he has imagined, he will never meet with a success unexpected in common hours.*
- Henry David Thoreau

## IRA COMPARISON CHART

|  | Traditional IRA | Roth IRA | Education IRA | Non-Deductible |
|---|---|---|---|---|
| Purpose | Retirement | Retirement | Education (tuition) | Retirement |
| Max. Contrib. | $3,000/person less other IRAs, except Education IRA | $3,000/person less other IRAs, except Education IRA | $500 per child combined | varies |
| Yearly Deadline | April 15 | April 15 | April 15 or end of tax year | April 15 |
| Who's Eligible? | Individuals with earned income; or non-working spouse | Earned income; non-income; or non-working spouse | Child under 18; by parent/grandparent | Earned income; non-income; or non-working spouse |
| Advantage | Contributions tax-deductible; growth tax-deferred; self-directed contributions | Tax-free growth/withdrawals after 5 years; no penalty on withdrawals before 59 1/2 if for education | No tax on earnings or withdrawals; transferable to another child or grandchild | Growth tax deferred; self-directed. |
| Disadvantage | Penalties for early withdrawals - no borrowing allowed. | Contribution not deductible | Contribution not deductible; for child's education only | Contribution not deductible; penalties and no borrowing allowed |

| | Tax-deferred | Tax-free | Tax-free for education | Tax-deferred |
|---|---|---|---|---|
| Earnings | Tax-deferred | Tax-free | Tax-free for education | Tax-deferred |
| Tax on Distributions | Treated as income 10% penalty before age 59 ½ * | Tax free - no penalty on withdrawals before 59 ½ if for education | Tax-free if for education - 10% penalty plus tax on balance | Tax on growth - 10% penalty before 59 ½ |
| Age Limit for Contributions | 70 ½ | None required | Child must be under 18 | 70 ½ |
| Mandatory Withdrawals Begin | 70 ½ | None required | Age 30 or rolled over to Education IRA | 70 ½ |
| Rollover | Yes | Yes | Yes, to sibling's IRA | Yes |
| Penalty for Excess Contributions | Yes | Yes | Yes | Yes |
| Penalty for Early Withdrawals | 10% | 10% before 59 ½ - none for education | 10% unless for educational purposes | 10% |

* There is no penalty before age 59 ½, if a distribution of up to $10,000 is used for your first home, for your children, grandchildren or qualified educational expenses.

> ### Financial Fitness Tip #19
> ### If you work for yourself, start a SEP or KEOGH

Keoghs work just like IRAs, only much, much better. They're for those of us who are self-employed. If you own a business or plan to start one, remember the following:

1.  Contribute to the maximum. There are two kinds of plans - defined benefit and defined contribution, and you'll have to check the IRS rules to determine which will allow you to get the best tax savings. Either way, you will be able to contribute much, much more than you ever could to an IRA - and reap massive AGI rewards. Go for maximum tax savings impact - when you are self-employed you need these since your income/cash flow is likely to be as high as your expenses.

2.  If you have employees, choose a profit-sharing Keogh. That's because you are required to include them in a Keogh if you start one for yourself. With a profit-sharing plan, you contribute only if you have profits. A great motivator and benefit to you in lean years. If you don't have employees, a money purchase plan, where you contribute a set number of dollars each year, will work fine.

3.  If you are over 50, choose a defined benefits plan. That's where you decide how much you're going to be withdrawing from your Keogh after you retire. The rules for determining what you can contribute for your employees, will vary depending on your individual circumstances. You *can* calculate this yourself by thinking of this as a word problem: How much do I need to contribute each year for XX years to retire at age XX, with an income of $XX,XXX from an investment paying

X%? Here's why you have a trustee - to help you with the calculation and do the paperwork once your contribution amount is defined.

4. Set up a Keogh trust to get the most profit from your Keogh dollars. Never ever put your Keogh money in a CD - the interest is usually terrible - the paperwork is easy, but you'll lose so much potential profit it just isn't worth it. Instead, the trust will allow you to invest your Keogh in any investment, so long as the law permits. You can even have the IRS review your plan in advance to make sure it's okay - get a letter of determination, Form 5300. Don't join a group master plan, offered by some banks, mutual funds, trade associations, and insurance companies - your investment choices are limited, and that means so are your profits.

5. If you hire your spouse, you can increase your maximum yearly contribution. Even though this is income for your spouse and has been declared on your taxes, it's tax deductible to you - an even trade. And your spouse's contributions are deductible on your return.

As of this writing, you can invest your Keogh in almost anything except collectibles or even a mortgaged property where the account might be considered collateral against the loan.

**Financial Fitness Tip #20**
**Make maximum contributions to your KEOGH plan**

Since the benefits are so substantial, you will want to make the maximum contributions to your Keogh plan. Your maximum contribution will depend on whether it is a *defined contribution plan* or a *defined benefit plan*.

If your Keogh is a defined contribution plan, your annual contributions and other additions in 2004 – except for earnings – to an account cannot exceed 100% of the compensation actually paid to the participant or $41,000 (whichever is less).

In the year 2004, the annual benefit for a defined benefit plan participant cannot exceed the lesser of 100% of the participant's average compensation for their highest three consecutive years or $165,000.

Make sure you speak with your accountant or CPA to make sure you receive the maximum benefits of this powerful investment vehicle.

---

**Financial Fitness Tip #21**
**Don't invest your KEOGH or IRA in a**
**tax shelter - it's silly!**

---

You can't take a tax deduction over and over on the same investment. Both your contribution to an IRA or Keogh *and* your earnings are already tax sheltered, so don't put them into tax-exempt securities of any kind, tax-sheltered limited partnerships, or annuities. Since the return on these before taxes is lower than other investments, why lose the profits? Instead, go for tax lien certificates, mutual funds, real estate options, or discounted mortgages.

---

**Financial Fitness Tip # 22**
**Rollover and keep those profits movin'**

---

You don't have to keep your Keogh or IRA in a bank - in fact, that's one of the worst places to keep it! Upgrade to better investments with rollover rules that really do give you substantial control over these important funds. Just make sure you roll over the funds directly into similar fund, plan, or from one trustee to another. If you withdraw the money yourself and then reinvest it, you might end up paying a withholding penalty and pay an additional early withdrawal penalty. OUCH!

 **<u>Financial Fitness Tip #23</u>**
**Get an independent trustee or open a self-directed account for better results**

There is no law that says you can't choose your own IRA or Keogh investments. All you need to do is open a self-directed account. You can do that with a brokerage firm, mutual fund family, or with the help of an independent trustee. This is the best way to make sure your funds are earning the maximum so you can take advantage of investment shifting (which I will discuss later) and with that, you have a full range of investment options.

You will need an independent trustee if you want to invest in tax liens, real estate, or discount mortgages – law requires it.

Here is a sample list of a few Self-Directed IRA Trustees to get you started. You can look in your telephone book or the Internet to find more of them.

| Name | Phone | Website |
|------|-------|---------|
| Entrust | 800-392-9653 | www.entrustadmin.com |
| UMB Bank | 800-996-2862 | www.umb.com |
| Millennium Trust | 800-258-7878 | www.mtrustcompany.com |
| Wash. Mutual | 800-331-3426 | www.wmfinancial.com |
| Fiserve Corp | 800-872-7882 | www.fiserve.com |

---

 **Financial Fitness Tip #24**
**Choose an investment option that fits right in with your long-term financial goals**

---

Many people feel that IRAs and Keoghs just aren't lucrative enough to give them the retirement income they desire - and if they keep their IRA at the bank, they're right. However, since you have the option to control your own IRA or Keogh investments why not investigate one of the following options and see if it fits in with the goal-setting exercises you completed back in Chapter One.

1. **Tax Lien Certificates** - This had to be my favorite investment of all time. So much so, that I have a whole chapter in this book relating to the subject. Tax lien certificates can be purchased for as little as $25 to as much as $100,000 per certificate. You can earn 18%, 25%, even up to 50% return backed by the government. Let the government finance your retirement!

2. **Mutual Fund Families** - Think of the possibilities of investment shifting with your IRA/Keogh. If you've made contributions over the years and are discouraged with the profits, try this. It's easy; most mutual fund families have an IRA/Keogh account option and they automatically assign you a trustee for a few bucks a year.

3. **Land Lease Limited Partnerships** - Great for high income and capital appreciation. A limited partnership buys real estate with the investment money and then leases it to a developer who builds a building. The building owners pay rent to the partnership, and this income isn't taxed because of the IRA/Keogh status of the investment. If the partnership sells the property and the profits are deposited in a tax-sheltered IRA/Keogh, no tax is due. Check these out carefully. Contact the real estate people in your area. Above all, watch out for scams!

4. **Real Estate Options** - They hold more risk and require more paperwork, but they can be lucrative and fun. You can use your IRA/Keogh to purchase vacant land or property which could appreciate in valued substantially - tax sheltered, of course. Or you can invest in a short-term real estate option - it gives you the exclusive right to buy the property at some time in the future. Your deposit holds the property - if you don't buy, you lose your option money, but if you buy, your option money is applied to the purchase price and you could reap enormous tax-sheltered profits on a lucrative purchase. You can do the similar option deal with residential rental properties like houses or condos. You buy an option from someone who wants to unload a property that isn't selling and then lease the property from the owner. You in turn sublease to someone to make the payments on the lease. Your trustee can help you manage the paperwork for the IRA/Keogh investment. If you make a profit on your option by selling it to someone else - a perfectly legal transaction - your profit is tax-sheltered.

## What About Withdrawals?

It's retirement money, okay? You're not supposed to withdraw it until you retire. If you take any money out of your IRA/Keogh, the money taken out is generally subject to federal tax at ordinary income tax rates up to 35%, and that's not including your state or local income tax. Here are some basic rules to remember about withdrawals:

- **Withdrawals Made Before Age 59 ½:** On top of the income tax you'll pay on any withdrawal, you will have to pay a 10 percent penalty. For example, if you withdraw $10,000 from your IRA, you'll be penalized $1,000 plus taxes dues. With the IRS, there is always an exception to almost any rule. The 10 percent penalty will not apply if you take a consistent income stream for five years or until you are 59½, whichever is longer. If you need a clarification of this rule, consult with your tax expert for any help with the calculations.

- **Withdrawals Between Age 59 ½ and 70 ½:** During this time frame, you will have the most freedom and flexibility with their IRA assets: you can withdrawal as much as you like (paying tax an all withdrawals, of course, assuming they were deductible contributions) or you can let your nest egg continue to grow, tax deferred.

- **Withdrawals Made After Age 70 ½:** You must start withdrawing your money at this time. Now that you've finally established a solid retirement fund, the IRS will come along and penalizing you for *not* taking money from your accounts. You will be taxed on up to *half* of what you should have taken out but didn't - this is on top on the tax you will owe for any sums not withdrawn.

There may be an additional penalty of 25% on the amount you withdraw, if the IRA/Keogh was established within to two years of the withdrawal.

To make penalty-free IRA withdrawals the life expectancy method works best. Unlike a 401(k) or 403(b) plan, which will allow you to borrow against your investment, your IRA does tie up your capital. If you want to start withdrawing before the age of 59½, here's how to do it:

Get the IRS Life Expectancy Table from IRS Publication 590 (found at www.irs.gov). Find your current age and check your life expectancy. Divide the balance in your account by the number of years the IRS thinks you are going to live. The next year, you would divide your remaining balance by your new life expectancy as the table projects it. Make sure you offset the income from the withdrawal with a tax plan that creates optimal deduction - you will pay tax on that income if you don't.

If you want to slow down your withdrawals and you are married, use the joint-life expectancy tables. Use the same calculations with the new life expectancy figures.

To get the largest possible payout each year, use a different method, the *amortization method*. You project the rate of return on your investments and then determine how much you would withdraw each year so your account is empty at the end of your life expectancy. You will have to prove to the IRS that the rate of return is a reasonable one. If your IRA is in a mutual fund with an annual return of 10%, it won't be difficult to prove a 10% payout to the IRS.

Of course, you can always take out a home equity loan, pay it with early withdrawals from your IRA, and get penalty-free money to make the payments on tax-deductible interest. Here the power of leverage works for you - you get use of the extra cash and a deduction to boot!

Don't forget that you can contribute to your IRA even while you're withdrawing money from it - and you do not have to tell the IRS why.

But what if you need some quick cash? If you are under the age of 59½ and need some quick cash, you may be able to get a loan against your retirement plan. Your Trustee has the forms available to you and the interest rate is nominal. A loan will give you access to your cash without worrying about an Early Withdrawal Penalty. Contact your tax professional for more information.

## A Note On Converting a 401(k) Pension Plan

If you're changing jobs and you've got a nice 401(k) plan, you can roll that plan over to your new employer's plan fairly easily. Whatever you do, **don't** withdraw that money yourself - you'll pay a whopping penalty to the IRS, even if you do end up reinvesting it. You must do a direct custodian-to-custodian transfer. Here's how:

1. Before you leave your job, ask for your employer for a "direct custodian-to-custodian transfer."
2. Fill out the form to roll the investment over into your new employer's 401(k). Make sure the new plan accepts transfers - a few don't. If it doesn't, roll it into an IRA.

*A billion here, a billion there,
and pretty soon you're talking about
real money.*
- Everett Dirkson

## <u>Summary of Chapter Five</u>

No those weren't financial steroids flowing through your financial muscles, you just followed the powerful wealth building techniques of tax-deferred and/or tax-deductible retirement plans. In this chapter, you learned to:

- Love the IRS – crazy but true.

- Determine which retirement plan suits your needs.

- Consider a self-directed IRA.

- Choose the type of investments for your retirement account

- Avoid withdrawing any money from your retirement account until you are retired – hence the name.

## Chapter Six

# *Slicing The Fat Off Your Insurance*

"The only good insurance salesman is a dead insurance salesman."
*Sign in medical claims office*

We all have insurance of one kind or another. We expect our employers to offer it as a benefit or we purchase insurance on our own. Like the commodities markets, insurance has long been described as a form of legalized gambling - one that we feel we can't live without. You can insure - or bet on - almost anyone and anything, pitting potential gains against loss or risk.

The three main categories of insurance are:

1. **Life Insurance**. This places a cash value on a person - returns are payable upon death to the beneficiaries noted on the policy.

2. **Health Insurance**. This pays medical expenses such as hospital, doctor, and dentist bills. Policies are also available to cover other medical expenses, such as eye care, prescriptions and orthodontic procedures. Disability and nursing home/hospice insurance are usually included in this category.

3. **Property/Casualty Insurance.** This covers about any other risk you (or the insurance companies) can imagine. This category includes Automobile insurance, homeowner's/renter's insurance, business insurance, rental car insurance and even flight insurance.

135

### Insurance as Gambling : The Bet You *Want* To Lose

In daily living there are many risks. Risk and fear are intimately linked. You worry about how you and your family will survive if something "bad" should happen. How would you live if a family member got seriously ill? How would you pay the hospital bills? What if they died? How would you pay for the funeral? What about car accidents, home robberies, and fires?

The news media heightens our fears with reports of yet another medical emergency, natural catastrophe, or robbery. The legal system plays into this by awarding huge settlements for injuries that occur on private property. The insurance industry thrives on this type of "free" publicity. Even the excessive settlements paid ends up working in the industry's favor. By preying on your fears, the industry creates a false sense of dependency on its products. It's easier for them to sell you on the idea of "security", and to guarantee a healthy cash flow for themselves.

Consider the commercials that many insurance companies run. They portray themselves as members of your family, friendly neighbors, or sturdy landmasses you can rely on in any situation - they "will always be there." But let's look at reality.

If you've ever tried to get a decent claim, you know one thing - if your family members or neighbors treated you the way the insurance industry does, you wouldn't answer your door when they came to visit. Insurance is big business, a business more interested in turning a profit than in responding to any human drama that you may experience.

When you buy an insurance policy, you are in fact gambling with the insurance company. You are betting that you will have a loss of some kind and the insurance company is betting that they will not have to pay on your claim. To win this bet, you have to lose. You expect to regain enough money to recover your loss and you hope the premiums you have "bet" do not exceed the amount of your loss.

It would seem that your odds of collecting are pretty even, but in all actuality, they are more like craps odds in Vegas. If the dice weren't loaded on the insurance companies' side, most insurers would go belly up. Most insurance policies are about as helpful as low value leverage - you lose more than you gain.

This brings us to Financial Fitness Tip #25:

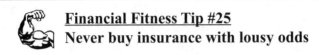

**Financial Fitness Tip #25**
**Never buy insurance with lousy odds**

Insurance companies create cash flow by selling policies. The more premiums they collect, the more money they make. Insurance products are designed to collect much more in premiums than will ever be paid out. Companies also increase their odds by limiting the conditions under which they will pay through excluding risks that you have the greatest chance of collecting on. They thrive on exceptions and loopholes. What the agent promiseth...the fine print taketh away.

How do insurance companies stack the deck in their favor?

- **By creating deductibles and/or elimination periods**. These limit the frequency of claims made on the policy. Since most of the claims against most policies are small and frequent, creating larger deductibles limits the liability of the insurance company.

- **By including "limited coverage" clauses**. These limit the amount of coverage available at the beginning of the policy and may dictate the length of time coverage remains in effect.

- **By finding "loopholes" to avoid paying a claim**. Claims adjusters, hired by the company, work hard to find reasons *not* to pay you. Adjusters will attempt to find a legal basis to reject your claim or lower the amount that they will pay you. I have heard of a *victim* of a car accident having the amount of his claim discounted by 20%. Why? In the opinion of the adjuster, "Claimant was 20% responsible for being *at* the intersection that the accident occurred." Appalling? Yes - but true.

- **By delaying or rejecting claims on account of incorrectly or incompletely prepared forms**. The adjuster will spit a claim back to you and it is your responsibility to resubmit the claim — filled out to the satisfaction of the adjuster. Each day that the insurance company does not have to pay out on a claim is another day that the company has use of your money for its purposes.

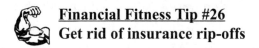

**Financial Fitness Tip #26**
**Get rid of insurance rip-offs**

Let's start with the worst value insurance. Unfortunately, this is also the kind you're most likely to be suckered into. It's natural. We worry. What if my car needed a major overhaul? How would I buy a new one? What if I lose my job - how will I make the payments on my car or house? How would my family survive? And so on. Insurance sales professionals are trained to play on these worries. This is where you are most vulnerable to the purchase of useless insurance.

Add-on policies or warranties are the most common example of lousy odds insurance. A good salesman will use every form of pressure that he can - he will even tell you outright lies, prey upon your fears as a responsible consumer and human being, and insinuate that the quality of the products you are buying need these extra warranties. How do you avoid paying extra money for these worthless contracts? As Nancy Reagan told us in the 1980's, "Just say NO!"

The following insurance rip-offs are prevalent in today's consumer arena. Each of these policies or warranties is designed to benefit everyone involved in the transaction - but you.
First you must identify these policies and then decide if they are the value that you were led to believe. Most of these policies duplicate what you already have covered by your own life, health and homeowner plans.

# Insurance Rip-Offs

| Type of insurance | What is it? | Personal financial benefits | Alternate plan? |
|---|---|---|---|
| Credit Life Insurance | Insurance policy that pays off a loan if the borrower dies | None | Add the value to your term life policy |
| Credit Disability Insurance | Policy that pays off a loan if the borrower is permanently disabled | None | Put this money into your savings, invest it, or add to your personal disability plan |
| Mortgage Life Insurance | Insurance that pays off a home mortgage if the borrower dies | None | Add the payoff value of your mortgage to your term life policy |
| Automobile Service Contracts | Extended warranties on automobiles— generally doesn't kick in until after manufacturer warranty has expired | None | Pay for outside repairs yourself - find a reliable inexpensive mechanic |
| Credit Card Insurance | Insurance on credit cards- covers credit card payments if borrower is unemployed or disabled | None | Add the value to your term life or disability plan |

## Extended Warranties & Service Contracts

Extended warranties and service contracts are available everywhere. Buy a TV, stereo, major appliance or car and you will be offered an extended warranty by the salesperson. The salesperson will attempt to coax you into buying this for your own protection.

In reality, this warranty is worthless as the paper it is written upon. An extended warranty is basically an add-on warranty, backed by the store that becomes effective after the manufacturer's warranty has expired. The catch is that you pay for it the entire time you own the object – even while the manufacturer's warranty is in effect.

A manufacturers warranty generally lasts for at least one year - and overrides the extended warranty or service contract you are paying for right now. Once in effect, store warranties and contracts don't cover the most common instances in which you'd need service, such as normal wear and tear. Additionally, if you have included the warranty or contract in your financing, you are paying interest on the amount for the term of your loan. What's this warranty really worth? Not much!

The salesperson collects a nice commission on each extended warranty or service contract sold. The store can do this because service contracts are virtually all profit. Repairs made under these contracts cost significantly less than the amount you will pay for the contract - sometimes virtually nothing.

Automobile service contracts can be even more costly. They do not cover normal wear and tear, towing, or a rental car for the period that your car is being repaired. Most contracts include a deductible that doesn't consider any of these items. You then are expected to pay for the repair yourself, and get reimbursed by the company that holds your contract. As if that's not enough, then you get the big surprise. The contract company will disallow many of the items that the garage included on the repair bill, and send you a check for the items that the contract covers (which usually isn't very much).

The table above outlines many of these *scam*-insurance coverages, and most of them bloat the payments on long-term purchase contracts. Go to your filing system. Find copies of these warranties, contracts, and service agreements. If you are still paying for them, **cancel them!**

When you draft the cancellation letter, include the date of purchase and the loan number. State that upon cancellation, you would like a refund on remaining portion of the contract. Be forewarned though, many contracts have a non-cancellation clause or high cancellation fees which may preclude getting a refund. Remember, the dealer will do whatever he can to retain his profit.

## Credit Life and Disability

Credit life and disability insurance is another high profit item for dealers and finance companies. Theoretically it is supposed to protect you, the borrower, if you should become disabled or die. Actually, it is just a way for financial institutions to ensure that they will get all of their money back (and then some). The policy is a form of decreasing term coverage. It covers only the remaining balance of your loan, yet the payments remain the same throughout the term of the loan.

Any type of loan is a target for this insurance rip off. Examine your contracts - it may have been added without your consent. The loan officer may even tell you that it is "required" as a term of your loan to take this insurance. This is untrue and against the law. Don't let the loan officer frighten you- in reality, the bank doesn't come and take everything from your family if you should die or be disabled. The bank is only concerned about getting repaid. All it requires is that the payments be made as originally promised, regardless of where the money originates.

If you are smart, you will include in your term life insurance the amounts to pay off all your debts - and your family will be taken care of. When you consider the probability of something dire happening to you while you have the loan, versus the amount of cash you are paying for this extra, overpriced insurance, it's more sensible to put this money into a mutual fund.

Remove this insurance from any of your existing loans. You can either speak to the loan officer personally or put the request in writing. If you have paid for this insurance up front, ask for a refund on the remaining insurance. If it has been included in your loan, ask that your payments reflect the deduction of this charge or that payments be taken off at the end of your loan.

## Credit Card Insurance Cancellation

Have you ever noticed that little box on the back of your credit card application? You know, it asks you if you would like insurance in case you cannot make your payments on the card. All they ask is that you initial the box. Credit Card Insurance is one of the highest profit forms of insurance. The premiums are based on the amount you have charged - your balance. Credit Card Insurance can add up to as much as an extra 8 percent per year on your unpaid balances.

It's very difficult to collect on Credit Card Insurance. Coverage may not begin until 30 days after you have become unemployed or disabled - and even then the balance on the card is not paid off. Payments are made only for the duration of your disability or unemployment.

If you have this insurance on any of your revolving charge cards, simply write a letter to the credit card company and ask for it to be removed. Make a note of when you sent the letter and follow up with your next statement to ensure that it has been removed.

## Declining or Canceling Mortgage Life

Mortgage life, like credit life insurance, is a declining term insurance. This means that at the end of the term, the value of the insurance is considerably less than at the beginning of the policy. However, you are forced to make the same premium payment for the duration of the policy.

If you are buying a house, decline this option when the lender offers it to you. If you have an existing mortgage with this insurance, cancel it. Why? You can add the value of your loan to your existing term life insurance, or take out another policy that will cover the mortgage in the eventuality of your unplanned demise. This will be significantly less expensive— and you can adjust the value of the insurance, hence minimizing your premium payments — as you pay off your loan.

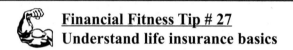

**Financial Fitness Tip # 27**
**Understand life insurance basics**

Life insurance— what is it and why do you need it? When you buy life insurance, you allow the insurance company to have use of the premium money you pay for as long as you are alive. After you die, the company passes your beneficiary the agreed upon value of the policy. Life insurance is important if your family would suffer financially upon your death. It protects your loved ones from loss of income or assets.

### Making Educated Life Insurance Decisions

Who should be covered by life insurance? Contrary to what insurance companies tell you, it's not necessary for everyone.

If you are a single person with no dependents, you do not need life insurance. Ask yourself, who would benefit from the policy? Should your parents? Generally, your parents do not need compensation for your death, unless they depend on you for financial support. If you have concerns about burial costs, buy a small policy to cover the cost of your funeral and make your parents the beneficiaries.

Your children do not need to be insured. It's not a reflection on your parenting abilities if you don't insure your children. No amount of money would compensate you for the emotional loss if your child died. So why would you want to purchase a high-priced, high-dollar policy on them? The probability that your child will die is very slim. The odds are so long, they are silly. It's wiser to purchase policies on an income-earning adult, not a dependent child.

If your spouse does not work and does not provide services in the home, like childcare, it is not necessary to insure him or her either. Remember, insurance is to protect against potential financial loss, not emotional loss.

## Term Life vs. Cash Value

Some employers offer, as a benefit, life insurance along with health insurance. Health costs are extremely difficult to control and are very costly for insurance companies. Life insurance policies attempt to make up for these lost profits.

If you change jobs, the company is required to offer you continuing health and life insurance coverage under the COBRA law. This law states that you are allowed to continue the same level of coverage for a period up to 18 months.

It is wise to decline this coverage unless you have an illness that could be considered a pre-existing condition— or are otherwise uninsurable. The rates that you are offered are significantly higher than the rates the company was paying for the same coverage - sometimes 1000% higher. That's because your policy has changed from a group policy to a personal policy - you, and you alone, are responsible for the payments. Once you are personally insured, it's likely that the life insurance has been changed from term, which is basically inexpensive, to whole life insurance, which is very expensive and does not provide any additional coverage.

## Maximize Protection, Minimize Cost

There are three major kinds of life insurance: Whole Life, Universal Life, and Term Life.

1. **Whole Life Insurance***:* This policy creates "cash value." You pay premiums to build up that cash value. Unfortunately, most of the time neither you nor your heirs see any of this value. This insurance is a one of the worst rip-offs, since you are guaranteed a fixed amount as a premium and as a death benefit. You are promised that you can borrow against the "cash value" of the policy. Unless you borrow against your cash value – which then would be deducted from your death benefit – you will never see it. It has been this way since 1888.

2. **Universal Life Insurance***:* This policy combines term insurance with an investment plan. You decide on the premium you want to pay. First the premium money goes to pay the cost of the insurance and then the balance goes to a tax-deferred investment plan. Sounds like a good idea? In a perfect world it is, but the insurance company charges higher than normal rates for the term life insurance and large commissions are taken from your premiums or cash value. If you decide to withdraw your cash value, the insurance company charges a huge surrender fee. This insurance is basically a rip-off.

3. **Term Life Insurance***:* This policy is plain everyday no-frills insurance. It protects your beneficiaries against financial loss. All of the premiums you pay go toward the policy. This is the best, simplest, highest value insurance.

Did you ever wonder why many of the tall buildings in your city have the names of insurance companies on them? Two reasons: Whole Life and Universal Insurance Life policies. Your hard-earned premiums pay for the buildings.

**Financial Fitness Tip #28**
**Never use life insurance as an investment vehicle**

As I'm sure you have already figured out, the potential returns you'll receive as your own money manager will far surpass that of any type of life insurance policy. Keep in mind those Universal Life insurance policies that guarantee you a rate of return are quoting that return only after fees and commissions have been paid – those returns are on the lower amount and not the face value of the policy. Make sure you read the fine print.

### What Really Works: Term

Life insurance was initially designed to replace the loss of income of a particular family member when they die. Unfortunately, for many families in America, both spouses are usually working. If this is the case in your household, both spouses need to be insured. Only purchase enough life insurance so that the proceeds, invested at 12%, would allow you to maintain the same lifestyle if that person would to die (see the chart which is included). For this reason alone, I do not recommend the purchase of insurance for children unless they greatly contribute to the family's income, which is generally not the case.

You should always purchase term insurance. Term insurance is strictly death insurance. There is no investment attached to this insurance policy. You would receive a much higher rate of return, without commissions, by following my safe high-yielding investment strategies outlined later on in this book.

**IMPORTANT NOTE:** *<u>NEVER</u> CANCEL YOUR EXISTING INSURANCE POLICIES UNTIL COVERAGE WITH YOUR NEW COMPANY HAS TAKEN EFFECT. OTHERWISE, YOU MAY GET CAUGHT WITHOUT COVERAGE AND WILL BE IN **BIG** TROUBLE.*

Since we all now agree that Term, instead of Whole or Universal Life, is the better choice, let me show you how much you can save – and eventually make – by switching coverages.

---

### <u>Male Age 35 Non-Smoker $250,000 Policy</u>

Whole Life Premium - $ 4,900/year
<u>Term Life Premium -   $   150/year</u>
Savings       $ 4,750/year

---

Just look at the money you are saving every year. But, it gets better. What if you were to spend the same amount of money every year, but just re-allocate this expenditure to something more profitable? In other words, take that $4,750 in yearly savings and put that amount aside every year and place it in one of the No-Load Mutual Funds (discussed in a later chapter) that earns **only** 20% per year. Since you are spending this money anyway, you won't miss it.

| Yearly Investment | Interest Rate | Yrs Invested | Return |
|---|---|---|---|
| $4,750 | 20% | 10 | $  123,304 |
|  |  | 15 | $  342,167 |
|  |  | 20 | $  886,768 |
|  |  | 30 | $5,613,937 |

You got to love the power of compounded interest. Obviously, you sooner you begin to save, the better off you will be.

Next, you may be thinking "But I want to begin living a better lifestyle now. I don't want to stash away that much money every year." Ok, then what would your returns look like if you made only a one-time investment – at the same 20% - instead of doing that every year?

| One-Time Investment | Interest Rate | Yrs Invested | Return |
|---|---|---|---|
| $4,750 | 20% | 10 | $ 29,411 |
|  |  | 15 | $ 73,183 |
|  |  | 20 | $182,104 |
|  |  | 30 | $1,127,537 |

As you can see, the numbers are pretty impressive. And yes, a 20% return in a No-Load Mutual Fund is realistic (I'll give example of the funds in a later chapter). Remember about the government guaranteed tax lien certificates that pay up to 50% per year? Add that to the equation and the returns become obscene.

### Create A New Life Insurance Plan

Be careful! Insurance salespeople will attempt to get you to add options that mean a larger commission for them with no additional protection for you. Two of the most common add-on options are *disability premium waivers* and *double-indemnity*.

*Disability insurance waivers* are basically the same as Credit Card Insurance or credit life disability insurance. They state that if you become disabled and unable to work, your premiums will be paid to the insurance company. Like Credit Card Insurance or Credit Life, this benefits the insurance company and not you. Most policies have a six-month disability minimum before coverage begins. If your policy has cash value, payments are taken from that anyway - it's stated in your policy - so this coverage is bogus.

*Double-indemnity*, or accidental-death coverage, doubles the face value of the policy if the insured dies an accidental death. If you have it, drop it. Instead, buy a greater value term life insurance policy that pays a larger amount for every type of death, not just accidents.

## LIFE INSURANCE INCOME REPLACEMENT

Determine your family income to find out how much life insurance each income producing family member should carry. Since your investment (passive) income will continue after your death, for the purposes of this exercise, only concern yourself with what I call *active income*.

1.  Total the amount of the income your family would not have if you or your spouse were not working.

| Income Producing Programs | Yearly Amount |
|---|---|
| Salary | $ _____ |
| Commissions and Bonuses | $ _____ |
| Social Security | $ _____ |
| Retirement Plan Income | $ _____ |
| Annuities | $ _____ |
| IRA Withdrawals | $ _____ |
| Life Insurance Policy Paid By Employer | $ _____ |
| Spouse's Income | $ _____ |
| Other Active Income | $ _____ |
| **Total Active Income** | $ _____ |

2.  Purchase enough life insurance so that the proceeds, invested at 12%, would allow you to maintain the same lifestyle if that person would to die.

## Life Insurance Planning Chart

|  |  | Yearly premium cost for first 10 years of amount of insurance shown in column B | | | | | | | |
| Your or Spouse's Current Income (A) | Approx. Amount invested at 12% that would replace income 100% (B) | Age 25 (C) | Age 30 (D) | Age 35 (E) | Age 40 (F) | Age 45 (G) | Age 50 (H) | Age 55 (I) | Age 60 (J) |
|---|---|---|---|---|---|---|---|---|---|
| $ 20,000 | 170,000 | 203 | 203 | 212 | 288 | 390 | 567 | 839 | 1,247 |
| 25,000 | 210,000 | 239 | 239 | 250 | 344 | 470 | 689 | 1,025 | 1,529 |
| 30,000 | 250,000 | 250 | 250 | 263 | 375 | 513 | 750 | 1,125 | 1,675 |
| 35,000 | 300,000 | 290 | 290 | 305 | 440 | 605 | 890 | 1,340 | 2,000 |
| 40,000 | 350,000 | 330 | 330 | 348 | 505 | 698 | 1,030 | 1,555 | 2,325 |
| 45,000 | 375,000 | 350 | 350 | 369 | 538 | 744 | 1,100 | 1,663 | 2,488 |
| 50,000 | 420,000 | 386 | 386 | 407 | 596 | 827 | 1,226 | 1,856 | 2,780 |
| 60,000 | 500,000 | 450 | 450 | 475 | 700 | 975 | 1,450 | 2,200 | 3,300 |
| 70,000 | 600,000 | 530 | 530 | 560 | 830 | 1,160 | 1,730 | 2,630 | 3,950 |

| | | | | | | | | | |
|---|---|---|---|---|---|---|---|---|---|
| 80,000 | 675,000 | 590 | 590 | 624 | 928 | 1,299 | 1,940 | 2,953 | 4,438 |
| 90,000 | 750,000 | 650 | 650 | 688 | 1,025 | 1,438 | 2,150 | 3,275 | 4,925 |
| 100,000 | 850,000 | 730 | 730 | 773 | 1,155 | 1,623 | 2,430 | 3,705 | 5,575 |
| 125,000 | 1,000,000 | 850 | 850 | 900 | 1,350 | 1,900 | 2,850 | 4,350 | 6,550 |
| 150,000 | 1,250,000 | 1,050 | 1,050 | 1,113 | 1,675 | 2,363 | 3,550 | 5,425 | 8,175 |
| 175,000 | 1,500,000 | 1,250 | 1,250 | 1,325 | 2,000 | 2,825 | 4,250 | 6,500 | 9,800 |
| 200,000 | 1,750,000 | 1,450 | 1,450 | 1,538 | 2,325 | 3,288 | 4,950 | 7,575 | 11,425 |
| 300,000 | 2,500,000 | 2,050 | 2,050 | 2,175 | 3,300 | 4,675 | 7,050 | 10,800 | 16,300 |
| 400,000 | 3,400,000 | 2,770 | 2,770 | 2,940 | 4,470 | 6,340 | 9,570 | 14,670 | 22,150 |
| 500,000 | 4,200,000 | 3,410 | 3,410 | 3,620 | 5,510 | 7,820 | 11,810 | 18,110 | 27,350 |
| 750,000 | 6,250,000 | 5,050 | 5,050 | 5,363 | 8,175 | 11,613 | 17,550 | 26,925 | 40,675 |
| 1,000,000 | 8,400,000 | 6,770 | 6,770 | 7,190 | 10,970 | 15,590 | 23,570 | 36,170 | 54,650 |

All rates are guaranteed 10 year level term. Rates are for example purposes only.
Rates shown are for non-smoking male in good health. Female rates are equal or less.

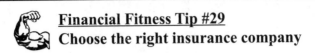

**Financial Fitness Tip #29**
**Choose the right insurance company**

How do you pick out the right insurance company? Consider these common sense requirements. First, you want low premiums. Second, you want to ensure that the company you pay premiums to today will be around to pay your beneficiaries tomorrow.

Avail yourself of the professionals who know about the insurance industry. *A.M. Best* is an independent organization that monitors insurance companies and rates them according to a set of financial stability criteria. Ratings which are acceptable are A-, A (Excellent), A+ (Superior) and A++ (Super Superior). Any company rated below A- should be eliminated from your list of potential insurance providers. Ratings below A- indicate that the company is less than stable financially and you do not want to invest your hard earned cash in them. You would be gambling on a leaky boat - even if you win, you might sink.

Don't be tempted to go with a company just because mom and dad did, or because it is very well known. Companies that have the greatest recognition factor do not necessarily have the best insurance deals. Often these companies charge higher premiums to cover their advertising costs. Do your homework – you may find another less known, comparably rated company that will provide the same coverage for less money.

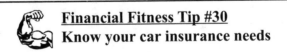

**Financial Fitness Tip #30**
**Know your car insurance needs**

Be prepared. Your agent may give you and earful. Why? You're taking money out of their pockets. Insurance salesmen are paid a commission for the business they write. The larger the premium, the larger the commission. In fact, they may have already spent the commission they made on you when you purchased your policy. So if you change your coverage and raise your deductible, your premium will be reduced. They may have to give back part of their commission that they earned from you back to the insurance company. This is called a *charge-back*. So they may try to talk you out of the changes that you want to make, in order to protect *your* interest of course. Stand firm and hold your ground.

This is one of the reasons why I started *Financial Fitness Monthly* (www.FinancialFitnessMonthly.com). Besides having a great offline newsletter, you have unlimited access to talk with one of our *Financial Fitness Trainers™*. Many times our subscribers call their Financial Fitness Trainer and then hand the phone to their insurance agents. The Financial Fitness Trainer will then inform your insurance agent the changes that you demand. Since many insurance agents become friends of the family throughout the years, you may not have the guts to take money out of your agents pocket and put it back into yours.

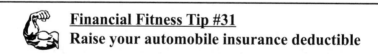

**<u>Financial Fitness Tip #31</u>**
**Raise your automobile insurance deductible**

By raising your deductible to $500, $1,000 or even higher, you may be able to reduce your premiums by 40-60%. Statistically, you will get in an accident once every twelve years.

If you are still worried about covering a high deductible, get a low interest rate credit card that will be used only in emergencies to cover insurance deductibles. Don't forget your emergency Slush Fund that should have six months of living expenses. You can always use that Slush Fund to take care of any deductibles.

You will have lower premiums with the higher deductibles, therefore, saving hundreds or even thousands of dollars per year.

Don't forget that even if you have a low deductible such as $100 or $150, any claim that you may file could dramatically raise your premiums or the insurance company could drop you all together. Not a very comforting thought.

In the meantime, shop around and get quotes from other insurance companies. Less than 25% of Americans actually shop around for auto insurance. By shopping around, you may be able to save an additional 5-30%.

Check to see if your insurance company offers discounts (i.e. multiple vehicles, good student, safe driver, anti-theft). Such discounts could save an additional 5-25%.

Another thought would be to contact the insurance company that carries your Homeowner Insurance. You'll be surprise on how aggressive they will be in order to get your Auto Insurance to be with them also. This option may save you even more money.

## Bodily Injury Liability

This covers any injuries to the driver or other people involved in an accident. On your Declaration page (the first page on your automobile insurance policy), liability coverage is denoted by a set of two numbers (i.e. 10/20, 50/100, 100/300). With all of the numbers, add three zeros – 10/20 becomes 10,000/20,000).

The first number is what the insurance company will pay for one person's injuries (including attorney fees). The second number states what the insurance company will pay per accident (including attorney fees).

This Bodily Injury Liability should cover your net worth if you were to be sued. Remember when you calculated your net worth in an earlier chapter? The coverage you need should only be 1.5 times your net worth. As an example, if your net worth is $10,000, the first number (of the liability coverage) should be $15,000.

If your net worth is only $10,000, there is no need to get 100/300 coverage. You would be overpaying for coverage that you don't need. Conversely, a homeowner would most likely need 100/300 coverage. Do not get any more coverage than that. If you need more than 100/300 coverage, it is wiser to get an Umbrella Policy for only a few hundred dollars a year – much cheaper than getting higher liability coverage from your auto insurance company.

Since I suggest the 1.5 times your net worth in liability insurance, what is the .5 for? The .5 should be enough to cover any attorney fees. I'm sure you'll agree that the attorneys will get their money regardless of what we receive.

## Property Damage

This coverage will insure you if you were to damage other people's property. Coverages start at the State minimum and usually go up to $50,000.

## Comprehensive

This coverage will insure you for any claims for theft, fire, glass or vandalism. Many people have deductible as low as $100 or $150 for this coverage. Again, the money you can save by raising this deductible could be as much as 60%.

## Collision

This coverage will insure you for any claims for Damage to your car in an accident – regardless if the other person is insure or not. Again, many people have deductible as low as $100 or $150 for this coverage.

The money saved and re-allocated by raising this deductible could be as much as 60%.

**Financial Fitness Tip #32**
**Drop you Comprehensive and Collision coverage if your vehicle is worth less than $2,500**

It is not cost effective to still pay for Comprehensive and Collision insurance if your vehicle is worth less than $2,500. The premiums do not outweigh the benefits of this coverage in that instance. There is no reason to continually pay for coverage that doesn't make good financial sense.

As you can tell by now, I'm showing ways to become more self-insured. Your Slush Fund or credit card should cover you if you need it.

## My New Automobile Policy

### Coverages to Replace

| Coverage | Current Limits | Desired Limits | Current Premiums | New Premiums | Notes |
|---|---|---|---|---|---|
| Bodily Injury/ Liability | | | | | Check for all possible discounts |
| Property Damage/ Liability | | | | | |
| Umbrella Liability | | | | | Optional for those needing needing high limits |
| Comprehensive Deductible | | | | | At least $500 |
| Collision Deductible | | | | | At least $500 |

## Coverages to Drop

| Coverage | Current Limits | Desired Limits | Current Premiums | New Premiums |
|---|---|---|---|---|
| No-Fault (PIP) | | | | -0- |
| Medical Payments | | | | -0- |
| Uninsured Motorist | | | | -0- |
| Emergency Road Service | | | | -0- |
| Car Rental Expense | | | | -0- |
| Accidental Death & Dismemberment | | | | -0- |
| Specialty Coverage | | | | -0- |

**TOTAL PREMIUM** $_____          -0-

**TOTAL AMOUNT SAVED** $_____

Even though most families have more than one car, let's say that you were **only** able to save $500 per year by re-designing your automobile policy. How much will that save – or make – you over time? Again, since you are spending this money anyway, you won't miss it.

| Yearly Investment | Interest Rate | Yrs Invested | Return |
|---|---|---|---|
| $500 | 20% | 10 | $ 12,979 |
| | | 15 | $ 36,018 |
| | | 20 | $ 93,344 |
| | | 30 | $ 590,941 |

As in the life insurance example, you may be thinking "But I want to begin living a better lifestyle now. I don't want to stash away that much money every year." Ok, then what would your returns be if you made only a one-time investment – at the same 20% - instead of doing that every year. Let's see:

| One-Time Investment | Interest Rate | Yrs Invested | Return |
|---|---|---|---|
| $500 | 20% | 10 | $ 3,096 |
| | | 15 | $ 7,704 |
| | | 20 | $ 19,169 |
| | | 30 | $118,688 |

As you can see, the numbers are still pretty impressive. Think of all of this money available to you for your retirement that can be accomplished with a little planning and discipline on your part.

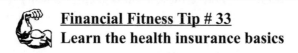

**Financial Fitness Tip # 33**
**Learn the health insurance basics**

As you see in the media, health insurance costs are constantly rising and this is one of the most expensive parts of your financial plan. Your financial future may depend on if you have the correct coverage if your health is seriously in danger.

You may be covered by a health plan by your employer, but your circumstances may change. It has been statistically shown that the average American changes employers seven different times in their lifetime. What would happen if you should lose your job due to corporate downsizing (not that this **ever** happens)? Your employer will allow you to keep your existing coverage for up to one year. What happens during this time, if you should get an ailment or condition that your new health insurance company considers a pre-existing condition? They can either insure you at a much higher rate or they may not cover you at all. Then what do you do?

A big misconception is that individual health insurance policies cost a lot of money. Generally speaking, that is true. This is why people are relieved when their employer will pick up the cost of some, if not all, of their monthly premium. It doesn't matter if you are getting overprice coverages or not. I heard of one employer's insurance company demand that all females are required to pay for maternity care. One lady who I spoke with was 57 years old at the time and was required to pay for maternity coverage.

The truth of the matter is that health insurance does not have to cost you a lot of money each month. There are many organizations across the country, including the subscribers of *Financial Fitness Monthly* (www.FinancialFitnessMonthly.com), which allows its members to have access to individual health insurance policies at group rates. This will circumvent any problems you may have in the future with employer changes or pre-existing conditions.

*Disability insurance* is designed to replace some or all of the income lost due to an injury or an ailment. Usually benefits will not be paid until the insured has been away from their job for 3-5 months (each disability plan varies). In most cases, people who are disabled usually return to work in 30-60 days; hence this form of overpriced insurance only benefits the insurance company, not the insured. The only situation where disability insurance makes sense is when the insured is in poor health and is accident-prone.

Think of disability insurance as going to a casino in Las Vegas. Casino "A" has a payout for their slot machines of 99%. Casino "B" has the shot machine payout of only .3215%. Which casino would you rather play at?

According to the Social Security Administration, you have a .5786% chance of becoming disabled and only a .3215% chance of becoming disabled to the point where Social Security will acknowledge that fact that you are indeed disabled.

Now that you know these facts, I'm sure that you are intelligent enough to figure out if disability insurance is for you.

Investigate your health insurance and disability coverage. If you have a group plan through your employer, check to see how good their plan really is. If you do not have health insurance now, begin to start shopping.

Turn the page to see how much money you can save if you re-allocated the money spent on disability insurance:

**Average cost for a healthy 43 year old male for a disability payout of $2,300 per month**

| Yearly Investment | Interest | Years | Return |
|---|---|---|---|
| $1,800 | 20% | 10 | $ 46,726 |
| | | 15 | $ 129,663 |
| | | 20 | $ 336,038 |
| | | 30 | $ 2,127,387 |

And what if you wanted to use this yearly investment to instead make extra principle payments on your mortgage – to accelerate your equity in your home? What would be the return if you only wanted to make a one-time investment of $1,800 to your retirement account?

| One-Time Investment | Interest | Years | Return |
|---|---|---|---|
| $1,800 | 20% | 10 | $ 11,145 |
| | | 15 | $ 27,733 |
| | | 20 | $ 69,008 |
| | | 30 | $ 427,277 |

Don't forget that money in your retirement account is tax-deferred. Yes, you **can** have a comfortable retirement.

## WHAT YOU WANT AND DON'T WANT IN YOUR
## HEALTH INSURANCE POLICY

| **Option** | **Don't Want** | **Want** |
|---|---|---|
| Rates | Higher Individual Rates | Lower Group Rate |
| Deductible | $250 | $1,000 |
| Stop Loss | 80/20 to $1,000 | 80/20 to $5,000 |
| Claim Payments | Reasonable and Customary | Regular |
| Claim Time | 6 Weeks | 14 Days |
| Company Sell | 1 or 2 States | 40 or more states |
| Company Rating | Below A | A or above |
| Coverages | Maternity<br>Dental<br>Supplemental Accident<br>Prescription Card | |

---

**Financial Fitness Tip # 34**
**Understand your homeowner's insurance**
**policy**

---

Your home is the most expensive purchase you may ever make in your life. You not only need to protect you home, but also it's furnishing and other valuables. Video tape the inside and outside of your house and store the videotape in a safe deposit box with all of your valuable papers. In case there is a problem with a claim, your videotape may help you recover if a claim is filed. Make sure your policy covers any computer equipment or jewelry, if applicable.

Purchase earthquake or flood insurance only if you are located in a government-designated earthquake zone or flood plain.

Make sure you purchase *replacement value* coverage and not *market value coverage*.

---

**Financial Fitness Tip # 35**
**Cancel PMI once you have at least 20%**
**equity in your home**

---

Lenders normally require PMI (Private Mortgage Insurance) if your down payment is less than 20% of the purchase price. This is an insurance policy that lenders require that you purchase in the event that you should default on your loan. If you refinance your home, you can expect to receive a refund of any unused premiums that your mortgage company required you to purchase.

If you have lived in your property for quite some time or you reside in an area that has significantly increased in value since you last appraisal, you can simply ask the insurance to cancel this policy. To protect the insurance company's interest, they may order an additional appraiser from an appraiser - that they specify – at your cost.

PMI usually cost $50 - $100 per month for every $100,000 that you borrow. According to *HomeGain*, approximately 2,700,000 homeowners where paying PMI needlessly in the year 2001. Make sure you don't make the same mistake.

Let's say that by canceling this insurance, you **only** save $50 a month ($600 per year) – which is the minimum that you would pay. How much would you save?

| Yearly Investment | Interest | Years | Return |
|---|---|---|---|
| $600 | 20% | 10 | $ 18,690 |
| | | 15 | $ 51,865 |
| | | 20 | $134,415 |
| | | 30 | $850,955 |

And what if you wanted to use this yearly investment to instead make extra principle payments on your car loan? What would be the return if you only wanted to make a one-time investment of $600 to your retirement account? Turn the page to see the shocking results.

| One-Time Investment | Interest | Years | Return |
|---|---|---|---|
| $600 | 20% | 10 | $ 3,715 |
| | | 15 | $ 9,244 |
| | | 20 | $ 23,003 |
| | | 30 | $142,426 |

Have I got your attention yet? Financial Fitness is nothing more than lowering your expenses and re-allocating those funds to a more profitable use.

# Homeowner's Insurance Quotes

## Premiums / Limits

|  | Company 1 | Company 2 | Company 3 |
|---|---|---|---|
| Company | _____ | _____ | _____ |
| Policy Type | _____ | _____ | _____ |
| House | _____ | _____ | _____ |
| Detached Buildings | _____ | _____ | _____ |
| Trees, Shrubs, Plants | _____ | _____ | _____ |
| Personal Property |  |  |  |
|    On-Premises | _____ | _____ | _____ |
|    Off-Premises | _____ | _____ | _____ |
| Additional Living |  |  |  |
|    Expenses | _____ | _____ | _____ |
| Comprehensive Personal |  |  |  |
| Liability | _____ | _____ | _____ |
| Medical Expense |  |  |  |
|    Payments | _____ | _____ | _____ |
| Scheduled Item |  |  |  |
| Endorsements |  |  |  |
|    Extended Thrift | _____ | _____ | _____ |
|    Inflation Guard |  |  |  |
|    Replacement Cost | _____ | _____ | _____ |
|    Other | _____ | _____ | _____ |
|  |  |  |  |
| Deductibles | _____ | _____ | _____ |
|  |  |  |  |
| **Total Annual** |  |  |  |
| **Premium** | _____ | _____ | _____ |

## Summary of Chapter Six

Geez, talk about liposuction for these bills that drain you ever month. In this chapter, you learned how to:

- Get rid of the insurance rip-offs.

- Determine how much life insurance you need and purchase term insurance.

- Shop around to find the best auto insurance premiums.

- Slice the fat from your auto insurance policy.

- Analyze my health insurance and dump the coverage options you don't need.

- Cancel PMI, if applicable.

- Re-allocate money that you're already spending to more profitable areas.

---

**Need some personal guidance with your insurance?**

**Go to: www.FinancialFitnessMonthly.com**

**and talk with one of our Financial Fitness Trainers**

---

## Chapter Seven

# Steer Clear Of the Automobile Money Treadmill

*If you can't convince them, confuse them.*
Harry S. Truman

If you are one of those people who are attached to the romance, glamour, and power associated with cars, you are not going to like this chapter. But if you want to become financially fit, you will just have to swallow hard, open your eyes, and accept the truth - one of the most common and damaging financial leaks is the monthly payment on new cars. Believe it or not, after income taxes and your home, automobiles are your biggest lifetime expense.

### The Myth of the Good Deal

What's your definition of a good deal? There are lots of books and hotlines out there that claim they can tell you how to get a good deal on a new car. Unfortunately, they can't. They can show you how to get the *best* deal on a new car - but not a *good* deal.

If I'm playing blackjack or poker, a good deal is one where I've got cards with winning potential. I love hearing people boast about the amazing deal they got at the car dealership. When you walk into a car dealership, you can be certain of only one thing - the dealer is the only one who gets a good deal.

Why? Like the fine print on credit card debt and some insurance products, automobile sales practices are basically a legalized scam. The finance manager at a car dealership - the guy who actually prints out your contract and puts the pen in your hand - can juggle numbers fast enough to confuse a professor of calculus. He holds all the cards, he only deals what he wants you to see - and he never

171

shows you what's up his sleeve. Who says you can't be financially fit? Car dealers!

### If It Feels Good... Watch Out!

Unlike a few years ago, when high-pressure sleaze tactics prevailed, today the car salesperson will be warm, friendly, and *lay* (or is it *lie*) like a rug while smiling at your kids. Instead of treating you like the mark in the con game, today's most successful car sales professionals will use emotional warfare. You're not just buying a car; you're buying a relationship with our team of professionals who have only your best interest in mind. Even before you buy the car, you will be introduced to the head of the shiny clean maintenance department, shown how carefully your car will be serviced, all to make you feel warm and fuzzy just like a member of the family.

Don't fall for it. Sure, this is a family - one great big dysfunctional family, and you are the codependent sucker. Like all screwed up families, this is one where confusion reigns. You will be told carefully selected bits of the truth, but not enough so you really know where you stand. You will be shown lots of numbers, but they will be incomprehensible. You will be encouraged to ask questions, but you won't get answers. Everyone will be trying to help you win, while they are making certain that you can't.

This confusion depends on the careful application of deception. Every new car has so many sneaky little costs built into the price that it's almost impossible to know how much money the dealer is making, and how much you are overpaying. The car dealer counts on these enormous covert profits— profits that are so well hidden, half the time even the sales people are clueless about them.

You can't bank on making the salesperson an ally in your struggle, even a salesperson you have known for twenty years. If you fight *not* to pay for phony charges, and win the battle, today most car dealerships are so greedy for profits that they will dock the salesperson's commission. *There are no winners in the trenches - only survivors.* Don't lose the war – fight.

### Your Car Is An Expense

You may love beautiful cars. That's understandable because so do I. But if you want to enjoy owning your cars, educate yourself how to do so without getting abused.

Don't lie to yourself with the same emotional ploys used in car advertising — "I deserve this." Never convince yourself that your car is an investment: "I might as well get a model that's loaded, and get more for it when I trade or sell!" Sorry. Your house appreciates over time, but an automobile never appreciates. As a car salesman who actually happens to be a friend once told me, "There's no such thing as equity in a car."

Forget the TV commercials that boast about high resale value. Resale value, as you will learn in this chapter, is about as real as Monopoly money - it's just part of playing the game. A car is at best depreciable - and at worst, it might as well be a completely perishable item. If you want to become financially fit, it's essential that you separate your emotions from reality, and the toughest place to do this is in the cheerful, friendly, seductive world of cars.

Face facts. An automobile is an expense. That means that owning and maintaining a car is a potential financial loss. Your home will eventually pay for itself simply because of appreciation. But when you overpay for a car, you might as well just turn on the faucet and let your money pour down the drain. You must make your car a less expensive expense.

This brings us to Financial Fitness Tip #36:

 **Financial Fitness Tip #36**
**Control all future car purchases by**
**paying only for what you want. Use high**
**value leverage, or cash to buy a car**

The following *Supercharged Car Buying Strategies* are all designed to help you regain control of that most out-of-control financial situation. Automobiles, like college, are hideously expensive - yet unlike college, you do have some negotiating room in any car purchase. Whether you buy from the new car dealer, the used car lot, or a private seller, if you end up paying the highest price on the street, you don't have to look farther than the nearest mirror for the sucker.

 **Financial Fitness Tip #37**
**Detach your emotions from your car purchases**

If you're lonely and you don't want to get a pet, go shop for a car. When you walk into the dealer's showroom, it's unlikely that you will be alone for more than about thirty seconds. Instant friendship and instant trouble.

Why? Car advertising and sales tactics manipulate your self-esteem in subtle, but powerful ways. Ask yourself if a new car might make you feel happy, sexy, safe, and competent. If so, the smell of a new car might be enough to make you giddy, and that can lead you to spend money foolishly, something you wouldn't do if you had not been mildly brainwashed in advance.

Even people who wouldn't normally abuse credit cards or buy on impulse will lose financial control in an automobile purchase transaction, while telling themselves that they are getting a "good" deal.

Americans are addicted to their automobiles. To become financially fit, you must control how, when, and why you buy cars. That's impossible if you are in the habit of getting a "good" deal on a new car every two years. So promise yourself right now that you will buy your next car unemotionally.

Pledge that you will do your research in the library or bookstore or at the next major auto show - not in the showroom with the salesman at your elbow. Make a solemn commitment to retain some control over the transaction - and to walk away from the dealership as soon as you feel yourself losing control. Don't pay the highest price on the street. Wean yourself from the emotional strokes of the dealer and arm yourself with facts.

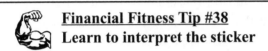

**Financial Fitness Tip #38**
**Learn to interpret the sticker**

You know what a car costs - right? It's all there on the sticker. There are two parts - *the MSRP (Manufacturer's Suggested Retail Price) and the "sucker" sticker, pasted next to the MSRP.* The MSRP is the manufacturer's price plus some dealer profit. The other price, the one on the sucker sticker, is the highest price you could possibly pay for that car at that dealership. Let's see what each set of charges on the sticker really means.

1.  MSRP is the base retail price of the car that the manufacturer thinks is fair, plus a dealer profit of 15 to 25 %.

2.  Underneath the base price is the options list. Options hold the biggest profit margins for the dealer - mark-ups of 75 to 200%. The more options on the car you buy, the bigger the dealer's profit.

3.  Next come dealer's prep and freight charges. Prep and freight are almost sheer profit for the dealer. He can charge you whatever he wants to, and most of the time, he does. Did you know it costs the dealer money to get the car to your town and then to fix it up so you can buy it? My goodness,

why should the dealer pay those costs? He's **only** making 20% on the base and 75% on the options! The dealer never pays $200 to $500 for prep and freight - only you do. The dealer did not have to build the car from parts that came off the truck - he probably spent $10 for a wash job by the porter, usually a kid, in the "Dealer Preparation Department." If the car was damaged on the truck or isn't running properly, the trucking company or manufacturer pays for it. The only fair price for prep and freight is NOTHING. When was the last time you paid a special charge for someone to dust the washers and dryers at the local appliance store?

The three items above add up to the sticker price. Right next to it is another price list.

4. The dealer sticker (often referred to affectionately as the "sucker" sticker) is a second retail price list pasted next to the manufacturer's sticker. It's printed to look just like the manufacturer's sticker. It contains charges that end up adding five to fifty percent pure profit for the dealer.

Usually the dealer sticker will say something like "LABEL IS NOT AN OFFICAL FACTORY OR GOVERNMENT STICKER. IT IS APPLIED BY YOUR DEALER." On this sticker the dealer lists anything he likes, using official sounding names like "dealer mark-up," "dealer adjustment," or "dealer market value." Here's where you pay for "clear coat paint" and "fabric protection." "Administration fee" - I guess that $200 pays for the paper your contract will be printed on.

Dealers and salespeople call these charges "*front-end loading*," profits they can build into the deal before you sit down with the finance manager to sign the paperwork. Consider all of these "front-end" items additional dealer profit - they are bogus items designed to inflate the price of the car.

**Financial Fitness Tip #39**
**Do not allow the salesperson to use the sucker sticker as a negotiation ploy**

The dealer's sucker sticker is the single most common reason people walk away from the dealership saying "Ha ha ha, I got a good deal!" But ask yourself this question: if the sucker sticker adds $4,000 to the price of the car and the salesperson then gives you a $1,500 discount, who's the sucker? Sure, you can *pretend* you got a good deal - you'll just never get financially fit pretending you're not a fool.

Add-ons or options that cost the dealer a pittance are stacked on this sticker. Oh boy, door guards. They cost the dealer $30 - why are you paying $399? Or how about that extra delivery charge? What are you paying for? Nothing. The real delivery charge is already built into the price. Yup, read the fine print right next to the MSRP: "Manufacturer's Suggested Retail Price ***Including*** Recommended Dealer Prep" (italics mine, of course).

Never negotiate the price of a car by looking at the dealer's personalized sticker. Look at the MSRP - and work from there. The only way to retain control in a car purchase is to know the difference between stuff you have to pay for and stuff you don't. Working from the MSRP means that at the very least you will not pay the highest possible price for the car you want. If the salesperson and the dealer want to make a sale, they will opt not to waste too much time trying to sucker you.

**Financial Fitness Tip #40**
**Don't pay for all cost, no value extras**

The dealer (or sucker) sticker lists lots of items you simply shouldn't pay for. The most common of these are rust proofing, fabric coating and paint sealant. Rust proofing or undercoating can cost you $200-$350 and paint sealant adds another couple of hundred dollars to the already inflated price.

As in all scams, false logic plays upon you. You don't want your car to rust out, especially if you endure terrible winters. And since you can finance it, why wouldn't you want to add this valuable protection to your car? The manufacturer has already painted an effective rustproof coating on the undercarriage of your car when it was built. It is more effective than anything the dealer will spray on. Don't pay to rustproof your car twice.

Fabric protection or fabric coating for the interior will add another $200-$300 to the bloated total. Dealer fabric coating is no more than the kid who staffs the "Dealer Prep Department" pulling your car into the garage and spraying the interior of the car with a couple of cans of Scotchguard. You can do this yourself in your own garage, since the chemicals they use are the same ones that you can buy in any department store, grocery, or auto supply.

Paint sealer is 100% profit for the dealer. Keep your car shiny without paint sealant by waxing your car every six months or so. If your paint begins to fade after a couple of years, many new products can "brighten" your paint job for under $20 and an hour of elbow grease. Or get your car detailed by a local body shop for about $100 every 12-18 months.

By the way, at the beginning of the infamous NADA (National Automobile Dealers Association) guide, known as the Blue Book, the editors actually say that much optional equipment has little or no value on older cars. This admission from the car industry is reason alone not to allow the salesperson to talk you into purchasing a car that's front-end loaded with bogus options.

If you are tough enough, you can get many options free by asking the dealer to remove them, and their price, from the car before you buy it. The salesperson will look at you with loathing, since you are not a sucker, but if you are willing to endure the change from friend to adversary, this strategy will work in most cases. Even if you don't get the options free, they will probably offer them to you at cost rather than lose the sale or remove them from the car. Here's where it pays to do your research. If you know what you really need and want in advance, you won't be as likely to fall for low-value goodies.

**Financial Fitness Tip #41**
**Never use low-value leverage to buy a car**

Leverage is a waste of money if it costs you dearly, especially on a big ticket item like a car. As with all other credit strategies, you must know your true interest rate when you purchase an automobile. Even more importantly, do not shop for a payment. Shop for the lowest overall price on the car you want.

You might say, "But my car payment is the single largest monthly payment I make – (after my mortgage). I've got to be able to afford that payment!" Of course. But don't buy the payment; buy the car.

How many times has this happened to you? You start talking with a salesperson about a car, and you're asked how much you want to spend per month. "Oh, about $300," you reply. The salesperson will find some reason to leave, will tell the finance manager what you are willing to spend, and return with "$325 a month and it's yours." You might be so glad they got close to your "price," you fall for this deal. Don't!

At a well-run, high-volume dealership the finance department alone can produce $100,000 a month in extra profit. The finance manager normally gets five to seven percent of that profit and is likely to use many types of sales strategies targeted to load you up with every high-profit item the dealer has to offer. All you have to do is sign on the dotted line.

Most buyers are so relieved to get close to the price and monthly payments they want and to be approved for a car loan so they are ready to agree to anything. When the finance manager says, "We can do it. But your payment will be $25 more," you are more than happy to agree. More false logic.

But remember, for each $25 per month the finance department can get from you by adding extras into your contract, the dealer makes up to $1,500 profit *over and above* the profit already built into the original car price.

The computer in the finance department is remarkable. It can take what you want to pay as your down payment and monthly payment, and voila'. It spits out a loan in which your payments will be exactly as ordered. Never buy anything just because you can afford the payment, especially not a car. For every extra dollar per month that you pay, it will cost you 60 times more—plus interest—once the car has been paid off (on a 60 month loan).

Remember the front-end loading we talked about earlier? There's also back-end loading. If the finance manager can get just another $25 per month from you, they will stuff your contract with "back-end" items like credit life insurance, credit disability insurance, an extended warranty, and maybe even a higher interest rate. If you finance your car for 48 months, that's $25 x 48, or an additional $1,200 you spend for the car—just because you told them how much you were willing to pay per month.

Sometimes those back-end items, on which you will pay interest for the life of your loan, can add another $5,000 to the price of your car. If you tell the finance department that you can spend another $12 per month on a 60-month contract, his computer will "decide" that your extended service contract should cost $720. If there was only five dollars per month left to play with, the exact same service contract will cost $300. Or if you don't buy all those extras, but still say you can afford that "extra" $25 per month, guess what—the APR on your contract will guarantee that you will spend that extra $25 every month for 60 months. Sneaky? Yes. Legal? Yes, it's legal. And it happens all the time. **This is not leverage - it's robbery!**

<u>Never</u> get financed by the dealer. The dealer is not a banker - he negotiates a deal with a bank, which then agrees to finance all the cars sold by this dealer for a fixed rate. If the dealer can get you to agree to a higher interest rate, he gets to keep the extra money. This is the same type of low value leverage that many credit cards trap you into, and you fall into that money pit because you buy something simply because you can afford the payment.

See the Smart Car Alternatives, especially Financial Fitness Tip #46, later in this chapter - it explains why short term financing, and not payment shopping, is a better overall financial strategy. It will also explain why you can protect your wealth building power by switching from a "new car mentality" to an alternative way of thinking.

Before you buy a car, go to your bank or credit union. Use the bank and credit strategies in this book to get rates and terms from a personal banker or your credit union loan officer. Do your homework and decide what you should pay for the car you want. Then get approved for a loan in that price range before you ever set foot in a car showroom. This gives you added negotiating power, since you already know you have the loan - it's as though you have the cash in your pocket. You will also know exactly what you will spend in interest.  In the unlikely event that the dealer won't sell you a car under these conditions, just walk away.  Car salespeople learn to say "next" all the time - so should you.

Remember this basis rule of thumb: If you buy a car based on the monthly payment, when you sign the purchase contract, you are probably paying 250% more than the car is worth. Add it all up. The MSRP, plus the front-end items (options on the manufacturer's sticker, the freight which really isn't freight, the sucker items), plus an extended service contract, credit life insurance, credit disability insurance, and probably an inflated interest charge.

Don't forget that they aren't the only car dealership in town that sells the car you want. You can always go to their competitor.

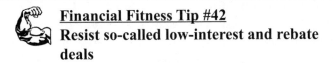

**Financial Fitness Tip #42**
**Resist so-called low-interest and rebate**
**deals**

The car industry is like the stock market - tricky and volatile. This month sales are up, the next month the store has a bunch of unsold cars and trucks. When demand is light, dealers have to find ways to sell more cars. The result: low interest rates and rebates, advertised aggressively. But as you know from the chapter on credit and leverage, the lender never really loses money.

Always be suspicious of a big rebate or super-low interest rates. The interest on a new car loan is about 5.5 percent on a 36-month loan – with the assumption that you have perfect credit. If your FICO score isn't 730 or above ("A" credit), expect to pay a higher rate. Yet dealers and manufacturers will bombard the public with slick ads offering interest rates cut from 50 to 100 percent. "Wow," you think, "Now is the time to buy. I know I'll get a great deal." Hence, the second most common reason fools rush in.

The truth is the car companies are not losing any profits with factory incentives, rebates, and low interest rates. The low interest rate results from what the loan industry calls a "buy-down," and it's no bargain for you.

Here's an example. Average overall profit on a car with options (not including dealer sticker items) is about 30%, split between the dealer (20%) and the manufacturer (10%). That means overall profit on a sticker price $25,000 car loaded with extras can be $7,500.

Even after this profit, the dealer still has lots of play with the numbers on the front or back end. These extras can add another $5,000 or more to the price of the car. Who would you rather be in this scenario? The dealer/manufacturer, with a total profit of $7,500 plus $5,000 for $12,500 in their pockets, - or you, borrowing $12,500 to buy this car? You'd rather be the dealer in this game, of course. If you're convinced you need and want this car, you won't feel good borrowing that $25,000 unless the dealer makes you feel good about it. Enter the low interest "incentive."

Here's how the low "buy-down" interest rate works. Let's say you are a wimp and agree to pay that $25,000 for the car, thinking "So what, I'm getting a break on the interest." To qualify for a "low" 2% rate, you must come up with a 20% down payment and agree to a short term on the loan - a maximum of 24 months. Or maybe you need a FICO score of 730 and above ("A" credit). You scrape up cash and a trade-in for $5,000.

Even with the interest buy down or rebate, your beautiful new car will depreciate by over 20% as soon as you drive it off the lot, and the dealer will be laughing all the way to the bank.

---

**<u>Financial Fitness Tip #43</u>**
**Trading in? Don't give them your keys!**

---

When you and the salesperson start to talk terms, if you have a trade-in the salesperson will ask for the keys to your car. You'll be told that the sales manager has to take your car for a drive. **Don't do it.** Why should you give your keys to a total stranger, even if you want to buy a car from him? The sales manager can tell, by just glancing at the exterior and mileage of your car, how much it is worth within about $25. What's this little drama all about?

This charade makes you a captive audience - you can't walk away from the deal until the sales rep lets you leave - hopefully in a new car. Many dealerships have a special parking area - out of sight from you and other buyers -where they take your car and park it.

With your undivided attention, the sales team can hold you "hostage" until you sign.

Sound extreme? Sure, but it will be done so subtly you may not notice until it's too late and you're tired, or bored enough to buy. This practice is not as common as it once was, but depending on how gullible you appear and how expensive a car you want - the odds are about even that it will be tried. The discomfort value of this tactic sells a lot of cars. That's why you shouldn't get all warm and fuzzy during the car buying process. Retain control of everything - including your keys and your checkbook.

 **Financial Fitness Tip #44**
**Make sure the Blue Book is the right color**

Ah, the legendary Blue Book - that biblical document which reveals the "wholesale" price of every car that has ever been built. Talk to a "gear-head" (and we all know one or two) and they will tell you that you shouldn't pay a penny more than the listed Blue Book price.

What exactly is the Blue Book? If you go to a dealer and ask to see the Blue Book he will pull a book, usually with a black or green cover, out of a drawer and begin to quote you prices. Unfortunately, this isn't really The Blue Book. This is a book that is printed expressly for the automobile industry which inflates the prices in the real Blue Book by hundreds of dollars. It's a wonderful toy to demonstrate what a wonderful price the dealer is giving you for your trade-in. Unfortunately, if you're taken in by it, you risk being sunk in a pit of confusion when the finance department starts spitting numbers at you.

The real Blue Book is printed by NADA (National Automobile Dealer's Association) and it lists the actual value of every available automobile. You won't be shown that real Blue Book at a car dealership. But if you do your homework you can go to the library or your bank and look at one - it has an orange cover. You can find it online for free at www.kellybluebook.com. Before you go shopping, look up your trade-in, as well as the car you want - and see what the true price of should be.

## If You *Must* Buy A New Car: Defensive Tactics
As you will see in the Smart Alternatives Section below, you can use your car dollar much more wisely - and with much less stress and hassle - if you resist buying a new car. But if you have your heart set on a new car, fresh from the showroom floor, remember these defensive tactics to save yourself hassles from the beginning:

**1. Do everything you can to buy the car with smart leverage - leverage *you* control.** That means getting a loan pre-approved by your bank or another lending institution. Remember that car interest is not deductible on your taxes - no way, no how. You might actually be better off getting a home equity loan for $20,000 and getting more car for your money, by coming in with cash and offering a price, and deducting the interest on your taxes. That's high value leverage.

**2. Don't assume the salesperson is your enemy.** The salesperson's job is to spend the time and effort necessary to schmooze you into being receptive to confusion. Car sales representatives have a saying: "If the customer wins, the salesman always loses." Most salespersons work for a pathetically low base salary - the only way they make a livable wage is by generating the right types of profits for the dealer each month. They don't want to waste your time - or theirs - trying to get you to dance, only to discover that you want to play power games.

If you walk in with cash or a pre-approved loan, say so. Tell the salesperson you are not willing to pay the highest price for the car. Tell him or her that you are not shopping for a payment. Explain that you've done your homework, and that you want to do this as quickly and painlessly as possible.

I have often accompanied friends who buy a car in this simple, straightforward way. They call a few dealers in advance, ask for the sales manager and explain themselves. They make an appointment, look at a few cars with a salesperson that has been prepped, choose a car, make a low offer, accept a slightly higher counter offer, nip the finance manager's spiel in the bud - and conclude the entire purchase in about an hour. The salesperson might make only $50-$100 commission (what salesmen call a *mini*), the dealer makes a small profit, no one is offended or manipulated - and you've bought that $25,000 car for $20,000 at a rate of interest which is acceptable and understandable.

**3.    Negotiate all options, phantom costs, and back-end items**. Don't try to get the car for cost. No dealer will sell you a car without some profit. Offer to pay a few hundred dollars over the MSRP for the car you want - and then try to get the options for cost. If you call a high volume dealership in advance, ask for the sales manager, and explain what you want, you might be pleasantly surprised. You might also find yourself pressured *after* you arrive at the dealership - but *applied* knowledge is power, and since you know what you are willing to spend, all you have to do is stand firm and be ready to exercise #4.

**4.    Be prepared to walk.** Unless you are buying - and can afford - some limited edition special collector's car, it's extremely unlikely that another dealership won't have exactly what you want, in the color and style you want, next week or next month. If you don't like what's happening, say so - and say, "buh-bye."

### The Smart Car Alternative Strategy
You are far better off financially buying the car you really love and want when it's used. I call this the Smart Car Alternative Strategy. Why is it smart? Because of the huge proportion of your overall wealth that is eaten up by your automobiles. Over your lifetime, you will

probably personally own five to fifteen different automobiles - that doesn't necessarily include your spouse and children. Based on what you've learned about the huge profits made by car dealers, the high insurance costs for new automobiles, and the wasted, non-deductible interest on car loans - how can anyone but movie stars and millionaires afford to burn so much money and still remain solvent?

True wealth sure isn't based on buying a new, overpriced mediocre automobile every three to five years. It is about getting the most from your money - and making more. If, like many Americans, one-fifth to one-fourth of your monthly expenses goes to paying for and maintaining cars, how can you possibly make investments? You're too busy driving bad investments.

Some of the biggest financial disasters I've ever seen are in people's garages. That's why I recommend that, with your very next car purchase, you give my Smart Car Alternative Tips a try. With these dozen helpful pointers you can buy a good car - probably even a better car than you could otherwise afford - and increase both your enjoyment and financial strength.

**The Smart Car Alternative Strategy simply means that you buy the car you really, really want when it's affordable for you.** That usually means buying it when it's about two years old. You might get it when it's only a year old - or, as in the case of my favorite car, when it's three years old - but you get to have it, own it, and enjoy it without suffering financially.

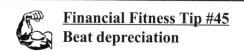

**Financial Fitness Tip #45**
**Beat depreciation**

A new car depreciates about 20% the moment you drive it off the lot. That means the $25,000 car you financed for $20,000 is now worth only $20,000. Hold on — it gets worse. With all the extras the finance manager talked you into when you negotiated your loan, you end up paying over $30,000 for a $25,000 car that is now worth less than $20,000. Yup - after owning your car one day, you now owe two and a half times what it is worth.

The Smart Car Alternative is to buy the car that you want, but wait until it is two to two and one-half years old - after its depreciated enough to be dirt-cheap.

"Why?" you ask. "Why would I want to buy a car without a warranty?" Come on. When you buy a two-year-old car, you can be reasonably sure you are buying a car that has all of its basic "bugs" worked out - courtesy of the original owner. What would you rather do? Pay 60% less for the same car, and keep the rest of that cash to cover any minor repairs that should come up? Or buy it new, and end up with a car worth less than 10% of its purchase price after you finish making your last payment?

Leverage is only valuable if it makes you financially stronger. This basic depreciation table shows how much weaker your "investment" is after a few years.

| Age Of Car (years) | Depreciation Of Purchase Price |
|---|---|
| 1 | 15% |
| 2 | 22% |
| 3 | 21% |
| 4 | 21% |
| 5 | 21% |

Don't let your cars drain you of your hard-earned cash. If you made an investment that did this poorly, if you bought a house that lost its value this quickly - well, you wouldn't make that same mistake twice

When you buy a car from an individual owner you can be sure of getting a good deal - if you are prepared. Why? No one advertises a car for sale unless they absolutely need to sell it.

I knew someone who bought an immaculate BMW, worth $10,000, for about $4,000. It was one of the best purchases they ever made - the car still runs beautifully, looks terrific, and cost them less than the down payment on a run of the mill new car. In the real estate business, I learned to buy "when there is blood running in the streets." That phrase is about 150 years old, but it is still true. Buying in a buyer's market guarantees that you will help someone unload something they can no longer afford - and you come out the winner.

Don't trick yourself into thinking that buying from a private individual is fraught with hassles and danger. It's in fact one of the easiest transactions in the world - unlike a car dealer, private sellers usually must divest themselves of an unwanted vehicle. That means they are ready, eager, and willing to make a deal. As long as you know how to determine what the car is worth, you can negotiate your way to driving the car of your dreams.

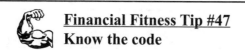

**Financial Fitness Tip #47**
**Know the code**

First decide exactly which model you would like to own. Then grab the classified section of your local newspaper, shopper, or auto trader magazine. With a bit of practice you can interpret these ads and find several cars that look good.

Classified ad users use contractions and code words to keep their advertising costs low - kind of like the personal ads if you are into that sort of thing. Here are the codes used in almost all U.S. newspapers.

| CODE | DEFINITION | CODE | DEFINITION |
|---|---|---|---|
| a/c, air | air conditioning | loaded | has many options |
| a/t, at, auto | automatic transmission | man trans | manual transmission |
|  |  | mt |  |
| cass | cassette tape player | mi | miles or mileage |
| cond | condition | mint | like-new condition |
| conv | convertible | orig owr | original owner selling |
| cpe | coupe (2 door) | obo | or best offer |
| cruise | cruise control | pb | power brakes |
| cu in | cubic inches (size of engine) | ps | power steering |
| cyl | cylinders (3,4,5,6 or 8) | pow seats | power seats |
| dlr | dealer is selling car | pw | power windows |
| exc | excellent condition | rdls, rads | radial tires |
| h/back, h/b | hatchback | rear dfg | rear defogger |
| hd | heavy duty suspension or shocks | sac | sacrifice |
| hdtp | hardtop | sed | sedan (4 door) |
| K | number of miles in thousands | snrf | sunroof |
| lk new | like new | vnyl | vinyl top |
|  |  | wrnty | warranty comes with car |

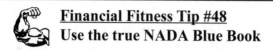

**Financial Fitness Tip #48**
**Use the true NADA Blue Book**

Now determine exactly, precisely, accurately what the car of your choice is worth. This is the maximum amount you will agree to pay - no matter what. Get yourself the NADA Official Used Car Guide - the one we talked about above, the one with the orange cover which all the auto dealers and bank loan officers use. Ask your personal banker to see his copy of this guide. Or if you would like to peruse the pages a bit longer, go to the public library or buy a copy at a major bookstore. To order the guide for yourself you can call 1-800-544-6232. It comes out monthly - so be prepared to act quickly.

You can also find the Kelly Blue Book online at www.kellybluebook.com. When you go to that website, you'll be able to find the value of the car you want to purchase, as well as the value of your own car. And best of all, its FREE.

Ever notice how your geographic location affects the price of everything you buy, from seafood to lawn fertilizer? Your car is no exception. The NADA Guide has nine editions published for the Central, Eastern, Midwest, Mountain, New England, Pacific Northwest, Pacific, Southwest, Southeastern, and Southwestern regions. By looking in the NADA guide for your region, you can establish the approximate value of any domestic or foreign car, van or light truck within $25.

First look up the model number and year of the car you want. Then find the columns marked **Av'g trd-in** (average trade-in) and **Av'g loan** (average loan). The average trade-in represents the price a dealer could get for the car at an auction. This price, after adjustments for options, condition and mileage, is also the maximum you will offer when you buy the car.

The current value of each option is listed at the end of each model-year. Most options add at least a little value to the car, but if certain ones are missing, they can actually *subtract* value from the car. These include (but are not limited to) those basic, can't live without them options like power steering, power brakes, and air-conditioning.

The figures listed in NADA assume the car is in good, clean condition - not perfect, but with no obvious damage, and in decent running order. Keep this in mind as you are looking at a prospective car.

The column marked *Av'g loan* displays the value of the car for the purpose of borrowing - the amount of money a lender will approve if you borrow to buy the car. Depending on whether you pay cash or borrow, the "right" price for the car is the NADA price minus the cost of putting the car back into good, clean, working condition.

Most banks will allow you to borrow the exact loan value shown in the NADA guide. This means if you can get the "right" price you need never make a down payment. Talk about high value leverage. Why would a bank allow you to take a loan with little or no down payment? Depending on how close you can negotiate the "right" price, you never owe much more than the value of the car. This is a smart, low risk loan for banks and credit unions. They win, and so do you.

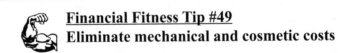

**Financial Fitness Tip #49**
**Eliminate mechanical and cosmetic costs**

Meet with the seller in a neutral place. Make an offer based on your homework and your assessment of the car. Then ask him or her to accompany you and take the car to a reputable mechanic, who should go over the car thoroughly and make a list of everything that needs repair now or soon.

Most repair shops will gladly do this if you if you agree to bring the car back for the work at a later date. Ask for an itemized estimate - a price for each needed repair. Sure, you will pay $50 to $75 for this service, but in the long run it will end up saving you money now and in the future. Never buy a car without going through this process. If the seller won't agree to it, simply say "next" and keep shopping.

Politely tell the seller that your offer was for a car that was in good condition, meaning that you expected everything to look okay and to work properly. Then present the seller with two choices:

1. Have the necessary work done. In turn, you agree to return next week with the agreed upon price.
2. Deduct the repair costs from the agreed upon price you and you will take the car now.

If the seller really wants to get rid of the car, he will take your immediate offer or negotiate for a mutually agreeable price.

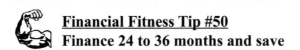

**Financial Fitness Tip #50**
**Finance 24 to 36 months and save**

Never finance a car loan for over 36 months. Of course the longer the term the smaller the payments - but remember what we've learned about shopping for a payment? The truth is that the longer the term of a loan, the more interest you pay, and the less value for your leverage.

When you shorten the term of a loan you reap a twofold benefit. First, you pay less total interest - and that means your car cost you a lot less. Second, a greater percentage of your payment goes directly to principle instead of interest. If you shorten the term of your loan, you also shorten the term of your leverage. By choosing a 36-month loan instead of a 60-month loan you can save about 17% of the cost of the car. With longer-term loans you can pay up to 25% more for the same car. This rule holds true whether you buy a new or used car.

What if you just can't afford the higher payment? Here is where buying a car even one year old can pay off handsomely. Your payments will probably not be any higher for the shorter term than if you had bought the new car for the longer term.

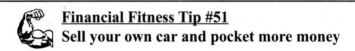

**Financial Fitness Tip #51**
**Sell your own car and pocket more money**

It's a fact, sad but true: When you trade-in your car you might as well give it away. Dealers really don't want your trade-ins. Trade-ins are difficult to resell in a used car lot. If your trade doesn't sell, the car goes to auction where is disposed of for a ridiculously low price. From the dealer's perspective, as long as your trade-in sits in his used car lot, he's not making any money. His profit sits there, unrealized.

The dealer doesn't like being inconvenienced in this way. Who pays for the dealer's inconvenience? You do. The dealer has many ways to make you pay, from using the original inflated mark-up to offset his "loss" to playing with the numbers of your loan contract with his trusty finance department computer.

If you were smart and found out the auction price of your trade-in before you bought a new car, you might have noticed that the trade-in offered by your dealer was about $1,000 less. Ask him about it and you may be told that there is no market for your car at this time. The dealer then takes your car, sells it at the auction price and pockets the $1,000 as sheer profit. The moral of this interesting story? Never trade in your old car. Sell it yourself and put the extra $1,000 in your pocket.

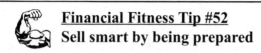

**Financial Fitness Tip #52**
**Sell smart by being prepared**

There are three simple things that will almost guarantee a profitable, easy sale of your car:

1. **Contact the loan officer at the financial institution that holds your current car loan. Ask what it would take for someone else to take over the loan.** The potential buyer will probably have to reapply. If their credit is good, the bank will usually be very glad to continue to handle the loan. Now you can put "Financing Arranged" in your ad, therefore widening the scope of calls you may get. If you have the model, year, and Vehicle Identification Number (VIN) ready when you talk to your potential buyer, all he or she has to do is go to your bank.

2. **Determine the price you are going to ask for the car**. Refer to the trusty NADA guide and find the average trade-in price. This is the very least you will take for your car. When you advertise, start your asking price $200 to $400 dollars above this. This gives you just enough room to negotiate with potential buyers.

3. **Glamorize, glamorize, glamorize! Cosmetics are just as important to a car buyer as the mechanical aspects.** Fix all the minor inexpensive items that are broken or worn on the car. Take your car to the local detail shop and have them give it the works. They will clean, wax and make

your car look and smell just like new. Do all those dirty jobs - the glove box and trunk, the scratches in the paint. Steam clean the engine and remove all of the corrosion from the battery cables. You might even buy inexpensive mats or seat covers if the floors and seats are worn. Tighten anything that shakes or rattles. If major repairs should be required, be honest in your ad and discount the price.

**Financial Fitness Tip #53**
**Control advertising, inquiries and**
**appointments**

1. **To advertise smart, buy a classified ad in your local newspaper or auto trader.** Avoid running the ad for the full week - it's not worth the cost. In your ad include all of the *key words* that make the buyer's eyes light up, like *must sell, like new, low mileage, financing arranged, financing available.* Include your phone number, the times that you will receive calls and the asking price in your ad. By including the asking price you will cut down the number of calls from people who are just looking.

2. **Set a specific time and date for prospective buyers to inspect the car.** Arrange to show the car to all of the prospective buyers at once. Ask prospects for their names and phone numbers. By simply doing this and telling the prospect that you must make a special effort to be there and that you would appreciate a call if he were unable to keep the appointment, you can prevent the no-show syndrome by about 50%.

3. **To prevent the stalling tactics of people who want to go home or think it over, show the car to as many people as you can**

**schedule at once.** They will wonder why everyone is interested in this one car. One car and several prospective buyers equal at least one bona-fide offer.

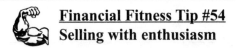

**Financial Fitness Tip #54**
**Selling with enthusiasm**

They will all ask you, so be prepared: "Why are you selling this car?" Be ready to give a reasonable, positive, enthusiastic answer. Tell an anecdote or two about what a great, reliable car it is, and how much you will miss it. Should a prospect point out a flaw, counter with a smile and say, "Sure, that's why you are getting such a great deal."

Most prospective buyers will want to test-drive the car. That's completely acceptable. Just never let them take your car without going along for the ride yourself. One of the biggest scams these days is a "prospective buyer" showing up and taking a car for a *permanent* test drive. Just because you're not sitting with a car salesman doesn't mean you should be a sucker.

Once you begin negotiations, most prospective buyers want to deal a bit. But don't haggle below your rock-bottom price. Simply and firmly tell the prospect that you cannot and will not go any lower. Encourage him to look for a better price if he thinks he can. Then remind him that he may lose the opportunity to buy this particular car if he waits too long. Does this sound familiar? You did learn something at the dealership.

Once you have come to an agreement, how should you accept payment? **Never take a personal check or a promise.** Once you have signed a bill of sale over to the new owner, you cannot repossess the car if the check bounces. Instead you will be stuck trying to collect on the check. The <u>only</u> acceptable methods of payment are cash or certified checks. Make this clear to the buyer before you sign the title over to him. If the buyer is financing the car, his bank will pay off your loan. If there is anything left over, the difference will come to you. Until these arrangements have been firmed up by your bank - and his -asks the buyer to give you a *cash* down payment of $200-$1,000. This is good faith money to take the car "off the market" until the purchase is completed.

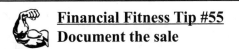

**Financial Fitness Tip #55**
**Document the sale**

If the buyer is financing the car through the bank, be sure they have the necessary insurance, license, and proof of ownership before they drive the car away. The bank will want to see this before they will process their loan. If they pay cash, and the necessary transfer papers have been signed, the buyer can take total possession of the car. Remember to remove your license plates before the car leaves your driveway. However, in some states such as California, the plates remain with the car.

Make sure you know your state's rules for the transfer of a title from one owner to another. Usually all owners listed on the front of the title must sign the back for the sale to be legal. Do not give the new buyer an unsigned title. If your name is still listed as legal owner, you could be liable for damages in the unlikely event of an accident. After signing the title, prepare and sign a bill of sale. Keep one copy for yourself and give one to the new owner. Here is sample - or you can purchase a form from a local office supplies store.

**Bill of Sale**

Sold to: _____ By _____

One _____
(year, make and model of car)

for $ _____ . Sold As Is.

Date _____

Your Signature _____

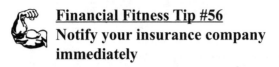

**Financial Fitness Tip #56**
**Notify your insurance company immediately**

Once you've sold your car and it is completely, totally, thoroughly in the new owner's name, cancel the insurance. Just make sure that your bank loan has been paid off before you cancel. As you learned in Chapter Six, you might end up liable for premiums and interest on an insurance policy that the lender purchases in the interim - and that can be outrageously expensive.

## Don't Forget!

Financial fitness means knowing the value of your dollar - and that's especially true of your car dollars. Don't forget to save on your car insurance costs using the tips in Chapter Six, and the car depreciation record-keeping skills in Chapter Four. You may not be able to drive "for free," but you should be able to cut your overall car expenditures by 50% or more using the combined power of these techniques - and that's money that will make you financially fit.

*If the automobile had followed the same development*
*as the computer, a Rolls-Royce would today cost $100,*
*get a million miles per gallon,*
*and explode once a year killing everyone inside.*
- Robert Cringely *InfoWorld*

## <u>Summary of Chapter Seven</u>

If you haven't already, you should be financially fit at this point. Purchasing a vehicle the correct way will pump up your retirement income in a big way. In this chapter, you learned how to:

- Change your view in the vehicle-purchasing arena. No F&I Manager will ever be able to *take you to the cleaners* ever again.

- Get financing approved ahead of time before you go shopping (if needed).

- Never finance a car over 36 months.

- Make an extra principal payment of your car loan in order to pay off the loan sooner.

- Sell your car yourself instead of trading it in.

# Chapter 8

## Legal Financial Steriods

*Let the government help finance your retirement.*
- Richard M. Krawczyk, Ph.D.

So-called *financial experts* have said for years that when you are younger, you can invest your money in higher-yielding high-risk investments. The theory behind this was that even if you lost all of your money, there would still be a number of years before your retirement so that you could play *catch-up*. And when you are approaching retirement age, your investments should be directed towards low-risk low-yielding conservative investments.

**I'm here to tell you today that they are all wrong!**

For years, I have searched and searched for a high-yielding secured investments. I was looking for a safe and secure investment that could be lucrative for both younger and older investors alike.

Wouldn't it be great if you could receive checks in your mailbox from the government? But these checks are not for T-Bills or municipal bonds. They are for Tax Lien Certificates (TLC).

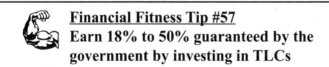

**Financial Fitness Tip #57**
**Earn 18% to 50% guaranteed by the government by investing in TLCs**

The practice of tax lien certificate sales is not a new one. They have been around for over 100 years. There are 3,300 counties in America. Each county needs tax dollars to operate. If these tax bills go unpaid, your local tax collector has the authority to seize your property and auction it off. Many times the property is sold for only amount of the back taxes owed.

Individuals either live in a *tax certificate* state or a *tax deed* state.

In tax certificate states, investor's don't receive the title of the property at the tax sale. You purchase the government lien for the back taxes. Your purchase of the government lien takes a lien position only second to an IRS lien. But, if an IRS tax lien were placed on a property **after** you purchased the tax certificate, your lien would hold a senior position, even higher than the IRS lien. It even has a senior position to a mortgage or deed of trust on the property. Before purchasing a tax lien certificate on a property, see if there are any IRS liens against the property.

When you purchase a TLC, the government allows you to receive all the tax money due, which include high interest, fees and penalties. As an example, TLC investors can purchase certificates in Iowa and receive 24% on their investments. In Michigan, you can earn as much as 50%.

If you live in a tax deed state, investors actually receive the deed to the property instead of a tax lien certificate. Depending on the state, there may be a right of redemption period for the homeowner. Please check the local rules for these states.

Why would you put your money in a passbook account or a CD at your local bank earning 1% to 6% when you can earn **10 times** more than the bank all by yourself?

**Financial Fitness Tip #58**
**No commissions are ever paid on TLCs -**
**which means more money in your pocket**

This is the best-kept secret in America today. Since no commissions are paid to anyone, stockbrokers, insurance agents and bankers won't tell you about them. Besides, why would your bank tell *you*? They "rent" your money at 1% to 6%, buy TLCs and then pocket the extra 15% or so for themselves. They would be losing money if they told you about them.

You may say that you feel safe putting your money in a bank because it's insured by the FDIC, right? Well, the government also secures TLCs. If the property owner does not make good on the back taxes owed, usually within two years (right of redemption for states may vary), you get the property.

Research has shown that 97% of all tax liens are paid off in the first two years. The reason for this is simple. Let's say that Joe doesn't pay his property taxes of $2,000. Investor Judy purchases a TLC on Joe's property. Joe happens to have a $100,000 mortgage on his property. After two years, do you actually think that Joe's mortgage company will lose their $100,000 interest in the property for $2,000? NO WAY! Guess who will pay off the TLC before the redemption period expires? The mortgage company does.

If you purchase a tax lien certificate and the owner sells the property during the redemption period, **you get paid**. If the owner pays the *taxman* for the back taxes before the end of the redemption period, **you get paid**. If the redemption period expires and the owner doesn't pay their back taxes, **you get the property**. YOU CAN'T LOSE! If you don't get a high rate of return on your investment, you get the property for the cost of their back taxes. That's equivalent to purchasing a property for only a **nickel to ten cents on the dollar**.

Tax certificates can range from $25 up to $100,000 or even more. The makes it an attractive investment for people of any age or financial condition.

If you are close to retirement age and you need to play *catch up*, this is a perfect way to do it. It's 100% guaranteed by the government and it's high-yielding.

If you are just starting out in your investment career, taking advantage of this type of investment can pay for the cost of college for when your children grow up and still plan for your eventual retirement.

A great way to make these investments is through your self-directed IRA. You will compound your money tax-free. You may also be able to withdraw some money from your IRA penalty-free if the money is used to pay college cost.

Here is a good example of IRA TLC investing. If Investor Don were to make a $2,000 investment into his IRA at the bank, the bank would pay about 3.75% interest. If he doesn't touch his investment, after 20 years, he would have $4,219. If Don would have a self-directed IRA in which he invested that same $2,000, assuming that he didn't touch his original investment and he invested in a TLC that only paid only 20%, he would have $76,675 in 20 years. And that's just on one-time investment of only $2,000. If you made a $2,000 yearly contribution for a few years and then stopped, the numbers would still be obscene.

The easiest way to get started is to call your county tax collectors office. If you live in a TLC state, ask what interest rate they are paying and how long the redemption period is. Since many states sell remaining TLCs after the auction, find out their policies regarding private sales. Ask to be put on their mailing list for their upcoming TLC auctions.

Small counties may only have 6,000 - 7,000 TLCs to sell, so check into your surrounding counties too. In larger counties, TLC auctions can last few weeks before all the TLCs are sold.

Would you like to take vacations tax-free? One of the ways to do this is to plan your vacation around TLC sales in other states. This is one avenue to increase your wealth as well as see other parts of the country, TAX-FREE.

This investment vehicle is a sure fire way to become financially fit quickly and safely.

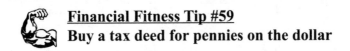

**Financial Fitness Tip #59**
**Buy a tax deed for pennies on the dollar**

If you're not interested in receiving a high rate of return in government guaranteed tax lien certificates, consider investing in *tax deeds*. In a Tax Deed state, you will receive the deed to the property immediately (some states have a redemption period, some don't) when you pay the back taxes. Again, that's equivalent to purchasing a property for only – **a nickel to ten cents on the dollar.**

Local tax collectors often negotiate private sales (usually in the amount of the back taxes owed) to dispose of this real estate. If the tax collector is in possession of a property on which the redemption period has already expired, you can purchase it and receive the deed immediately, even in a certificate state.

| **CERTIFICATE STATES** | | **DEED STATES** |
|---|---|---|
| Alabama | 12% | Alaska |
| Arizona | 16% | Arkansas |
| Colorado | 9% (above Federal Reserve) | California |
| Florida | 18% | Delaware |
| Illinois | 18% | Georgia |
| Indiana | 10-25% | Hawaii |
| Iowa | 24% | Idaho |
| Kentucky | 12% | Kansas |
| Louisiana | 5%+ | Maine |
| Maryland | 12-24% | Minnesota |
| Massachusetts | 18% | Nevada |
| Michigan | 15-50% | New Mexico |
| Mississippi | 17% | New York |
| Missouri | 10% | Ohio |
| Montana | 10% | Oklahoma |
| Nebraska | 14% | Oregon |
| New Hampshire | 18% | Pennsylvania |
| New Jersey | 18% | Texas |
| New York | 14% | Utah |
| North Carolina | 12% | Virginia |
| North Dakota | 12% | Washington |
| Rhode Island | 12% | Wisconsin |
| South Carolina | 8% | |
| South Dakota | 12% | |
| Tennessee | 10% | |
| Vermont | 12% | |
| West Virginia | 12% | |
| Wyoming | 18% | |
| District of Columbia | varies | |
| Puerto Rico | varies | |

Some rules for TLC investing. Each state and county's rules may be slightly different.

## SEMINOLE COUNTY, FLORIDA
## TAX CERTIFICATE SALE GUIDELINES

1. The 2003 Tax Certificate Sale will begin at 9:00 a.m., May 28, 2003 in the County Commission Chambers at the west end of the County Services Building, and will continue on a day to day basis until all certificates are sold. There will normally be a one-hour recess for lunch from 12:00 to 1:00 p.m.
2. Bidding is for the rate of interest only and may commence at the maximum rate of 18% and bid inversely to 0% in minimum quarter of a percent increments. Face value of certificate is: tax, plus cost, as advertised. The advertised figure is the amount due for each certificate purchased.
3. Bidders are asked to wait until the auctioneer has finished calling an item before bidding.
4. The first bid recognized by the auctioneer is the official bid.
5. Established bidders are required to deposit 10% of their intended purchases. New bidders are required a minimum deposit of $1,000 or 10% of the expected total above $10,000. The only exceptions to this deposit requirement are those individuals intending to purchase a single certificate. In these cases a bidder number will be assigned with a minimum deposit of $100 or 10% of the certificate, if higher. A bidder number will not be assigned until the buyer completes and files with the Tax Collector's Office IRS Form W-9. For further bidder information, call the Delinquent Tax Department at (407) 665-7641.
6. Purchase of a Tax Certificate in **no way** permits the certificate holders to enter the property or intimidate the landowner. The landowner has a period of two years from the date the tax became

delinquent to redeem the Tax Certificate. Payments of certificates are processed by the Office of the Tax Collector **only**.

Tax Certificates must represent taxes that are two years delinquent before a Tax Deed Application may be made, and also require that if any other taxes are outstanding, they be paid by the tax deed applicant.

7.  In the event a resolvable error is discovered in the Tax Certificate, it may be canceled or corrected by authority of the Department of Revenue. In this case, 8% interest per annum will be paid, except as revised by law or court order.

8.  The life of the Tax Certificate is seven years.

9.  The bidder name given at the sale is the name that will appear on the Tax Certificate. All required correspondence would be mailed to the address given at registration. Subsequent changes of address must be sent in writing to the Office of the Tax Collector.

10. After payment of balance due, all successful bidders will receive an electronic certificate listing. This list will be certified by the Tax Collector's Office as an accurate record of all purchases. Bidders requiring verification of specific certificate ownership may request a letter or list of confirmation be provided to a third party.

11. All Tax Certificates that are transferred **must** be recorded in the Office of the Tax Collector. There is a $4.50 fee for each transfer.

12. A lien created through the sale of a tax certificate may not be foreclosed or enforced in any manner except as prescribed in F.S. Chapter 197.

13. If a tax certificate you purchase becomes involved in bankruptcy, the court should notify and mail you the proper forms. During bankruptcy proceedings, the court will order the interest stayed from the time of filing until final determination. Florida Statutes are clear and in most cases they have guided the federal bankruptcy court. However, interest rates have been reduced and there is no assurance of what the courts may rule in the future.

*With money in your pocket, you are wise*
*and you are handsome and you sing well too.*
- Yiddish Proverb

## <u>Summary of Chapter Eight</u>

If you didn't consider the chapter on IRAs a financial *steroid*, this chapter will definitely do it for you. In Chapter Eight, you learned to:

- Determine if investing Tax Lien Certificates is for you.

- Decide if you feel more comfortable in Tax Lien Certificates or Tax Deeds.

- Determine the state that you wish to invest your retirement funds.

- Contact the Tax Assessor in the county that you wish to make purchases to be put on their mailing list.

# Chapter 9

## *How Discounted Mortgages Can Increase*

## *Your Level of Financial Fitness*

*Every man is enthusiastic. One man is enthusiastic for thirty*
*minutes, another man has it for thirty days, but it is the man who*
*has it for thirty years who makes a success in life.*
- William B. Butler

If your interested in another high-yielding investment, and don't mind doing a little digging to locate and manage them, this chapter is for you. We'll now explore discounted mortgages - another lucrative investment you'll never find at a bank, brokerage firm, or financial planners office. This investment can guarantee both unusually high income and growth potential.

If you don't have the financial resources available to you to purchase discounted mortgages, don't worry. Read this chapter anyway. This will give you enough knowledge to be able to broker discounted mortgages and **MAKE CASH NOW!**

 **Financial Fitness Tip #60**
**If you can handle some risk and a little**
**extra work, go for discounted mortgages**
**to maximize your profits**

Yes, these are some risks involved in discounted mortgages - although I will give you some tips for mitigating them.

## The Discounted Mortgage Investment

A discounted mortgage is usually a second mortgage that you purchase on your own steam. You have to locate it, negotiate for it, buy it and manage the sale. So it does take some work. The beautiful part is that you can earn 30% on your investment, virtually guaranteed, if you do your homework.

The discounted mortgage originated in the early eighties, when high interest rates made it difficult for some people to sell their homes. Sellers began to allow buyers to assume their existing mortgage, which has a low interest rate, and then a second mortgage as the down payment. Since sellers really don't like mortgages-they just want their money all at once - lots of sellers are looking for ways to receive a lump sum of cash out of their mortgage. They prefer this to the interest payments that often trickle in instead.

This is where your opportunity comes in. Sellers don't go out on the street trying to unload their mortgages. After all, who's out there to buy them? There's no knowledge regarding mortgages, and no obvious market. So many sellers will take 30% to 50% off the face value of the mortgage — the "discount" — and you and the seller negotiate a purchase price from there. You usually start by offering 60% of the face value — that's 60 cents on the dollar.

If the seller sells you an interest only $10,000 mortgage at 60% of the face value, you pay $6,000 for it. Say the mortgage term is over in five years, at that time you get the entire face value, or $10,000— that's a $4,000 return. If the mortgage had an interest rate of 12%, that would have been paid to you over five years, or $1,200 per year. You invested $6,000, and you made $1,200 annually, which comes out to a 20% return. Your interest profit ($1,200 x 5 years or $6,000) added to your discount profit ($4,000) equals your total profit— in this case $10,000 on your $6,000 investment. That's over a 30% return.

You may not even have to wait many years to get your total return back. Since homeowners refinance occasionally or sell their home in a few years, you may receive your investment back even quicker.

The math is relatively easy, once you work it out a few times, and the return is staggering. It's also a guaranteed return as long as you make smart purchases. The trick to the discount mortgage isn't in the investment itself - it's locating a mortgage to purchase.

### How To Find The Discounted Mortgage Seller

Use these techniques to locate discounted mortgages. You'll have to do a little legwork to do it. Is it worth it? How does a 30% return sound?

1. **The County Courthouse:** In the real estate records room of your county courthouse, you can research transactions in their file room or microfiche archive. Look for second mortgages on residential properties. The holders of the second mortgages (or deeds of trusts) are the previous owners of the property. You need the following information:
   - Who is the *Mortgagee* - that's the seller
   - Who is the *Mortgagor* - that's the person making the payments
   - *Address* - you need to look at the property
   - *Amount of the Mortgage*
   - *Terms* - payments, due date, interest rate

   Sometimes the second mortgage will be called a "deed of trust" or "second deed of trust."

   Compile a list of about 15 properties that fit your purchase price. Calculate the discount - you'll be buying the mortgages at 30% to 40% less than their face value.

2. **Put an Ad in the Newspaper:** Ads like "CASH FOR MORTGAGES" or "I'LL BUY YOUR MORTGAGE FOR

CASH" will generate a few good calls a week. Run them in the classified section. Your investment in the ad is, by the way, tax-deductible.

3. **Real Estate Professionals:** Here is where the power of networking can bring high-profit leads. Since someone who wants to sell a mortgage doesn't really know how to find a buyer, a real estate agent often gets the call. Make friends with some real estate agents. Ask them for referrals. You can get an endless supply of free leads in this way.

## How To Buy The Discounted Mortgage

Call the mortgagee or send them a letter. Identify yourself and explain that you know they hold a mortgage on the property in question. Then just explain that you are an investor who wants to buy the mortgage for cash. "Would you be interested in selling your mortgage?"

About 80% of them will say yes. Make an appointment, and negotiate by starting at 60% of the face value. Most will jump at your offer, since most people need cash flow right now. About one-third of mortgage holders will close at a 30% to 40% discount just to get their hands on the money.

You will need an attorney to transfer the mortgage and record it at the courthouse, so you have first claim on the property - or any other loans or mortgages that follow.

## How To Minimize The Risks Of Discounted Mortgages

There is only one basic risk with a discounted mortgage: the mortgagor (the one making the payments) defaults and you'll have to foreclose on the property. Plan for this unlikely contingency. Here's where using a good real estate attorney can save you frustration, time and possibly your investment.

### *Use A Good Attorney*

Make sure you choose an attorney who is familiar with real estate in your area. It's best to simply develop a plan that sets foreclosure proceedings in motion if the mortgagor is one day late on payments. Decide you will do this, develop a procedure, and stick with it. That's not harsh. You'd be surprised how few attempted foreclosures ever even get to foreclosure if papers are served right away. You don't give inertia a chance to set in if you are firm and swift in showing you mean business. Think about the swift kicks you've had to give yourself throughout this book to keep your head in the game.

Your attorney will suggest one of three plans. In the first, you go ahead and make the payments current yourself so the mortgagee (the seller) doesn't foreclose before you. In the second, you get a quitclaim deed from the mortgagor showing you as holder of the deed to the property. It saves the mortgagor the ordeal of foreclosure and will preserve his/her credit rating as well. Or should the foreclosure occur and the property goes to auction, bid an amount equal to the first mortgage plus the amount owed on the second mortgage - that way, if someone outbids you, you get all of your investment back. If no one does, you'll need to put 10% in escrow and you've got 30 days to finance the balance or sell the property, and the banks are usually happy to help you by lending you money to do that.

### *Get a Credit Report*

One way to hedge your bets in advance is to check the credit rating of the mortgagor. After all, good credit usually creates more good credit. If the seller really wants you to buy the mortgage, you'll be offered some sort of payment history - if not, ask for it. What you're looking for is a *seasoned* mortgage, one with a long payment history.

## *Set Limits On What You'll Finance*

Also, mortgage companies use a calculation, called an LTV (Loan to Value) ratio, for figuring out the upper limit of financing they will offer on the market value of any property. You should have your own LTV ratio also—make yours 80%. To decide how much you'd be willing to borrow to keep the property, calculate 80% of its appraised value. Then add up all the mortgages on the property - including yours. If that number is more than 80% of the appraised value, don't buy the mortgage.

## *The Discounted Mortgage As Part Of Your Investment Plan*

If the high returns and the challenge of making deals appeals to you, the discount mortgage gives you lots of benefits without excessive risk. If you've got a substantial amount of cash to invest, say over $15,000, get a taste for the process by locating some mortgages. Even if you're not ready to buy, try it out. For people who like to be out on the street— people who have done outside sales, for example— making their own decisions on how to play a deal, this is a lot more fun than reading a prospectus. I know, as a real estate junkie myself, I love the idea of getting a great return by working such a simple, hands-on plan.

No matter what, don't invest more than 40% of your capital in discounted mortgages, since your money isn't liquid and it could be tied up anywhere from two to ten years.

> *Bankers are brokers.*
> - Richard M. Krawczyk, Ph.D.

*The art of being rich is found not in saving,*
*but in being at the right spot at the right time.*
- Ralph Waldo Emerson

## Summary of Chapter Nine

In general, discounted mortgages confuse people because they just don't understand them. If you're in a financial position to do so and don't mind putting in your time at the financial gym, this may be a great investment vehicle for you. In this chapter, you learned:

- Being the banker could be more profitable than the customer.

- To determine if you wanted to spend the time to pump up your financial muscles with discounted mortgages.

# Chapter 10

## *Investment Shifting Your Way*

## *To Financial Fitness*

*Rollin' rollin' rollin', keep those doggies movin'.*
Rawhide Theme
*The Blues Brothers*

If you have followed every Financial Fitness Tip so far, you are already more financially fit than at least 90% of the population. You should pat yourself on the back. Since momentum is everything, let's get to Financial Fitness Tip #61:

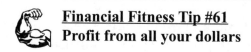

**Financial Fitness Tip #61**
**Profit from all your dollars**

That's right, every single one of them - even short-term cash. Now that your investments are coming into a clearer focus, we should now concentrate a little more on basic investment principles - which will insure maximum profits are realized. This leads us to our next Financial Fitness Tip:

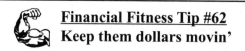

**Financial Fitness Tip #62**
**Keep them dollars movin'**

Remember, making a large income doesn't guarantee financial fitness. Multi-millionaires go broke every day—just look at Wayne Newton or Willie Nelson. The problem has nothing to do with how much they earn, but everything to do with what they do with their money, how leveraged they are, and who they trust with the management of their cash. Donald Trump is one of the more inventive and savvy entrepreneurs to come along in a while, hit success after success. Yet, even he almost lost it all when he rushed ahead even though the financial environment was not conducive to his creative strategies. I'm happy to say that "The Donald" is back on top again and even bigger than ever!

Financial Fitness is based on loving, nurturing, and coaxing maximum value out of the money you have - whether it's $10 or $10 million. Think of investing as cultivating a lush, gorgeous and highly productive garden. It doesn't matter how small the garden is, or how large. The point is why plant something and then neglect it? Why grows herbs and then let them go to seed? Why grow fruit that ends up rotting on the vine? Why exercise your body if you continue to have a bad diet? It's stupid, right? Go out there and pull up a few weeds, check to see which plants need to be thinned out, plant in rotation, invest in some extra fertilizer for the stuff that's really going good, balance perennials with annuals. Then sit back and enjoy.

Not every plant does well every year. Not every crop grows in every climate. You can't call some investments good and some investments bad without looking at them in context. To keep your money movin' in the direction of maximum profit, you've got to understand some basics of why you should move it, how you should move it, and most importantly, *when* to move it.

I'm certain that if the average American understood these simple principles and used them consistently, the average American would be financially fit. Financial fitness can be achieved without so-called high-risk vehicles. You can do it by knowing when to shift your money from mutual funds to stocks and from stocks to bonds and back again, rollin' down the trail of these good old standbys.

It's not scary. It's not intimidating. It does require learning some simple principles and basic skills, woven into a technique for making educated judgments about when your dollars might make more for you someplace else.

 **Financial Fitness Tip #63**
**Investment Shifting will make your decision easy**

*Investment Shifting* - sounds sophisticated, doesn't it? Don't worry, it's not. It's simply a methodology for earning anywhere from 12% to 20% or more per year safely, no matter what the interest rates out there are doing. That's a nice return. What's even nicer is you don't have to spend all day checking fund quotes to master the technique.

 **Financial Fitness Tip #64**
**Investment Shifting to maximize profit**

By using the follow guideline, simply pick a mutual fund that suits your needs. Let the economy (regardless of its condition) determine which mutual fund you should invest in.

- If the prime rate is consistently above 9.5%, invest your money in a money market fund.
- If the prime rate is consistently below 9.5%, invest in a stock mutual fund.
- If the prime rate is high and coming down, invest in a bond fund.

By checking the business section of your local newspaper or even online, you will be able to find the prime rate. When there is any speculation of change in the prime rate, it is usually reported by the national television and print media.

The flexibility and diversity of mutual funds means that you have all of the benefits of investing in stocks, bonds or money market funds, without all of the risk of investing in just one single company, bond type or money market account. Memorize the simple Investment Shifting Strategy outlined above and you already know everything you need to know to become a confident investor.

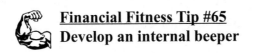

**Financial Fitness Tip #65**
**Develop an internal beeper**

Over a short period of time, you'll develop an internal beeper that alerts you to changes in interest rates. Just pay attention to the financial news on the radio or TV and watch for the prime rate. Once you become sensitized to them, you can shift your investments and never get caught off guard. If necessary, you can sell your shares outright and purchase funds outside of your current mutual-fund family – or just invest your money in something else like real estate. And don't forget, your retirement account can also invest in mutual funds.

# Prime Rate Investment Chart

B - BOND FUND
S - STOCK FUND
M - MONEY MARKET FUND

| DATE | RATE | INVEST |
|------|------|--------|
| **1972** | | |
| 24-Jan | 5 | S |
| 31-Jan | 4.75 | S |
| 5-Apr | 5 | S |
| 26-May | 5.25 | S |
| 2-Oct | 5.75 | S |
| 27-Dec | 6 | S |
| **1973** | | |
| 27-Feb | 6.25 | S |
| 26-Mar | 6.5 | S |
| 18-Apr | 6.75 | S |
| 7-May | 7 | S |
| 25-May | 7.25 | S |
| 8-Jun | 7.5 | S |
| 25-Jun | 7.75 | S |
| 3-Jul | 8 | S |
| 9-Jul | 8.25 | S |
| 18-Jul | 8.5 | S |
| 30-Jul | 8.75 | S |
| 6-Aug | 9 | S |
| 13-Aug | 9.25 | S |
| 22-Aug | 9.5 | M |
| 28-Aug | 9.75 | M |
| 18-Sep | 10 | M |
| 24-Oct | 9.75 | B |

| DATE | RATE | INVEST |
|------|------|--------|
| **1974** | | |
| 20-Jan | 9.5 | B |
| 11-Feb | 9.25 | S |
| 19-Feb | 9 | S |
| 25-Feb | 8.75 | S |
| 22-Mar | 9 | S |
| 29-Mar | 9.25 | S |
| 3-Apr | 9.5 | M |
| 5-Apr | 9.75 | M |
| 11-Apr | 10 | M |
| 19-Apr | 10.25 | M |
| 25-Apr | 10.5 | M |
| 2-May | 10.75 | M |
| 6-May | 11 | M |
| 10-May | 11.25 | M |
| 17-May | 11.5 | M |
| 26-Jun | 11.75 | M |
| 5-Jul | 12 | M |
| 7-Oct | 11.75 | B |
| 21-Oct | 11.5 | B |
| 28-Oct | 11.25 | B |
| 4-Nov | 11 | B |
| 14-Nov | 10.75 | B |
| 25-Nov | 10.5 | B |

# Prime Rate Investment Chart

B  -  BOND FUND
S  - STOCK FUND
M - MONEY MARKET FUND

| DATE | RATE | INVEST |
|------|------|--------|
| **1975** | | |
| 9-Jan | 10.25 | B |
| 15-Jan | 10 | B |
| 20-Jan | 9.25 | S |
| 28-Jan | 9.5 | S |
| 3-Feb | 9.25 | S |
| 10-Feb | 9 | S |
| 18-Feb | 8.25 | S |
| 24-Feb | 8.5 | S |
| 5-Mar | 8.25 | S |
| 10-Mar | 8 | S |
| 18-Mar | 7.75 | S |
| 24-Mar | 7.5 | S |
| 20-May | 7.25 | S |
| 9-Jun | 7 | S |
| 18-Jul | 7.25 | S |
| 28-Jul | 7.5 | S |
| 12-Aug | 7.75 | S |
| 15-Sep | 8 | S |
| 27-Oct | 7.25 | S |
| 5-Nov | 7.5 | S |
| 2-Dec | 7.25 | S |
| **1976** | | |
| 12-Jan | 7 | S |
| 21-Jan | 6.75 | S |
| 1-Jun | 7 | S |
| 7-Jun | 7.25 | S |
| 2-Aug | 7 | S |
| 4-Oct | 6.75 | S |
| 1-Nov | 6.5 | S |
| 13-Dec | 6.25 | S |

| DATE | RATE | INVEST |
|------|------|--------|
| **1977** | | |
| 13-May | 6.5 | S |
| 31-May | 6.75 | S |
| 22-Aug | 7 | S |
| 16-Sep | 7.25 | S |
| 7-Oct | 7.5 | S |
| 24-Oct | 7.75 | S |
| **1978** | | |
| 10-Jan | 8 | S |
| 5-May | 8.25 | S |
| 26-May | 8.5 | S |
| 16-Jun | 8.75 | S |
| 30-Jun | 9 | S |
| 31-Aug | 9.25 | S |
| 15-Sep | 9.5 | M |
| 28-Sep | 9.75 | M |
| 13-Oct | 10 | M |
| **1979** | | |
| 19-Jun | 11.5 | M |
| 27-Jul | 11.75 | M |
| 18/16 | 12 | M |
| 18/28 | 12.25 | M |
| 19/07 | 12.75 | M |
| 19/14 | 13 | M |
| 19/21 | 13.25 | M |
| 28-Sep | 13.5 | M |
| 9-Oct | 14.5 | M |
| 23-Oct | 15 | M |
| 1-Nov | 15.25 | M |
| 9-Nov | 15.5 | M |
| 16-Nov | 15.75 | M |
| 30-Nov | 15.5 | M |
| 7-Dec | 15.25 | M |

## 1979(continued)

| | | |
|---|---|---|
| 27-Oct | 10.25 | M |
| 1-Nov | 10.5 | M |
| 6-Nov | 10.75 | M |
| 17-Nov | 11 | M |
| 24-Nov | 11.5 | M |
| 26-Dec | 11.75 | M |

## 1980

| | | |
|---|---|---|
| 19-Feb | 15.75 | M |
| 26-Feb | 16.5 | M |
| 1-Feb | 16.75 | M |
| 4-Mar | 17.25 | M |
| 7-Mar | 17.75 | M |
| 14-Mar | 18.5 | M |
| 19-Mar | 19 | M |
| 1-Apr | 19.5 | M |
| 3-Apr | 20 | M |
| 18-Apr | 19.5 | M |
| 2-May | 18.5 | B |
| 7-May | 17.5 | B |
| 16-May | 16.5 | B |
| 27-May | 14.5 | B |
| 30-May | 14 | B |
| 6-Jun | 13 | B |
| 13-Jun | 12.5 | B |
| 20-Jun | 12 | B |
| 7-Jul | 11.5 | B |
| 24-Jul | 11 | B |
| 5-Sep | 12 | M |
| 12-Sep | 12.25 | M |
| 19-Sep | 12.5 | M |
| 26-Sep | 13 | M |
| 1-Oct | 13.5 | M |

## 1980 (continued)

| | | |
|---|---|---|
| 17-Oct | 14 | M |
| 29-Oct | 14.5 | M |
| 6-Nov | 15.5 | M |
| 17-Nov | 16.25 | M |
| 21-Nov | 17 | M |
| 26-Nov | 17.75 | M |
| 2-Dec | 18.5 | M |
| 5-Dec | 19 | M |
| 10-Dec | 20 | M |
| 16-Dec | 21 | M |
| 1-Dec | 21.5 | M |

## 1981

| | | |
|---|---|---|
| 9-Jan | 20 | M |
| 3-Feb | 19.5 | B |
| 23-Feb | 19 | B |
| 24-Feb | 18.5 | B |
| 10-Mar | 18 | B |
| 17-Mar | 17.5 | B |
| 25-Mar | 17 | B |
| 21-Apr | 17.5 | B |
| 26-Apr | 18 | B |
| 4-May | 19 | M |
| 11-May | 19.5 | M |
| 19-May | 20 | M |
| 22-May | 20.5 | M |
| 2-Jun | 20 | M |
| 8-Jul | 20.5 | M |
| 15-Sep | 20 | M |
| 22-Sep | 19.5 | M |
| 5-Oct | 19 | B |
| 13-Oct | 18 | B |
| 2-Nov | 17.5 | B |
| 9-Nov | 17 | B |
| 16-Nov | 16.5 | B |
| 24-Nov | 16 | B |
| 1-Dec | 15.75 | B |

# Prime Rate Investment Chart

B - BOND FUND
S  - STOCK FUND
M - MONEY MARKET FUND

**1982**

| | | |
|---|---|---|
| 2-Feb | 16.5 | B |
| 17-Feb | 17 | B |
| 23-Feb | 16.5 | B |
| 20-Jul | 16 | B |
| 29-Jul | 15.5 | B |
| 2-Aug | 15 | B |
| 16-Aug | 14.5 | B |
| 18-Aug | 14 | B |
| 20-Aug | 13.5 | B |
| 7-Oct | 13 | B |
| 13-Oct | 12 | B |
| 22-Nov | 11.5 | B |

**1983**

| | | |
|---|---|---|
| 11-Jan | 11 | B |
| 28-Feb | 10.5 | B |
| 8-Aug | 11 | M |

**1984**

| | | |
|---|---|---|
| 19-Mar | 11.5 | M |
| 6-Apr | 12 | M |
| 8-May | 12.5 | M |
| 25-Jun | 13 | M |
| 27-Sep | 12.75 | M |
| 16-Oct | 12.25 | M |
| 29-Oct | 12 | B |
| 8-Nov | 11.75 | B |
| 28-Nov | 11.25 | B |
| 20-Dec | 10.75 | B |

**1985**

| | | |
|---|---|---|
| 15-Jan | 10.5 | B |
| 20-May | 10 | B |
| 18-Jun | 9.5 | S |

**1986**

| | | |
|---|---|---|
| 7-Mar | 9 | S |
| 21-Apr | 8.5 | S |
| 11-Jul | 8 | S |
| 26-Aug | 7.5 | S |

**1987**

| | | |
|---|---|---|
| 31-Mar | 7.75 | S |
| 1-May | 8 | S |
| 15-May | 8.25 | S |
| 4-Sep | 8.75 | S |
| 7-Oct | 9.25 | S |
| 0/22 | 9 | S |
| 5-Nov | 8.75 | S |

**1988**

| | | |
|---|---|---|
| 2-Feb | 8.5 | S |
| 11-May | 9 | S |
| 14-Jul | 9.5 | S |
| 11-Aug | 10 | M |
| 28-Nov | 10.5 | M |

**1989**

| | | |
|---|---|---|
| 10-Feb | 11 | M |
| 24-Feb | 11.5 | M |
| 5-Jun | 11 | B |
| 10-Jul | 10.5 | B |

**1990**

| | | |
|---|---|---|
| 8-Jan | 10 | B |

**1991**

| | | |
|---|---|---|
| 2-Jan | 9.5 | S |
| 1-Feb | 9 | S |
| 1-May | 8.5 | S |
| 13-Sep | 8 | S |
| 6-Nov | 7.5 | S |
| 20-Dec | 6.5 | S |

**1992**

| | | |
|---|---|---|
| 2-Jul | 6 | S |

**1993**

No Changes

**1994**

| | | |
|---|---|---|
| 23-Mar | 6.25 | S |
| 18-Apr | 6.75 | S |
| 17-May | 7.25 | S |
| 16-Aug | 7.75 | S |
| 17-Nov | 8.5 | S |

**1995**

| | | |
|---|---|---|
| 1-Feb | 9 | S |
| 13-Jul | 8.75 | S |
| 20-Dec | 8.5 | S |

**1996**

| | | |
|---|---|---|
| 31-Jan | 8.25 | S |

**1997**

| | | |
|---|---|---|
| 26-Mar | 8.5 | S |

**1998**

| | | |
|---|---|---|
| 30-Sep | 8.25 | S |
| 16-Oct | 8 | S |
| 18-Nov | 7.75 | S |

**1999**

| | | |
|---|---|---|
| 30-Jun | 8 | S |
| 25-Aug | 8.25 | S |
| 16-Nov | 8.5 | S |

**2000**

| | | |
|---|---|---|
| 2-Feb | 8.75 | S |
| 22-Mar | 9 | S |
| 16-May | 9.5 | S |

**2001**

| | | |
|---|---|---|
| 3-Jan | 9 | S |
| 31-Jan | 8.5 | S |
| 21-Mar | 8 | S |
| 18-Apr | 7.5 | S |
| 15-May | 7 | S |
| 27-Jun | 6.75 | S |
| 21-Aug | 6.5 | S |
| 17-Sep | 6 | S |
| 2-Oct | 5.5 | S |
| 6-Nov | 5 | S |
| 11-Dec | 4.75 | S |

**2002**

| | | |
|---|---|---|
| 6-Nov | 4.25 | S |

**2003**

| | | |
|---|---|---|
| 25-Jun | 4 | S |

Investment Shifting works because the rate of return on the three most basic securities—stocks, bonds and money market securities— is driven by general interest rates. If interest rates go up, the value of these investments change. Some go up. Some go down. Consider, if you will, the following:

## The Benefit of Predictability

If the interest rate goes down, money market instruments go down too. If interest rates go up, stocks and bonds will go up too. Anywhere from 80% to 98% of the value of a stock, bond, or money market instrument is driven by interest rate changes. That means you can safely assume a direct, stable correlation between a shift in interest rates and a change in the value of these investments. Thus, the first benefit of investment shifting technique: changes in the value of your investments are predictable.

## The Benefit of Safety

Because it's driven by interest rates, investment shifting will work for these basic types of securities, all of which are tried and true investment vehicles: mutual fund families, your 401(k) or other retirement fund, an IRA or SEP, and tax-sheltered annuities you control. To maximize safety, the second investment shifting benefit, you invest in groups of stocks, bonds, or money market instruments— not in single stocks and bonds.

Why? On a given day, depending on what Congress, the President, other financial markets, the weather, or the planets do, any given stock can rise or fall dramatically. But on a given day, about 80% of all stocks, bonds and money market instruments will behave completely predictably in response to interest rates. What would you rather bet on? Choosing one single stock and hoping it won't change in price - or buying a little bit of a whole bunch of different stocks, 80% of which will be obedient to the laws of interest rates?

rather bet on? Choosing one single stock and hoping it won't change in price - or buying a little bit of a whole bunch of different stocks, 80% of which will be obedient to the laws of interest rates?

## The Benefit of Good Timing

The final benefit is that combining predictability and safety, investment shifting allows you to choose what type of fund will do best, and when, so you can outperform the overall markets. Instead of putting your money in one place and leaving it there to earn five, six, or eight percent, you can make simple logical moves that yield more like 20% or more.

*Conservative* investments are often lazy investments - places to stash cash, not places to create profit. They are actually very risky because your money slowly but surely erodes in the safe, secure vehicles. Inflation is no respecter of *conservative* strategies. Don't fall for the safe-secure syndrome. The most conservative investment is the one that preserves and increases the value of your money safely, simply, and predictably.

Best of all, investment shifting doesn't require you to move your money more than a couple of times a year (sometimes only every couple of years). You move your money after interest rates go up or down, so you don't have to read Tarot cards to decide where your money should go. The technique requires minimal attention and no risk at all. Just use your intelligence and enthusiasm. and get ready to make a profit.

## A Word On Greed

Greed is not good for amateurs, and let's face it, you wouldn't be reading this book unless you were an amateur, part-time wealth builder. That's okay - most people are part-time investors. In the context of investing, you are greedy if you try to double your money in less than one year through speculation. Speculation is defined as trying to predict the way a market will go based on some future event that may or may not happen. Those times when a butterfly flaps its wings in Tokyo and the markets go wild. What would Ben Franklin say? The cons outweigh the pros.

Speculation, like gambling, can be fun, exciting, and lucrative, but only if you can afford to lose your investment. That's not for you— at least not now. Shift your investments based on what's already happened, not on what might happen. It's safer, it's easier, it's less stressful, and it works.

### Choosing Mutual Funds

There are well over 8,000 different mutual funds on the market. Sounds intimidating? Relax. All those funds mean you can breathe a sigh of relief. Instead of having to find one stock that will meet your investment goals, you can choose from diversified mutual funds that offer a wide variety of management philosophies, track records, fees, and risk factors. The advantages to mutual funds are numerous:

- You can invest in the markets without thousands of dollars
- Even with a small amount of cash, you can invest in several types of funds for strategic wealth building
- You don't have to pay huge commissions to brokers
- You benefit from the skill of some of the best professional fund managers in the country.
- You can enjoy instant diversification. A mutual fund is made up of at least 100 different securities
- You enjoy liquidity. Mutual funds are obligated to redeem your shares promptly, usually within 24 hours. Some even allow you to write checks against your account.
- Dividend and interest distributions are made monthly; capital gains can be taken or reinvested.
- It's easy to shift investments from one type of fund to another within the same family.
- You are in control of your investment— not some salesperson trying to make a commission off their particular product.

It was recently reported by ABC News that 95 million investors own mutual fund shares having a market value of over $7 trillion. How is that for safety in numbers?

Mutual funds work and have worked consistently for many types of investors with many different goals. The trick is matching the goal of the fund with your own financial goals. You can choose from blue-chip stock funds, value funds, small-capital stock funds, growth funds, investment-grade bond funds, junk-bond funds, overseas funds, gold funds, sector funds, and the kitchen sink fund.

Which one will work for you? Go back to goal-setting exercise session. Look at your financial objectives. What kind of return will you need to achieve that college fund or new house or retirement income? Do a little math, and then do a lot of research. Make a commitment to investigate, evaluate, and get rollin'.

Mutual fund performance is listed in the newspaper on a daily basis. Look for the NAV (net asset value) of the fund, which is the current value per share. That's what it will cost you to buy a share. What's performing best? The performance shows the percentage change of the NAV over a period of time. Naturally, you want to investigate funds that show you positive returns. Then call, write, or browse the Internet for information on various funds and fund family that intrigues you.

A great place to go online is Morningstar (located at www.morningstar.com). This site is a great resource for mutual fund investing.

Gather information so you can see which fund's objectives really match your own.

### The No-Load Advantage

To load or not to load. That is the question.

A *no-load fund* does not charge you a commission to buy shares or withdraw your funds. As a beginner, a no-load fund probably makes sense. Load funds will charge you a commission of up to nine percent, on either your principle or earnings, - and when you're just starting out, your goal is to practice the *Investment Shifting Strategy* with ease and confidence. Calculating those commissions can make the process tricky, and it's not initially necessary to embarking on your investment journey.

Don't confuse commissions (loads) with management fees. Even no-load funds will charge you a small fee, about one percent annually, for doing research on their stocks, choosing them, monitoring the markets for you, record keeping and detailed monthly statements. If you're thinking logically, you'll see that with a no-load fund you get a lot for your one percent. The NAV you see in the newspaper has already deducted the management fee - one less calculation to worry about.

Don't let anyone tell you that a load or sales commission increases your chance for profit. Don't forget the wealth-creation basics. If you have to pay someone to make money for you, you are splitting up your profits. It's one thing if you own a business and pay an employee to work for you, but it's quite another if you're paying a brokerage firm, broker, insurance agent, or financial planner just for the privilege of helping you buy some shares. Eliminate the middleman and save up to nine percent in commission fees.

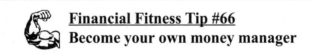

**Financial Fitness Tip #66**
**Become your own money manager**

The Investing Shifting Strategy is the simplest and safest method for knowing *when* to do it. *How* to do it? Remember the no-load advantage we talked about earlier? To get comfortable with managing your own investments, it makes sense not to have to pay a fee every time you want to shift your money.

Every week, new mutual fund families find new ways of making money for you, and themselves. If you end up paying a fee to move your money outside the family, it gets complicated trying to decide whether you are better off taking your money outside. Fee structures tend to get more, not less, complicated. If you are starting out with a small amount of money, keep it simple, and go with a no-load fund.

There are a few cases when a load fund makes sense. A one-time load may pay off, depending on the fees involved, the potential return in a load fund, and how long you're going to keep your investment in a particular place.

So do a little math. Front-end loads are deducted only once – up front. It might be worth it if you want to get into something new and lucrative with a small amount of principal, like a sector fund (e.g. technology) you want to explore. Most load funds have slightly lower expense ratios (how much of your investment you tend to lose if you leave your money there for more than five years) than no-loads.

No matter what, it's really smart to just stay away from loads of more than 4.5%. That front-end *hit* is deducted right at the beginning. If you invest $1,000 in a fund with a six percent load, only $940 of your money goes to work for you. The bottom line is that the fund now has to earn over six percent that year, just so you can get your money back.

It's never worth it to pay a load for a bond fund. Bond funds tend to have much lower expense ratios than any other kind of fund. If you're investing for retirement, some load funds will waive the load if you're buying the investment through your IRA – a nice deal.

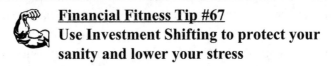

**Financial Fitness Tip #67**
**Use Investment Shifting to protect your**
**sanity and lower your stress**

With Investment Shifting, you don't have to be one of those frantic investors calling their fund company from their cell phone in a panic. Even after your internal prime rate *beeper* goes off, the markets respond predictably but not instantaneously. Things move within a couple of weeks, not minutes. This gives you time to assess, do some research and adjust.

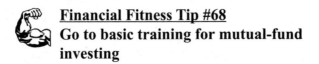

**Financial Fitness Tip #68**
**Go to basic training for mutual-fund**
**investing**

Now for some basics that will put you in a position of strength whenever you talk to a broker, financial planner, banker or security salesperson:

***FIXED INCOME FUNDS*** – These are government securities, municipal bond funds and corporate bond funds. The managers of these funds are trying to do what the name implies: create a sizable and stable flow of investment income to their share/bondholders.

    **Government Security Funds** – These group together a bunch of different U.S. securities like T-bills, long-term notes and bonds, and government agency issues. These are considered among the safest for principal investment because your shares are backed by the full faith and credit of the USA. That almost completely eliminates the risk of default, although there is a risk that your principal may not be worth very much depending on how the prime rate swings.

Government prices react inversely to interest rates more than any other investment. The value of your portfolio will react inversely also. The trade-off is that your fund managers will take steps to maintain a stable *net asset value* (NAV), but even then, the power of prime rates will have an impact. So use Investment Shifting to minimize the risk of interest rate erosion of the value of these funds.

**Municipal Bond Funds** – To get a nice high current income from these – and it's free from federal taxes and in some cases, state and local taxes too. These are great funds for people in high tax brackets who would like some current tax-free income. The yields will still be lower than they would be for taxable funds – if you don't make allowances for the impact of taxation. So you'll have to calculate a tax-free vs. taxable equivalent yield. Sounds scary? Don't worry. All this means is you have to compare apples to apples. You have to figure out how much you would get after taxes from a taxable instrument and then compare it to a tax-free fund.

To do this, divide the current yield of any tax-free fund by 1.00 minus your marginal tax rate. Use this number to see whether you're getting a better return.

**CORPORATE BOND FUNDS** – These are invested in debt securities like corporate bonds and debentures, convertible bonds, notes, or commercial paper. These usually have higher yields than High-Quality Funds and High-Yield Funds.

**High-Quality Funds** – These invest in corporate bonds that carry the top four bond ratings. That means a Baa or higher from Moody's, or a BBB or higher from Standard & Poors. These are *blue chip* bond funds, nice if you want current income and safety of principal.

**High-Yield Funds** – Sometimes referred to as *junk bonds*, these combine low-grade, high-yield corporate bonds with some stocks. Even though the lower grade of bonds (BBB/ Baa or lower) implies a higher risk, the yield is also higher. Your principal remains stable and you get the benefit of high current income.

*EQUITY FUNDS* – Let's face it. Equity investing is exposed to some price volatility. These are shares of corporate common stock, grouped into mutual funds designed to mitigate most of the risk of investing in single shares. You've got a much greater opportunity for profit with these than you do with bonds, but your principal is also in a slightly riskier position. Historically, these funds have produced the highest long-term returns, particularly when the economy is growing and interest rates stay at reasonable levels.

**Growth & Income Funds** – These are groups of blue-chip stocks. They tend to regain their value after weal market periods and seem to grow continuously over the years. It is always advisable to include blue-chip stocks in most portfolios, because even though they go up and down, they don't tend to go down and stay down. This is a big advantage if you want the benefits of stocks without some of the risk.
**Growth Funds** – Groups of common stocks that are likely to hit substantial capital growth, they simply aren't as mature or stable as blue chips. But they are generally chosen from high

quality companies – and are much more likely to grow quicker than blue chips. That means you get shares that rise in value faster, without excess risk.

**Aggressive Growth Funds** – These are made up of securities that are excellent candidates for rapid capital appreciation. Here is where you'll find stocks of small companies with promising new products or technologies, companies that are in turnaround after some financial setbacks, and those *bargain* companies – the ones selling at way below book value. Yes, these funds have much higher volatility and risk, and are for investors who don't panic easily.

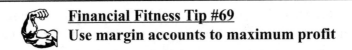

**Financial Fitness Tip #69**
**Use margin accounts to maximum profit**

So far I've talked about non-leveraged investments: taking your own money and making profits from it. To increase your investment capital – and your potential for return – why not take advantage of leveraged investing? You already do that when you get a mortgage for your home. A *mutual-fund margin account* can help you do just that.

A margin account is actually a line of credit. You can use it to borrow money using the shares you already own as collateral. Basically, you can borrow money at a lower rate and invest it at a higher rate.

"Sounds smart," you say. "But is it safe?" It is as safe as any leveraged investment used wisely. All margin accounts have something called a *minimum margin requirement*. That is the amount of collateral you must maintain on your loan. Since your collateral is actually the shares you own, it is possible that if you borrow to invest in more, and the shares drop in value below the minimum margin

requirement, you will receive a *margin call*. That means you are going to
have to come up with more collateral.

Sounds scary? Don't worry. If you invest in mutual-funds,
the price of your shares would have to drop a whopping 50% *before*
there is a margin call. During the worst stock market drop in history
(remember Black Monday?), the average stock market mutual fund
dropped only 16%. Fidelity and Magellan, the mutual-fund giants,
were too large to move fast enough. That makes buying pretty safe
and potentially lucrative for you.

Just make sure that the interest rate you pay on the margin
account is only a couple of points above the prime. Most people don't
know that the interest is tax-deductible up to the total amount of your
investment income.

Depending on SEC rules, you can borrow up to 50% of the
market value of your shares with a mutual fund margin account. This
is good news if you want to use your margin account to free up capital
for other investments. You can use your mutual fund shares as
collateral for a personal loan and borrow up to 50% of their market
value.

Not all mutual funds offer margin accounts. Discount firms
such as Fidelity and Charles Schwab offer ways for you to margin
these share of more than 200 mutual funds.

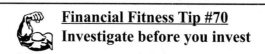

**Financial Fitness Tip #70**
**Investigate before you invest**

With the advent of recent government investigation regarding mutual
funds, make sure you check sources like the Internet to see if the
mutual fund family that you are interested in is not in violations of
any security irregularities. Your due diligence will save you money
and heartache in the long run.

## Fund Contact Information:

| Fund Name | Website | Telephone |
|---|---|---|
| American Century | http://www.americanfunds.com | 800.345.2021 |
| PIMCO | http://www.pimcofunds.com | 800.927.4648 |
| Reagons Morgan Keegan | http://www.morgankeegan.com | 800.366.7426 |
| Pioneer | http://www.pioneerfunds.com | 800.225.6292 |
| Buffalo | http://www.buffalofunds.com | 800.492.8332 |
| Wasatch | http://www.wasatchfunds.com | 800.551.1700 |
| FBR | http://www.fbr.com | 888.888.0025 |
| Oberweis | http://www.oberweis.net | 800.323.6166 |
| Bjurman, Barry | http://www.bjurmanbarry.com | 800.227.7264 |
| Bridgeway | http://www.bridgewayfunds.com | 800.661.3550 |
| CGM Focus | http://www.cgmfunds.com | 800.345.4048 |
| Burnham | http://www.burnhamfunds.com | 800.874.3863 |
| Alpine | http://www.alpinefunds.com | 888.785.5578 |

## Government Long Term Bonds

| Fund Name (Ranked by 3yr Return) | Symbol | 1999 % | 2001 % | 2003 % | Front Load | Deferred Load | Expense Ratio % | Total Assets | Min Invest. |
|---|---|---|---|---|---|---|---|---|---|
| American Cent. Target Mat 2020 Adv | ACTEX | -5.1 | 16.3 | 0.7 | None | None | 0.84 | 167 | $2,500 |
| American Cent. Target Mat 2010 Adv | ACTRX | -7.1 | 10.4 | 1.9 | None | None | 0.84 | 245 | $2,500 |
| American Cent. Target Mat 2015 | ACTTX | — | 6.1 | 1.6 | None | None | 0.84 | 142 | $2,500 |
| Vanguard Long-Term US Treasury | VUSTX | -8.7 | 4.3 | 1.1 | None | None | 0.28 | 2,072 | $3,000 |
| Dreyfus US Treasury Long-Term | DRGBX | -8.1 | 2.5 | 5.9 | None | None | 0.80 | 102 | $2,500 |

## High Yield Bonds

| Fund Name (Ranked by 3yr Return) | Symbol | 1999 % | 2001 % | 2003 % | Front Load | Deferred Load | Expense Ratio % | Total Assets | Min Invest. |
|---|---|---|---|---|---|---|---|---|---|
| Regions Morgan Keegan Select Hi Inc I | RHIIX | — | 18.0 | 11.6 | None | None | 0.91 | 635 | $1,000 |
| Regions Morgan Keegan Select Hi Inc C | RHICX | — | 17.1 | 10.9 | None | None | 1.64 | 635 | $1,000 |
| Buffalo High-Yield | BUFHX | 2.0 | 10.6 | 17.3 | None | None | 1.03 | 206 | $2,500 |
| BlackRock High Yield Bond Instl | BHYIX | 8.7 | 7.1 | 23.3 | None | None | 0.70 | 581 | $5,000 |
| BlackRock High Yield Bond Svc | BHYSX | 8.4 | 6.7 | 22.9 | None | None | 1.00 | 581 | $5,000 |

## Small Cap - Growth Stock Fund

| Fund Name (Ranked by 3yr Return) | Symbol | 1999 % | 2001 % | 2003 % | Front Load | Deferred Load | Expense Ratio % | Total Assets | Min Invest |
|---|---|---|---|---|---|---|---|---|---|
| William Blair Small Cap Growth N | WBSNX | — | 26 | 51.2 | None | None | 1.62 | 354 | $5,000 |
| Wasatch Core Growth | WGROX | 19.4 | 28.8 | 35.2 | None | None | 1.29 | 1,424 | $2,000 |
| Wasatch Ultra Growth | WAMCX | 17.5 | 18.3 | 40.8 | None | None | 1.71 | 585 | $2,000 |
| Wasatch Small Cap Growth | WAAEX | 40.9 | 24.2 | 37.6 | None | None | 1.31 | 1,262 | $2,000 |
| Baron Small Cap | BSCFX | 70.8 | 5.2 | 40.3 | None | None | 1.36 | 1,051 | $2,000 |

## US Stock Funds

| Fund Name (Ranked buy 3yr Return) | Symbol | 1999 % | 2001 % | 2003 % | Front Load | Deferred Load | Expense Ratio % | Total Assets | Min Invest. |
|---|---|---|---|---|---|---|---|---|---|
| Alpine U.S. Real Estate Equity Y | EUEYX | -17.6 | 25.2 | 70.8 | None | None | 1.72 | 73 | $1,000 |
| FBR Small Cap Financial A | FBRSX | - 5.4 | 23.9 | 34.2 | None | None | 1.56 | 509 | $2,000 |
| CGM Focus | CGMFX | 8.5 | 47.7 | 52.7 | None | None | 1.20 | 653 | $2,500 |
| CGM Realty | CGMRX | 2.6 | 5.1 | 81.4 | None | None | 1.30 | 605 | $2,500 |
| Fifth Third Microcap Value Instl | MXAIX | 21.6 | 22.9 | 58.3 | None | None | 1.40 | 189 | $ 100 |

**Note:**
Top 5 performing funds (based on a 3 year total return **annualized** - five year history shown) in each category with minimum investment of under $5,000, total expense fees under 1.75%, and no up front or deferred fees (NO LOAD). Funds also had to manage over 50 million.

All data was gathered based on 10/31/03

Total Assets column is based on Millions of dollars.

*Are you up for the Challenge?* **www.FinancialFitnessChallenge.com**

## Summary of Chapter Ten

WOW! Talk about strengthening your financial muscles. Let's summarize what I've taught you learn in this final chapter:

- Using my Investment Shifting Strategy will make you rest much easier at night.

- You learned how to develop an internal beeper.

- You can become your own money manager.

- You went through mutual fund basic training.

- You now know how to use margin account to leverage your way to financial fitness.

- Investigate thoroughly before making an investment.

## The Next Phase of Financial Fitness

I'd like to congratulate you on completing this book. As you learned, dealing with your finances can be fun and exciting – as opposed to a trip to a dentist.

This book has touched on just a few of my basic strategies in order to make you financially fit.

Some of you may want to take your education on financial fitness to a whole new level. Then again, some of you have be overwhelmed what I taught you so far. Whatever you do, don't freak out and don't get stressed out. I have two solutions to your problem:

1. I have developed a home study course titled *Financial Aerobics™ – 30 Days to Financial Fitness™* (www.FinancialAerobics.com). This is one of the official products of the *Financial Fitness Challenge™* (www.FinancialFitnessChallenge.com). This course is a 30-day program for people that would like a little more structure than just reading a book. If you follow the exercises outlined in that course, you will be more financially fit than you can imagine!

2. In realizing that some people need a little hand-holding, I developed a program that I call Financial Fitness Monthly™ (www.FinancialFitnessMonthly.com). In addition to receiving an offline newsletter, you'll also be able to speak on the phone with one of my *Financial Fitness Trainers™* for an **unlimited** amount each and every month. It is a monthly subscription service, so you can pay as you go without paying for something you'll never use.

245

Don't forget to enroll in the *Financial Fitness Challenge*™. If money won't motivate you, I don't know what will.

Do me a favor and drop me a note. I would love to hear all about the success you've achieved using my strategies. Feel free to include a picture and/or video of yourself. You never know, we may feature your story one of our upcoming television shows.

To your continued success…

Richard M. Krawczyk, Ph.D.

Dr. Richard's Success Stories
PO Box 15458
Beverly Hills, CA 90209

successstories@FinancialUniversity.com

# *Glossary*

248

**Adjustable Life Insurance** - A form of whole life insurance that allows you to increase or decrease coverage by raising or lowering coverage as your needs change.

**Annually Renewable Term (ART)** – A term insurance policy that expires in one year. Just before year is up, you will receive a renewal notice for the next year's premium. An ART policy is the most cost effective. As you get older, your chances of dying increase so your premiums will go up.

**Automobile Insurance** - Protects innocent victims of accidents, caused by a vehicle, from serious financial loss.

**Beneficiary** - The person that is designated by the insured to receives the proceeds of the policy in the event of the insured's death.

**Bodily Injury** - Covers injury to people in other cars, pedestrians and passengers in the policyholder's car. The policyholder and family members are also covered while driving someone else's car, including rental cars. Covers legal defense and any damages up to the limits stated in the policy.

**Collision Insurance** - Covers damage to your car in the event of a collision with another vehicle or object no matter who is at fault.

**Comprehensive Insurance** - Pays for losses due to theft, damage from fire, glass breakage, falling objects, explosions, etc.

**Death Benefit** - The amount of money that the beneficiary receives when the insured dies; also known as the *face value* of the policy.
**Decreasing Term Insurance** - A policy where the face value of the policy decreasing over time while the premiums remain the same. Credit Life and Mortgage Life are examples of this type of policy. Policies are usually overpriced by as much as 400%.

**Double Indemnity** - A provision in a policy when the insurance company will pay double the face amount if the insured's death is cause by an accident.

**Duplicate Coverage** - Applies to benefits where an insured is covered by several policies with one or more companies, providing the same type of benefits, and often resulting in over-insurance. No insured can recover twice from the same loss.

**Endowment Insurance** - A contract providing for payment of the face amount at the end of a fixed period, at a specific age of the insured or at the insured's death before the end of the stated period.

**Fees and Commissions** - Charges for administrative and selling expenses levied against your face value or premiums.

**Life Insurance** - The risk insured against is the death of a particular person (the insured) upon whose death within a stated term (or whenever death occurs, if the contract provides), the insurance company agrees to pay a stated sum or income to the beneficiary.

**Load** - The sales commission paid on an investment.

**Management Fee** - The fee charged by a mtual fund for doing research on their stocks, choosing them, monitoring the markets for you, record keeping and detailed monthly statements.
**Modified Life Insurance** - A form of whole life insurance in which the premium is low in the early years and rises after a designated period of time.

**NAV (Net Asset Value)** - The current value per share. That's what it will cost you to buy a share of the mutual fund.

250

**No-Fault Insurance** - Allows you to recover losses from your own insurance company even if someone else is at fault, but requires you to give up the right to sue. Should not be taken unless required by state law.

**No Load Fund** - A mutual fund that does not charge you a commission to buy shares or withdraw your funds.

**Non-Participating Policies** - The insured is not entitled to share in the divisible surpluses of the insurance company. No dividends are paid.

**Paid-up Insurance** - The insured pays for the policy in full or over a period of years, after which no further premiums are due.

**Participating Policies** - The insurance company refunds a part of the premium payments if the company has a surplus of earnings.

**Policy Term** - The period in which the policy is in force.

**Premium** - Periodic payments required to keep the policy in force.

**Property Damage Liability** - Covers damage to someone else's car or property caused by the policyholder's car.

**Single Premium Life** - A form of whole life policy that requires a payment one single premium payable in a lump sum.

**Settlement Option** - Various forms of settlement in lieu of receiving proceeds in a lump sum payment.

**Surrender Charge** - A charge that the insured must pay if they wish to cancel their policy before a specific amount of time.

**Term Life Insurance** - Least expensive form of life insurance that provides protection for a limited number of years.

**Umbrella Liability** - Inexpensive supplemental liability policy that covers all personal liabilities. The more assets you accumulate, the more important personal liability becomes.

**Uninsured / Underinsured Motorist Coverage** - Covers injury other due to you. Nothing more than high-priced combination of life insurance and hospitalization insurance that is a complete waste of money.

**Universal Life Insurance** - A policy that combines an investment plan with term insurance. All premiums are deposited in the cash value account only after the company deducts its fees, commissions and monthly administrative cost. The interest rate on the investment plan varies. Many times advertised rates are only guaranteed for the first year only. Read the fine print.

**Variable Life Insurance** - A form of whole life insurance that allows you to invest the savings portion or *cash value* portion of your policy in stocks, bonds or mutual funds. Due to fluctuating market condition, these funds may increase or decrease in value.

**Whole Life Insurance** - Referred to sometimes as ordinary or straight life insurance. This insurance continues during the insured's lifetime and provides for payment of the amount insured at death or at the age of 100, whichever is first. In the United States, the insurance company keeps the *cash value* when you die. In Canada, the beneficiary receives both the face amount and the cash value when the insured dies.

# *Appendix I*

## Tax Lien Certificate State Contact Information

**Tax Deeds and Tax Lien certificates are offered in most states. Use the contact information below to find out more information in the state you choose.**

## ALASKA
Tax Deed Sales only
http://www.tax.state.ak.us/abouttax/contact.asp
Tax Collector
550 West 7th Avenue, Ste. 500
Anchorage, AK. 99501
1.907.269.6620

## ALABAMA
http://www.ador.state.al.us/advalorem/index.html
Alabama Real Estate Commission
Montgomery, AL 36106-3674
334.242.5544

## ARIZONA
http://www.revenue.state.az.us/
State Dept. of revenue
400 W. Congress, Tucson AZ 85701
602.542.3529
800.352.4090

## ARKANSAS
Tax deed sale
http://www.accessarkansas.org/
Benton County Tax Collector's office
479.271.1040
215 East Central, Ste. 101
Bentonville, AR. 72712

**CALIFORNIA**
http://www.boe.ca.gov/
1.800.400.7115
Los Angeles County Tax Collector
225 N. Hill St.
Los Angeles, CA 90012
213.974.2111

http://www.oc.ca.gov/treas/contact_us.htm
Treasurer-Tax Collector
Santa Ana, CA 92701
714.834.6229

http://www.oc.ca.gov/treas/
The Treasurer-Tax Collector
12 Civic Center Plaza
Santa Ana, CA 92701
714.834.3411

**COLORADO**
http://www.co.larimer.co.us/treasurer/taxsale.htm
200 W. Oak Street
Fort Collins, CO. 80521
970.498.7032

**CONNECTICUT**
http://www.drs.state.ct.us/forms/forms.html
Tax Collector
450 Capitol Avenue
Hartford, CT. 06106-1308

**DELAWARE**
http://www.state.de.us/revenue/
Division of Revenue
820 N. French Street
Wilmington, DE 19801
302.577.8200

**FLORIDA**
http://sun6.dms.state.fl.us/dor/
FL Dept. of Revenue
1379 Blountstown Hwy.
Tallahassee FL. 32304-2716
850.488.6800

**GEORGIA**
http://www2.state.ga.us/departments/dor/doroff.shtml
Atlanta Regional Office
4245 International Parkway
Hapeville, GA. 30345
404.968.0480

**HAWAII**
http://www.state.hi.us/tax/taxforms.html
Department of Taxation
P.O. Box 259
Honolulu, Hawaii 96809-0259
800.222.7572

**IDAHO**
http://www2.state.id.us/tax/index.html
Idaho State Tax Commission
PO Box 36
Boise, ID 83722-0410
800.972.7660

**ILLINOIS**
http://www.revenue.state.il.us/
Willard Ice Building
Springfield, IL 62702
800.732.8866

**INDIANA**
http://www.in.gov/dor/
Department of Revenue
100 N. Senate Ave.
Indianapolis, IN 46204
317.232.2240

**IOWA**
http://www.state.ia.us/tax/
Tax Collector
1305 E. Walnut
Des Moines, Iowa 50319
515.281.4040
800.367.3388

**KANSAS**
http://www.ksrevenue.org/forms-perstax.htm
Customer Relations
915 SW Harrison St.
Topeka, KS 66625-0001
877.526.7738
785.296.4937

**KENTUCKY**
http://revenue.state.ky.us/individual-2002.htm
Kentucky Revenue Cabinet
200 Fair Oaks Lane
Frankfort, KY 40620
502.564.4581

**LOUISIANA**
http://www.rev.state.la.us/sections/taxforms/default.asp
One Lakeshore Dr. Ste. 1550
P.O. Box 3702
Lake Charles, LA 70629
337.491.2504

**MAINE**
http://www.state.me.us/revenue/homepage.html
Property Tax Division
14 Edison Dr.
Augusta Maine 04332
207.287.2011

**MARYLAND**
http://www.marylandtaxes.com/default.asp
Baltimore
301 W. Preston St.
Room 206
Baltimore City, MD
410.767.1995

**MASSACHUSETTS**
http://www.dor.state.ma.us/forms/formsIndex/taxformsPERSONAL.htm
Massachusetts
PO Box 7010
Boston, MA 02204
800.392.6089

**MICHIGAN**
http://www.michigan.gov/emi/0,1303,7——,00.html
Michigan Dept. of Treasury
Lansing, MI. 48922
517.636.5320

**MINNESOTA**
http://www.taxes.state.mn.us/
Property Tax Division
Minnesota Dept. of Revenue
Mail Station 3340
St. Paul, MN 55146-3340
651.296.2286

**MISSISSIPPI**
http://www.mstc.state.ms.us/taxareas/property/main.htm
Mississippi Dept. of Revenue
P.O. Box 23338
Jackson, MS 39225-3338
601.923.7390

**MISSOURI**
http://www.dor.mo.gov/tax/forms/
Division of Taxation & Collection
301 West High St. Room 330
Jefferson City, MO 65101
573.751.3505

**MONTANA**
http://www.state.mt.us/revenue/css/contact/default.asp
Department of Revenue
P.O. Box 5805
Helena, MT. 59604-5805
406.444.6900

**NEBRASKA**
http://www.revenue.state.ne.us/index.html
Nebraska Dept. of Revenue
301 Centennial Mall South
PO Box 94818
Lincoln, NE 68509-4818
800.742.7474

**NEVADA**
http://tax.state.nv.us/taxnew/forms.htm
Department of Taxation
Grant Sawyer Office Building
555 E. Washington Ave
Ste 1300
Las Vegas, NV 89101
702.486.2300

**NEW HAMPSHIRE**
http://www.state.nh.us/revenue/
New Hampshire Dept. of Revenue
45 Chenell Drive
PO Box 457
Concord, NH 03302-0457
603.271.2191

**NEW JERSEY**
http://www.state.nj.us/
NJ Division of Taxation
One Port Center
2 Riverside Drive
Camden, NJ 08103
609.292.6400

**NEW MEXICO**
http://www.state.nm.us/tax/
Taxation and Revenue Department
1100 S. St. Francis Dr.
Sante Fe, NM 87504-0630
505.827.0700

**NEW YORK**
http://www.tax.state.ny.us/
Manhattan District Office
86 Chambers Street, 2nd Floor
New York, NY 10007-1826
800.835.3554

**NORTH CAROLINA**
http://www.dor.state.nc.us/forms/index.html
North Carolina Department of Revenue
PO Box 25000
Raleigh, North Carolina, 27640-0640
877.252.3052

**NORTH DAKOTA**
http://www.state.nd.us/taxdpt/misc/contacts.html
Office of State Tax Commissioner
State Capitol
600 E Boulevard Ave.
Bismarck ND 58505-0599
800.366.6888

**OHIO**
http://www.state.oh.us/tax/index.html
Tax Commissioner's Office
30 E. Broad Street, 22nd Floor
Columbus, Ohio 43215
1.614.995.0729

**OKLAHOMA**
http://www.oktax.state.ok.us/
State of Oklahoma
Connors Building, Capitol Complex
2501 N. Lincoln Blvd.
Okla. City, OK 73194
405.521.3160

**OREGON**
http://www.dor.state.or.us/ptd.html
Oregon Dept. of Revenue
955 Center St. NE.
Salem, OR 97301-2555

**PENNSYLVANIA**
http://www.revenue.state.pa.us/revenue/cwp/browse.asp?a=190&bc=0&c=32875
PA Dept. of Revenue
Cricket Field PLZ
615 Howard Ave, Ste. 204
Altoona PA 16601-4867
1.814.946.7310

**RHODE ISLAND**
http://www.tax.state.ri.us/
Rhode Island Division of Taxation
One Capitol Hill
Providence, RI. 02908
401.222.1040

**SOUTH CAROLINA**
http://www.tax.state.ri.us/
South Carolina Dept. Of Revenue
3 Southpark Cir.
Ste. 202
Charlestown, S.C. 29407
843.852.3600

**SOUTH DAKOTA**
http://www.state.sd.us/drr2/forms.htm
South Dakota
Department of Revenue
445 East Capitol Ave.
Pierre, SD. 57501-3185
605.773.3311

**TENNESSEE**
http://www.tennessee.gov/revenue/index.html
Dept. of Revenue
Andrew Jackson Building, Room 1200
Nashville, TN 37242-1099
615.741.2461

**TEXAS**
http://www.window.state.tx.us/taxinfo/proptax/ptaxpubs.html
Comptroller of Public Accounts
Property Tax Division
P.O. Box 13528
Austin, Texas 78711-3528
800.252.9121

**UTAH**
http://tax.utah.gov/index.html
Utah State Tax Commission
210 N. 1950 West
Salt Lake City, Utah 84134
1.800.662.4335

**VERMONT**
http://www.state.vt.us/tax/index.htm
VT Department of Taxes
Property Valuation & Review
PO Box 1577
Montpelier, VT 05601-1577
1.802.828.2777

**VIRGINIA**
http://www.tax.state.va.us/
Virginia Department of Taxation
Office of Customer Services
PO Box 1115
Richmond, VA 23218-1115
804.367.8031

**WASHINGTON**
http://dor.wa.gov/content/forms/forms_main.asp
Wadhington State Department of Revenue
Property Tax Division
PO Box 47471
Olympia, WA 98504-7471
800.647.7706

**WEST VIRGINIA**
http://www.wv.gov/
Property Tax Division
P.O. Box 2389
Charleston, West Virginia 25328-2389
1.800.982.8297

**WISCONSIN**
http://www.dor.state.wi.us/
Wisconsin Dept. of Revenue
2135 Rimrock Road
Madison WI. 53713
608.266.2772

**WYOMING**
http://revenue.state.wy.us/
Tax Collector
Herschler Bldg. 2nd Floor
West, 122 West 25th st.
Cheyenne, WY 82002-0110
1.307.777.7961

# *Appendix II*

## Sample List of Mutual Fund Families

## Fund Family Terms

**Family**: The name of the mutual fund family.

**Fund Name**: The name of the individual fund in the particular fund family.

**Symbol**: The Dow Jones symbol for the mutual fund. Just type in the symbol of the mutual fund at any investment website such as www.Morningstar.com to view the details of that fund.

**Asset Mil**: The size of that fund's assets in the millions.

**Min. Inv.**:  The minimum investment required to fund the account. Additional funding of the account may be lower.

**Loads**:

>    **In**: This is the commission percentage taken out of your initial investment when you first open your account.
>
>    **Out**: This is the commission percentage taken out of your investment when you withdraw from your account.
>
>    **"C"**: Denotes a closed fund.

**Withdrawal Options**: The methods that can be used to withdraw funds from your account.

>    **Phone** (P):  Funds can be withdrawn over the phone.
>
>    **Internet** (W): Funds can be withdrawn over the Internet at the fund family's website.
>
>    **Check** (C): Fund family will supply checks which can be used to with withdraw money.
>
>    **Income** (I): The option to receive a monthly check as income from your mutual fund account. Amount varies with the fund.

**Annual Return:** Indicates the percentage growth or decline in the value of the mutual fund for each year listed. The year 2003 is Year-To-Date (YTD) as they were calculated on 10/31/03.

# Types of Funds

| | |
|---|---|
| BL | BANK LOAN |
| C | CONVERTIBLE |
| CA | CONSERVITATE ALLOCATION |
| DE | DIVERSIFIED EMERGING MKTS |
| DPA | DIVERSIFIED PACIFIC/ASIA |
| EMB | EMERG. BOND MARKETS |
| ES | EUROPEAN STOCK |
| FLB | FOREIGN LARGE BLEND |
| FLG | FOREIGN LARGE GROWTH |
| FSMG | FOREIGN SMALL/MID GROWTH |
| FSMV | FOREIGN SMALL/MID VALUE |
| GNR | GLOBAL NATURAL RESOURCES |
| HYB | HIGH YIELD BOND |
| HYM | HIGH YIELD MUNICIPAL |
| IG | INTERMEDIATE GOVERNMENT |
| ITB | INTERMEDIATE TERM BOND |
| JS | JAPAN STOCK |
| LAS | LATIN AMERICAN STOCK |
| LB | LARGE BLEND |
| LG | LARGE GROWTH |
| LGO | LARGE GOVERNMENT |
| LOG | LONG GOVERNMENT |
| LV | LARGE VALUE |
| MA | MODERATE ALLOCATION |
| MB | MULTISECTOR BOND |
| MCB | MID CAP BLEND |
| MCG | MID CAP GROWTH |
| MCI | MUN I CALIFORNIA INT/SH |
| MCL | MUNICIPAL CALIFORNIA LONG |
| MCIS | MUNI CALIFORNIA INT/SH |
| MCV | MIDCAP VALUE |
| MF | MUNICIPAL FLORIDA |
| MM | MUNI MASSACHUSETTS |
| MMI | MUNI MINNESOTA |
| MNS | MUNI NATIONAL SHORT |
| MNI | MUNI NATIONAL INTERMEDIATE |
| MNJ | MUNI NEW JERSEY |
| MNL | MUNI NATIONAL LONG |
| MNYI | MUNI NEW YORK INT/SH |
| MNYL | MUNI NEW YORK LONG |
| MO | MUNI OHIO |
| MP | MUNI PENNSYLVANIA |
| MSSI | MUNI SINGLE STATE INT/SH |
| MSSL | MUNI SINGLE STATE LONG |
| PAJ | PACIFIC/ASIAN EX-JAPAN |
| SC | SPECIALTY COMMUNICATIONS |
| SB | SMALL BLEND |
| SF | SPECIALTY FINANCIAL |
| SG | SHORT GOVERNMENT |
| SH | SPECIALTY HEALTH |
| SNR | SPECIALTY NATURAL RESOUR. |
| SPM | SPECIALTY PERCIOUS METAL |
| SRE | SPECIALTY REAL ESTATE |
| ST | SPECIALTY TECHNOLOGY |
| STB | SHORT-TERM BOND |
| SU | SPECIALTY UTILITIES |
| SV | SMALL VALUE |
| UB | ULTRASHORT BOND |
| WA | WORLD ALLOCATION |
| WB | WORLD BOND |
| WS | WORLD STOCK |

## AIM

http://www.aimfunds.com

| ASSET | SYMBOL | TYPE | MIL | MIN INV | LOAD IN | LOAD OUT | P | W | C | I | 1999 | 2000 | 2001 | 2002 | 2003 (YTD) |
|---|---|---|---|---|---|---|---|---|---|---|---|---|---|---|---|
| Aggressive Growth A | AAGFX | MCG | 2,332 | 1,000 | 5.5 | 0 | Y | Y | N | Y | 45.1 | 3.0 | -26.0 | -22.7 | 23.0 |
| AIM Balanced A | AMBLX | MA | 2,325 | 1,000 | 4.75 | 0 | Y | Y | N | Y | 19.0 | -4.2 | -11.3 | -17.9 | 12.6 |
| AIM Basic Value A | GTVLX | LV | 5,869 | 1,000 | 5.5 | 0 | Y | Y | N | Y | 32.0 | 20.3 | 0.1 | -23.1 | 24.0 |
| Capital Development A | ACDAX | MCG | 1,008 | 1,000 | 5.5 | 0 | Y | Y | N | Y | 27.8 | 9.8 | -8.7 | -21.7 | 28.4 |
| Constellation A | CSTGX | LG | 7,876 | 1,000 | 5.5 | 0 | Y | Y | N | Y | 44.4 | -10.4 | -23.6 | -24.8 | 23.9 |
| Developing Markets A | GTDDX | DE | 245 | 1,000 | 4.75 | 1 | Y | Y | N | Y | 61.5 | -33.5 | -1.8 | -9.1 | 45.7 |
| Emerging Growth A | EMEAX | MCG | 150 | 1,000 | 5.5 | 0 | Y | Y | N | Y | X | X | -20.3 | -33.9 | 41.8 |
| European Small Company A | ESMAX | EUROPE | 47 | 1,000 | 5.5 | 0 | Y | Y | N | Y | X | X | -21.6 | 2.5 | 48.3 |
| Global Aggressive Growth A | AGAAX | WS | 861 | 1,000 | 4.75 | 0 | Y | Y | N | Y | 70.6 | -22.0 | -25.6 | -16.6 | 29.4 |
| Global Financial Services A | GFSAX | SF | 223 | 1,000 | 4.75 | 0 | Y | Y | N | Y | 24.2 | 26.4 | -9.2 | -17.5 | 24.3 |
| Global Health Care A | GGHCX | SH | 760 | 1,000 | 4.75 | 0 | Y | Y | N | Y | 5.5 | 52.1 | 4.7 | -22.7 | 11.8 |
| AIM Global Trends A | GTNDX | WS | 166 | 1,000 | 4.75 | 0 | Y | Y | N | Y | 51.9 | -7.9 | -17.0 | -9.6 | 28.4 |
| AIM Global Value A | AWSAX | WS | 17 | 1,000 | 5.5 | 0 | Y | Y | N | Y | X | X | -1.5 | -8.1 | 22.8 |
| AIM High-Yield A | AMHYX | HYB | 1,216 | 1,000 | 4.75 | 0 | Y | Y | N | Y | 2.1 | -23.8 | -3.6 | -10.4 | 24.3 |
| Intermediate Government A | AGOVX | IG | 1,147 | 1,000 | 4.75 | 0 | Y | Y | N | Y | -1.9 | 9.4 | 6.1 | 10.0 | 0.2 |
| International Emerging Gr A | IEGAX | FSMG | 79 | 1,000 | 5.5 | 0 | Y | Y | N | Y | X | X | -10.5 | -2.7 | 59.0 |
| Large Cap Basic Value A | LCBAX | LV | 229 | 1,000 | 5.5 | 0 | Y | Y | N | Y | X | 21.7 | 1.3 | -23.2 | 21.6 |
| AIM Libra A | ALAFX | MCG | 42 | 1,000 | 5.5 | 0 | Y | Y | N | Y | X | X | X | X | 42.5 |
| AIM Mid Cap Basic Value A | MDCAX | MCB | 94 | 1,000 | 5.5 | 0 | Y | Y | N | Y | X | X | X | -17.7 | 29.4 |
| AIM Mid Cap Growth A | AMCAX | MCG | 219 | 1,000 | 5.5 | 0 | Y | Y | N | Y | X | -10.1 | -21.2 | -31.9 | 34.5 |
| AIM New Technology A | ANTAX | ST | 55 | 1,000 | 5.5 | 0 | Y | Y | N | Y | X | X | -43.0 | -45.3 | 48.1 |
| AIM Opportunities II A | AMCOX | MCG | 194 | 1,000 | 5.5 | 0 | Y | Y | N | Y | 125.6 | 10.1 | -22.3 | -19.9 | 23.2 |
| AIM Premier Equity A | AVLFX | LB | 9,120 | 1,000 | 5.5 | 0 | Y | Y | N | Y | 29.9 | -15.0 | -13.0 | -30.9 | 19.0 |
| AIM Real Estate C | AIRCX | SRE | 428 | 1,000 | 0 | 1 | Y | Y | N | Y | -3.5 | 28.3 | 9.5 | 8.1 | 27.4 |
| AIM Short Term Bond C | STBCX | STB | 332 | 1,000 | 0 | 0 C | Y | Y | Y | Y | X | X | X | X | 2.2 |
| AIM Small Cap Growth A | GTSAX | SG | 1,813 | 1,000 | 5.5 C | 0 C | Y | Y | Y | Y | 90.6 | -0.7 | -13.8 | -28.0 | 34.7 |
| Tax-Free Intermediate A | AITFX | MNI | 477 | 1,000 | 1 C | 0 C | Y | Y | Y | Y | 0.1 | 8.2 | 4.5 | 9.6 | 3.0 |
| AIM Weingarten A | WEINX | LG | 2,813 | 1,000 | 5.5 | 0 | Y | Y | N | Y | 34.9 | -20.4 | -34.1 | -31.5 | 25.4 |

* WITHDRAWAL OPTIONS

ANNUAL RETURN

## AIM
http://www.aimfunds.com

| | SYMBOL | TYPE | ASSET MIL | MIN INV | LOAD IN | LOAD OUT | WITHDRAWAL OPTIONS P | W | C | I | ANNUAL RETURN 1999 | 2000 | 2001 | (YTD) 2002 | 2003 |
|---|---|---|---|---|---|---|---|---|---|---|---|---|---|---|---|
| Asia Pacific Growth A | ASIAX | PAJ | 132 | 1,000 | 5.5 | 0 | Y | Y | N | Y | 68.0 | -22.4 | -5.8 | -10.8 | 40.6 |
| AIM Basic Balanced B | BBLBX | MA | 138 | 1,000 | 0 | 5 | Y | Y | N | Y | X | X | X | -11.6 | 14.7 |
| AIM Blue Chip A | ABCAX | LG | 2,959 | 1,000 | 0 | 0 | Y | Y | N | Y | 25.6 | -9.3 | -22.9 | -26.4 | 19.6 |
| AIM Charter A | CHTRX | LB | 3,329 | 1,000 | 5.5 | 0 | Y | Y | N | Y | 33.9 | -14.7 | -23.1 | -16.1 | 15.7 |
| Demographic Trends B | ADDBX | LG | 561 | 1,000 | 0 | 5 | Y | Y | N | Y | X | -17.8 | -32.5 | -33.2 | 32.4 |
| Dividend Fund A | LCEAX | LB | 50 | 1,000 | 5.5 | 0 | Y | Y | N | Y | X | X | X | -12.9 | 18.3 |
| European Growth A | EADAX | ES | 443 | 1,000 | 5.5 | 0 | Y | Y | N | Y | 66.6 | -3.3 | -24.7 | -9.7 | 28.2 |
| AIM Floating Rate B | XAFRX | BL | 252 | 500 | 0 | 3 | Y | Y | N | Y | 5.5 | 5.0 | -1.5 | 2.7 | 6.1 |
| AIM Global Energy A | GTNAX | SNR | 40 | 1,000 | 4.75 | 0 | Y | Y | N | Y | 18.7 | 0.8 | -17.0 | 6.2 | 14.4 |
| AIM Global Growth A | AGGAX | WS | 546 | 1,000 | 4.75 | 0 | Y | Y | N | Y | 52.2 | -22.2 | -30.1 | -19.9 | 20.1 |
| Glbl Sci and Tech A | GTTCX | ST | 525 | 1,000 | 4.75 | 0 | Y | Y | N | Y | 108.1 | -38.9 | -54.2 | -44.0 | 50.3 |
| AIM Global Utilities A | AUTLX | SU | 141 | 1,000 | 5.5 | 0 | Y | Y | N | Y | 34.2 | -2.5 | -28.3 | -26.0 | 10.1 |
| Hi IncMuni Bond A | AHMAX | HYM | 144 | 1,000 | 4.75 | 0 | Y | Y | N | Y | -7.6 | 3.8 | 6.9 | 7.2 | 4.4 |
| AIM Income A | AMIFX | ITB | 715 | 1,000 | 4.75 | 0 | Y | Y | N | Y | -2.9 | -1.1 | 3.6 | 2.3 | 8.3 |
| Internation Core Equit C | IAVCX | FLB | 110 | 1,000 | 0 | 1 | Y | Y | N | Y | 21.6 | -11.0 | -16.8 | -12.9 | 16.7 |
| Internation Growth A | AIIEX | FLG | 1,600 | 1,000 | 5.5 | 0 | Y | Y | N | Y | 55.1 | -25.7 | -22.4 | -14.2 | 19.2 |
| AIM Large Cap Growth A | LCGAX | LG | 323 | 1,000 | 5.5 | 0 | Y | Y | N | Y | X | 8.5 | -36.1 | -26.5 | 25.8 |
| Limited Mat Treasury I | ALMIX | SG | 596 | 1 MIL | 0 C | C | Y | Y | N | Y | 2.9 | 7.2 | 7.7 | 4.9 | 1.2 |
| Mid Cap Core Equit A | GTAGX | MCB | 2,801 | 1,000 | 5.5 | C | Y | Y | N | Y | 37.1 | 18.8 | 0.5 | -11.1 | 20.8 |
| AIM Municipal Bond A | AMBDX | MNI | 419 | 1,000 | 4.75 | 0 | Y | Y | N | Y | -2.4 | 8.6 | 3.8 | 8.3 | 3.2 |
| AIM Opportunities I A | ASCOX | SG | 410 | 1,000 | 5.5 | 0 | Y | Y | N | Y | 84.2 | 23.0 | -9.3 | -24.8 | 31.5 |
| AIM Opportunities III A | LCPAX | LG | 173 | 1,000 | 5.5 | 0 | Y | Y | N | Y | X | 30.9 | -26.6 | -26.0 | 16.5 |
| AIM Premier Equity II B | VIIBX | LG | 71 | 1,000 | 5.5 | 0 | Y | Y | N | Y | X | X | -18.8 | -30.3 | 16.2 |
| AIM Select Equity A | AGWFX | LB | 515 | 1,000 | 5.5 | 0 | Y | Y | N | Y | 41.5 | -1.8 | -25.6 | -29.6 | 23.6 |
| AIM Small Cap Equity A | SMEAX | SG | 460 | 1,000 | 5.5 | 0 | Y | Y | N | Y | X | X | 8.9 | -19.2 | 36.1 |
| AIM Summit | SMMIX | LG | 1,914 | 50 | 3.33 | 0 | Y | Y | N | Y | 50.8 | -14.7 | -33.8 | -30.1 | 27.6 |
| AIM Total Return Bond B | TBRDX | ITB | 86 | 1,000 | 0 | 5 | Y | Y | N | Y | X | X | X | 7.7 | 3.2 |

* WITHDRAWAL

**AIM FUND REPRESENTATIVE: HOUSTON, TEXAS 800.959.4246**

\* Mutual-Funds have different share classes: class A, B, C, R and others. Each class has their own requirements. Speak with your investment specialist, or the fund representative to assist you further. In general you can't write checks from your retirement account. Additional funding into your account varies with each share class slightly. In general deposits are $50.00 for IRAs and $25.00 for automatic investing and 401k, and other savings plans. Converting from one share class to another may allow you to dodge the entrance and redemption fees, as well as lower the annual fees. It is absolutely necessary to familiarize yourself with the prospectus of each fund before investing.

Check-writing is allowed only with Aim Money-Market funds, Aim Cash Reserves fund (AIMXX), and Aim Tax-Exempt Cash fund.(ACSSX)

You may redeem class A shares only by check from AIM Tax-Exempt Cash Fund and AIM Cash Reserve Shares of the AIM Money Market Fund only.

## AMERICAN FUNDS

http://www.americanfunds.com

| | SYMBOL | ASSET TYPE | MIL | MIN INV | LOAD IN | LOAD OUT | P | W | C | I | 1999 | 2000 | 2001 | 2002 | 2003 (YTD) |
|---|---|---|---|---|---|---|---|---|---|---|---|---|---|---|---|
| US Government Sec A | AMUSX | IG | 2,853 | 250 | 3.75 | 0 | Y | Y | N | Y | -1.6 | 11.9 | 6.4 | 9.0 | 1.0 |
| New World A | NEWFX | DE | 1,752 | 250 | 5.75 | 0 | Y | Y | N | Y | X | -20.9 | -4.0 | -4.6 | 32.1 |
| Washington Mutual A | AWSHX | LV | 58,196 | 250 | 5.75 | 0 | Y | Y | N | Y | 1.2 | 9.1 | 1.5 | -14.9 | 17.4 |
| Invmt Co of Amer A | AIVSX | LV | 60,063 | 250 | 5.75 | 0 | Y | Y | N | Y | 16.6 | 3.8 | -4.6 | -14.5 | 17.7 |
| American Mutual A | AMRMX | LV | 10,691 | 250 | 5.75 | 0 | Y | Y | N | Y | -0.1 | 9.1 | 6.7 | -12.2 | 16.1 |
| Fundamental Invs A | ANCFX | LV | 19,346 | 250 | 5.75 | 0 | Y | Y | N | Y | 24.6 | 4.3 | -9.6 | -17.3 | 21.2 |
| Inc Fund of Amer A | AMECX | MA | 34,170 | 250 | 5.75 | 0 | Y | Y | N | Y | 0.5 | 10.0 | 5.4 | -4.4 | 16.4 |
| American Balanced A | ABALX | MA | 24,053 | 250 | 5.75 | 0 | Y | Y | N | Y | 3.5 | 15.9 | 8.2 | -6.3 | 16.8 |
| Tax-Exempt Fund CA A | TAFTX | MCI | 642 | 1,000 | 3.75 | 0 | Y | Y | N | Y | -2.0 | 11.2 | 3.8 | 8.1 | 2.9 |
| Tax-Exempt Bond A | AFTEX | MNI | 3,239 | 250 | 3.75 | 0 | Y | Y | N | Y | -2.3 | 9.7 | 5.6 | 8.4 | 3.3 |
| High-Inc Muni Bond A | AMHIX | HYM | 1,140 | 250 | 4.75 | 0 | Y | Y | N | Y | -2.3 | 7.3 | 6.2 | 6.2 | 4.5 |
| New Perspective A | ANWPX | WS | 28,862 | 250 | 5.75 | 0 | Y | Y | N | Y | 40.1 | -7.2 | -8.3 | -16.1 | 25.6 |
| Capital World Bd A | CWBFX | WB | 1,066 | 250 | 3.75 | 0 | Y | Y | N | Y | -2.2 | 1.5 | 1.5 | 16.5 | 12.0 |
| American Hi Inc Tr A | AHITX | HYB | 8,704 | 250 | 3.75 | 0 | Y | Y | N | Y | 7.6 | -3.2 | 7.4 | -3.6 | 24.6 |
| Intm Bd Fd of Amer A | AIBAX | STB | 5,162 | 250 | 3.75 | 0 | Y | Y | N | Y | 1.0 | 10.1 | 6.9 | 7.1 | 1.8 |
| Bond Fund of Amer A | ABNDX | ITB | 16,429 | 250 | 3.75 | 0 | Y | Y | N | Y | 2.3 | 6.2 | 7.2 | 6.1 | 9.5 |
| New Economy A | ANEFX | LG | 6,935 | 250 | 5.75 | 0 | Y | Y | N | Y | 45.9 | -16.2 | -17.3 | -26.0 | 32.1 |
| Grth Fund of Amer A | AGTHX | LG | 57,370 | 250 | 5.75 | 0 | Y | Y | N | Y | 45.7 | 7.5 | -12.3 | -22.0 | 25.9 |
| Amcap A | AMCPX | LG | 11,686 | 250 | 5.75 | 0 | Y | Y | N | Y | 21.8 | 7.5 | -5.0 | -18.7 | 24.3 |
| Tax-Exempt Fund VA A | TFVAX | MSSI | 221 | 1,000 | 3.75 | 0 | Y | Y | N | Y | -2.5 | 10.1 | 4.5 | 8.9 | 2.4 |
| Tax-Exempt Fund MD A | TMMDX | MSSI | 191 | 1,000 | 3.75 | 0 | Y | Y | N | Y | -2.3 | 8.2 | 5.1 | 8.3 | 2.9 |

## AMERICAN FUND REPRESENTITIVE: SANTA ANA, CA. 800.421.0180

* Each class has their own requirements. Deposit minimums after the account is set up are approximately $50 for each fund.

Checkwriting is not allowed with retirement accounts.

American Funds does have a money-market type account with check-writing privelages on their Cash Management Trust America, TaxExempt Money Market Fund, and the US Treasury Fund of America.

## AMERICAN CENTURY
http://www.americancentury.com

| | SYMBOL | ASSET TYPE | MIL | MIN INV | LOAD IN | LOAD OUT | *WITHDRAWAL OPTIONS P | W | C | I | 1999 | 2000 | 2001 | 2002 | (YTD) 2003 |
|---|---|---|---|---|---|---|---|---|---|---|---|---|---|---|---|
| Ginnie Mae Inv | BGNMX | IG | 1,767 | 2,500 | 0 | 0 | Y | Y | Y | Y | 1.0 | 10.4 | 7.4 | 8.3 | 1.0 |
| Target Mat 2020 Inv | BTTTX | LGO | 167 | 2,500 | 0 | 0 | Y | N | N | Y | -18.3 | 30.7 | -1.5 | 27.4 | 0.9 |
| Balanced Inv | TWBIX | MA | 600 | 2,500 | 0 | 0 | Y | Y | N | Y | 10.1 | -2.7 | -3.7 | -9.5 | 14.7 |
| CA Lg-Term T/F Inv | BCLTX | MCL | 496 | 5,000 | 0 | 0 | Y | N | N | Y | -5.2 | 14.8 | 4.2 | 8.6 | 2.4 |
| CA Int-Term T/F Inv | BCITX | MCIS | 449 | 5,000 | 0 | 0 | Y | N | N | Y | -1.1 | 10.0 | 4.3 | 8.8 | 2.0 |
| CA High-Yld Muni Inv | BCHYX | MCL | 345 | 5,000 | 0 | 0 | Y | N | N | Y | -3.3 | 12.5 | 4.7 | 9.1 | 3.6 |
| Century Utilities Inv | BULIX | SU | 139 | 2,500 | 0 | 0 | Y | N | N | Y | 11.5 | 4.0 | -21.1 | -27.4 | 16.7 |
| Real Estate Inv | REACX | SRE | 323 | 2,500 | 0 | 0 | Y | N | N | Y | -2.7 | 27.2 | 10.6 | 5.5 | 30.6 |
| Tax-Free Bond Inv | TWTIX | MNI | 602 | 5,000 | 0 | 0 | Y | N | N | Y | -0.9 | 9.8 | 5.2 | 9.1 | 2.5 |
| Life Sciences Inv | ALSIX | SH | 156 | 2,500 | 0 | 0 | Y | N | N | Y | X | X | -7.8 | -28.2 | 19.7 |
| Global Growth Inv | TWGGX | WS | 252 | 2,500 | 0 | 0 | Y | N | N | Y | 86.1 | -5.8 | -25.7 | -20.3 | 27.8 |
| Global Gold Inv | BGEIX | SPM | 640 | 2,500 | 0 | 0 | Y | N | N | Y | -3.2 | -24.0 | 34.1 | 73.0 | 31.9 |
| International Bd Inv | BEGBX | WB | 530 | 2,500 | 0 | 0 | Y | N | N | Y | -10.4 | -1.2 | -1.7 | 23.5 | 11.1 |
| Intl Growth Inv | TWIEX | FLG | 3,048 | 2,500 | 0 C | 0 C | Y | N | N | Y | 64.4 | -15.0 | -26.8 | -19.3 | 17.4 |
| Intl Discovery Inv | TWEGX | FSMG | 1,183 | 10,000 | 0 C | 0 C | Y | N | N | Y | 88.5 | -14.2 | -21.8 | -12.8 | 43.6 |
| Small Cap Value Inv | ASVIX | SV | 1,318 | 2,500 | 0 C | 0 C | Y | N | N | Y | -0.9 | 39.4 | 30.5 | -11.4 | 25.5 |
| Veedot Inv | AMVIX | MCG | 241 | 10,000 | 0 | 0 | Y | N | N | Y | X | -1.4 | -20.2 | -22.1 | 37.5 |
| Value Inv | TWVLX | MCV | 2,405 | 2,500 | 0 C | 0 C | Y | N | N | Y | -0.8 | 18.3 | 12.9 | -12.7 | 19.0 |
| Vista Inv | TWCVX | MCG | 1,291 | 2,500 | 0 | 0 | Y | N | N | Y | 119.1 | -1.0 | -27.6 | -20.9 | 36.3 |
| Heritage Inv | TWHIX | MCG | 1,302 | 2,500 | 0 | 0 | Y | N | N | Y | 51.3 | 17.4 | -25.6 | -16.0 | 18.5 |
| Equity Income Inv | TWEIX | MCV | 2,343 | 2,500 | 0 | 0 | Y | N | N | Y | -0.2 | 21.9 | 11.3 | -5.0 | 14.9 |
| New Oppor Inv | TWNOX | MCG | 318 | 10,000 | 0 C | 0 C | Y | N | N | Y | 148.0 | -18.2 | -29.6 | -22.6 | 24.3 |
| Giftrust Inv | TWGTX | MCG | 896 | 2,500 | 0 | 0 | Y | N | N | Y | 87.3 | -16.5 | -35.4 | -21.4 | 18.6 |
| Ultra Inv | TWCUX | LGO | 22,808 | 2,500 | 0 | 0 | Y | N | N | Y | 41.5 | -19.9 | -14.6 | -23.2 | 22.8 |
| Select Inv | TWCIX | LGO | 4,069 | 2,500 | 0 | 0 | Y | N | N | Y | 22.2 | -8.7 | -18.2 | -22.8 | 18.5 |
| Growth Inv | TWCGX | LGO | 4,973 | 2,500 | 0 | 0 | Y | N | N | Y | 34.7 | -14.7 | -18.7 | -26.1 | 19.7 |
| Short-Term Govt Inv | TWUSX | SG | 959 | 2,500 | 0 | 0 | Y | Y | N | Y | 1.9 | 7.7 | 7.1 | 5.3 | 0.7 |
| Small Company Inv | ASQIX | SB | 322 | 2,500 | 0 | 0 | Y | N | N | Y | 9.8 | 8.9 | 2.1 | -4.0 | 42.8 |
| Equity Growth Inv | BEQGX | LB | 1,311 | 2,500 | 0 | 0 | Y | N | N | Y | 18.5 | -11.0 | -11.0 | -20.3 | 22.5 |

## AMERICAN CENTURY

http://www.americancentury.com

| | | ASSET | | MIN | LOAD | | * WITHDRAWAL OPTIONS | | | | ANNUAL RETURN | | | | (YTD) |
|---|---|---|---|---|---|---|---|---|---|---|---|---|---|---|---|
| | SYMBOL | TYPE | MIL | INV | IN | OUT | P | W | C | I | 1999 | 2000 | 2001 | 2002 | 2003 |
| Income & Growth Inv | BIGRX | LV | 4,689 | 2,500 | 0 | 0 | Y | Y | N | Y | 18.0 | -10.5 | -8.4 | .19.4 | 21.0 |
| High-Yield Muni Inv | ABHYX | HYM | 15 | 5,000 | 0 | 0 | Y | Y | N | Y | -2.0 | 7.2 | 6.5 | 9.7 | 4.0 |
| Government Bond Inv | CPTNX | IG | 587 | 2,500 | 0 | 0 | Y | Y | N | Y | -2.0 | 12.5 | 6.8 | 11.0 | 1.2 |
| Capital Val Inv | ACTIX | LV | 93 | 10,000 | 0 | 0 | Y | Y | N | Y | X | 9.8 | 6.8 | -13.7 | 18.6 |
| Large Co Val Inv | ALVIX | LV | 306 | 2,500 | 0 C | 0 C | Y | Y | N | Y | X | 9.7 | 7.5 | -13.5 | 19.4 |
| Intl Opport Inv | AIOIX | FSMG | 2 | 10,000 | 0 | 0 | Y | Y | N | Y | X | X | X | -5.2 | 66.2 |
| Emerging Markets Inv | TWMIX | DE | 155 | 10,00 | 0 | 0 | Y | Y | N | Y | 106.2 | -30.1 | -8.7 | -18.8 | 47.0 |
| Inflat-Adj Bd Inv | ACITX | IG | 408 | 2,500 | 0 | 0 | Y | Y | N | Y | 1.7 | 12.0 | 7.6 | 14.7 | 6.3 |
| Technology Inv | ATCIX | ST | 202 | 2,500 | 0 | 0 | Y | Y | N | Y | X | X | -35.6 | -40.9 | 47.9 |
| Target Mat 2030 Inv | ACTAX | LOG | 13 | 2,500 | 0 | 0 | Y | Y | N | Y | X | X | X | 28.7 | -1.6 |
| Target Mat 2025 Inv | BTTRX | LOG | 139 | 2,500 | 0 | 0 | Y | Y | N | Y | -20.7 | 32.7 | -2.7 | 27.3 | -0.6 |
| Target Mat 2015 Inv | BTFTX | LOG | 142 | 2,500 | 0 | 0 | Y | Y | N | Y | -14.6 | 26.6 | 0.7 | 26.8 | 1.8 |
| Target Mat 2010 Inv | BTTNX | LOG | 245 | 2,500 | 0 | 0 | Y | Y | N | Y | -11.8 | 22.6 | 4.3 | 23.5 | 2.1 |
| Target Mat 2005 Inv | BTFIX | IG | 374 | 2,500 | 0 | 0 | Y | Y | N | Y | -5.8 | 13.3 | 8.5 | 14.6 | 1.7 |
| Strat Alloc: Mod Inv | TWSMX | MA | 1,045 | 2,500 | 0 | 0 | Y | Y | N | Y | 22.3 | 0.3 | -4.3 | -9.5 | 16.9 |
| Strat Alloc: Con Inv | TWSCX | CA | 508 | 2,500 | 0 | 0 | Y | Y | N | Y | 11.2 | 4.9 | 0.9 | -4.9 | 10.7 |
| Strat Alloc: Agg Inv | TWSAX | LB | 536 | 2,500 | 0 | 0 | Y | Y | N | Y | 33.8 | -2.5 | -9.3 | -14.0 | 21.1 |
| New Oppor II Inv | ANOIX | SG | 4 | 10,000 | 0 | 0 | Y | Y | N | Y | X | X | X | -15.9 | 35.6 |
| High-Yield Inv | ABHIX | HYB | 72 | 2,500 | 0 | 0 | Y | Y | N | Y | 5.9 | -14.1 | 3.2 | 2.7 | 16.0 |
| Global Nat Res Inv | BGRIX | GNR | 18 | 2,500 | 0 C | 0 C | Y | Y | N | Y | 26.5 | 5.6 | -5.2 | -2.9 | 9.0 |
| FL Municipal Bd Inv | ACBFX | MF | 57 | 5,000 | 0 | 0 | Y | Y | N | Y | -0.6 | 9.8 | 4.7 | 9.3 | 2.5 |
| Equity Index Inst | ACQIX | LB | 823 | 5 MIL | 0 | 0 | Y | Y | N | Y | X | -9.3 | -11.9 | -22.2 | 20.8 |

AMERICAN CENTURY FUND REPRESENTATIVE: KANSAS CITY, MO. 800.345.8765

*Check writing priviledges are available for Money-Market Mutual-Fund (BCTXX), Capital Preservation Fund (CPFXX).
Minimum additional deposit is generally $50.

# FIDELITY
http://www.fidelity.com

| | SYMBOL | ASSET TYPE | MIL | MIN INV | LOAD IN | LOAD OUT | * WITHDRAWAL OPTIONS P | W | C | I | 1999 | ANNUAL RETURN 2000 | 2001 | 2002 | (YTD) 2003 |
|---|---|---|---|---|---|---|---|---|---|---|---|---|---|---|---|
| Fidelity Trend | FTRNX | LB | 835 | 2,500 | 0 | 0 | Y | Y | N | Y | 40.7 | -7.2 | -12.4 | -20.9 | 20.9 |
| Fidelity Large Cap Stock | FLCSX | LG | 677 | 2,500 | 0 | 0 | Y | Y | N | Y | 30.2 | -14.5 | -17.8 | -23.0 | 18.9 |
| Fidelity Independence | FDFFX | LG | 4,651 | 2,500 | 0 | 0 | Y | Y | N | Y | 47.0 | 1.7 | -27.2 | -15.8 | 18.5 |
| Europe Capital Appreciation | FECAX | ES | 394 | 2,500 | 0 | 0 | Y | Y | N | Y | 23.8 | -5.8 | -13.1 | -15.0 | 24.8 |
| Equity-Income II | FEQTX | LV | 11,526 | 2,500 | 0 | 0 | Y | Y | N | Y | 4.4 | 7.5 | -7.2 | -15.4 | 25.0 |
| Structured Large Cap Value | FSLVX | LV | 22 | 2,500 | 0 | 0 | Y | Y | N | Y | X | X | X | -17.2 | 17.4 |
| Advisor Growth & Income T | FGITX | LB | 1,791 | 2,500 | 3.5 | 0 | Y | Y | N | Y | 25.0 | -13.0 | -8.9 | -19.1 | 18.5 |
| Advisor Equity Income Instl | EQPIX | LV | 4,748 | 2,500 | 0 | 0 | Y | Y | N | Y | 3.8 | 9.9 | -1.9 | -15.2 | 19.8 |
| Fidelity Equity-Income | FEQIX | LV | 21,446 | 2,500 | 0 | 0 | Y | Y | N | Y | 7.2 | 8.5 | -5.0 | -17.2 | 19.7 |
| Inflation-Protected Bond | FINPX | IG | 655 | 2,500 | 0 | 0 | Y | Y | N | Y | X | X | X | X | 6.7 |
| Spartan Government Income | SPGVX | IG | 928 | 25,000 | 0 | 0 | Y | Y | N | Y** | -2.1 | 12.8 | 6.9 | 11.5 | 1.2 |
| Intermediate Government | FSTGX | IG | 1,155 | 2,500 | 0 | 0 | Y | Y | N | Y*** | 0.6 | 10.3 | 7.9 | 10.2 | 1.1 |
| Fidelity Government Income | FGOVX | IG | 3,804 | 2,500 | 0 | 0 | Y | Y | N | Y*** | -2.3 | 12.6 | 6.7 | 10.9 | 1.1 |
| Fidelity Europe | FIEUX | ES | 1,282 | 2,500 | 0 | 0 | Y | Y | N | Y | 18.7 | -9.1 | -16.0 | -25.5 | 33.0 |
| Fidelity Destiny II | FDETX | LB | 4,920 | 50 | 8.67 | 0 | Y | Y | N | Y | 25.4 | -13.8 | -9.4 | -15.4 | 12.7 |
| Advisor Growth Opport T | FAGOX | LB | 5,835 | 2,500 | 3.5 | 0 | Y | Y | N | Y | 3.9 | -18.3 | -15.1 | -22.4 | 22.5 |
| Fidelity Ginnie Mae | FGMNX | IG | 4,745 | 2,500 | 0 | 0 | Y | Y | N | Y*** | 1.3 | 10.7 | 7.2 | 8.7 | 1.5 |
| Fidelity Fifty | FFTYX | LB | 940 | 2,500 | 0 | 0 | Y | Y | N | Y | 45.8 | -4.5 | -12.4 | 0.3 | 16.6 |
| Fidelity Growth & Income II | FGRTX | LB | 231 | 2,500 | 0 | 0 | Y | Y | N | Y | 8.1 | -3.9 | -9.2 | -17.1 | 19.3 |
| Fidelity Spartan 500 Index | FSMKX | LB | 9,073 | 10,000 | 0 | 0 | Y | Y | N | Y | 20.7 | -9.1 | -12.1 | -22.2 | 21.1 |
| Fidelity Export & Multinational | FEXPX | LB | 919 | 2,500 | 0 | 0 | Y | Y | N | Y | 41.8 | 1.5 | 0.7 | -18.7 | 23.6 |
| Fidelity Advisor Small Cap T | FSCTX | SG | 1,632 | 2,500 | 3.5 | 0 | Y | Y | N | Y | 68.5 | -17.6 | -3.9 | -20.4 | 32.7 |
| Fidelity Four-in-One Index | FFNOX | LB | 418 | 10,000 | 0 | 0 | Y | Y | N | Y | X | -7.7 | -10.0 | -16.0 | 21.0 |
| Fidelity Advisor Balanced T | FAIGX | MA | 1,745 | 2,500 | 3.5 | 0 | Y | Y | N | Y | 4.5 | -5.7 | -1.9 | -9.1 | 14.5 |
| Spartan MA Municipal Income | FDMMX | MM | 1,824 | 10,000 | 0 | 0 | Y | Y | Y | Y** | -2.1 | 11.8 | 4.4 | 9.7 | 3.4 |
| Fidelity Puritan | FPURX | MA | 20,646 | 2,500 | 0 | 0 | Y | Y | N | Y | 2.9 | 7.8 | -1.1 | -7.9 | 14.7 |
| Fidelity Balanced | FBALX | MA | 8,863 | 2,500 | 0 | 0 | Y | Y | N | Y | 8.9 | 5.3 | 2.3 | -8.5 | 21.8 |
| Spartan NJ Municipal Income | FNJHX | MNJ | 544 | 10,000 | 0 | 0 | Y | Y | N | Y | -1.5 | 11.4 | 4.2 | 9.8 | 3.1 |
| Spartan CT Municipal Income | FICNX | MSSI | 437 | 10,000 | 0 | 0 | Y | Y | Y | Y | -2.1 | 11.0 | 4.9 | 10.0 | 3.0 |

## FIDELITY
http://www.fidelity.com

| | SYMBOL | ASSET TYPE | MIL | MIN INV | LOAD IN | LOAD OUT | *WITHDRAWAL OPTIONS P | W | C | I | ANNUAL RETURN 1999 | 2000 | 2001 | 2002 | (YTD) 2003 |
|---|---|---|---|---|---|---|---|---|---|---|---|---|---|---|---|
| Spartan PA Municipal Income | FPXTX | MP | 290 | 10,000 | 0 | 0 | Y | Y | N | Y | -2.2 | 11.0 | 5.0 | 9.1 | 3.2 |
| Latin America | FLATX | LAS | 219 | 2,500 | 0 | 0 | Y | Y | N | Y | 54.9 | -17.5 | -6.0 | -20.9 | 43.4 |
| Spartan Short-Int Muni Inc | FSTFX | MNS | 1,815 | 10,000 | 0 | 0 | Y | Y | Y | Y | 1.6 | 6.2 | 5.7 | 6.5 | 2.4 |
| Fidelity Global Balanced | FGBLX | WA | 115 | 2,500 | 0 | 0 | Y | Y | N | Y | 23.0 | -6.0 | -8.2 | -6.1 | 22.2 |
| Fidelity Freedom Income | FFFAX | CA | 1,543 | 2,500 | 0 | 0 | Y | Y | N | Y | 7.2 | 6.3 | 2.2 | -0.3 | 5.7 |
| Fidelity Freedom 2040 | FFFFX | LB | 874 | 2,500 | 0 | 0 | Y | Y | N | Y | X | X | -13.5 | -19.7 | 24.3 |
| Fidelity Freedom 2030 | FFFEX | MA | 3,532 | 2,500 | 0 | 0 | Y | Y | N | Y | 28.5 | -5.1 | -11.7 | -17.3 | 22.0 |
| Fidelity Freedom 2020 | FFFDX | MA | 6,091 | 2,500 | 0 | 0 | Y | Y | N | Y | 25.3 | -3.0 | -9.1 | -13.7 | 19.4 |
| Spartan OH Municipal Income | FOHFX | MO | 424 | 10,000 | 0 | 0 | Y | Y | N | Y | -2.8 | 11.7 | 4.7 | 9.7 | 3.5 |
| Spartan MI Municipal Income | FMHTX | MSSI | 551 | 10,000 | 0 | 0 | Y | Y | Y | Y | -2.6 | 11.2 | 4.8 | 9.8 | 4.0 |
| Spartan FL Municipal Income | FFLIX | MF | 538 | 10,000 | 0 | 0 | Y | Y | N | Y | -2.7 | 10.8 | 5.3 | 9.2 | 2.9 |
| Fidelity Freedom 2010 | FFFCX | CA | 6,342 | 2,500 | 0 | 0 | Y | Y | N | Y | 19.0 | 0.7 | -4.3 | -6.9 | 13.4 |
| Fidelity Freedom 2000 | FFFBX | CA | 1,476 | 2,500 | 0 | 0 | Y | Y | N | Y | 12.2 | 4.0 | -0.1 | -1.8 | 7.2 |
| Fidelity Asset Manager: Income | FASIX | CA | 1,018 | 2,500 | 0 | 0 | Y | Y | N | Y | 5.7 | 3.6 | 1.3 | -0.5 | 12.8 |
| Fidelity Asset Manager: Growth | FASGX | MA | 3,612 | 2,500 | 0 | 0 | Y | Y | N | Y | 14.0 | -3.6 | -7.2 | -14.1 | 15.7 |
| Fidelity Select Computers | FDCPX | ST | 975 | 2,500 | 0 | 0 | Y | Y | N | Y | 81.0 | -31.2 | -27.3 | -42.1 | 62.6 |
| Fidelity Select Software & Comp | FSCSX | ST | 793 | 2,500 | 0 | 0 | Y | Y | N | Y | 93.2 | -20.5 | -7.0 | -23.4 | 29.2 |
| Select Network & Infrastruct | FNINX | ST | 75 | 2,500 | 0 | 0 | Y | Y | N | Y | X | X | -50.3 | -49.5 | 57.7 |
| Fidelity Destiny I | FDESX | LG | 3,324 | 50 | 0 | 0 | Y | Y | N | Y | 5.0 | -20.1 | -17.3 | -22.8 | 19.3 |
| Fidelity Convertible Securities | FCVSX | C | 1,731 | 2,500 | 8.67 | 0 | Y | Y | N | Y | 44.1 | 7.2 | 0.5 | -13.9 | 22.2 |
| Fidelity Blue Chip Growth | FBGRX | LG | 21,244 | 2,500 | 0 | 0 | Y | Y | N | Y | 24.3 | -10.5 | -16.6 | -25.3 | 19.1 |
| Fidelity Asset Manager | FASMX | MA | 10,998 | 2,500 | 0 | 0 | Y | Y | N | Y | 13.6 | 2.4 | -3.9 | -8.1 | 12.5 |
| Fidelity Utilities | FIUIX | SU | 855 | 2,500 | 0 | 0 | Y | Y | N | Y | 26.8 | -20.5 | -15.2 | -26.6 | 16.0 |
| Spartan CA Municipal Income | FCTFX | MCL | 1,517 | 10,000 | 0 | 0 | Y | Y | Y** | Y | -2.8 | 12.5 | 4.7 | 8.5 | 3.0 |
| Select Utilities Growth | FSUTX | SU | 203 | 2,500 | 0 | 0 | Y | Y | N | Y | 26.0 | -13.5 | -21.9 | -30.4 | 20.8 |
| Advisor Equity Growth Instl | EQPGX | LG | 10,216 | 2,500 | 0 | 0 | Y | Y | Y** | Y | 37.0 | -11.0 | -17.7 | -30.2 | 27.8 |
| Spartan NY Municipal Income | FTFMX | MNYL | 1,425 | 10,000 | 0 | 0 | Y | Y | N | Y | -3.3 | 12.9 | 4.4 | 10.9 | 3.4 |
| Select Multimedia | FBMPX | SC | 179 | 2,500 | 0 | 0 | Y | Y | N | Y | 44.1 | -23.0 | -1.0 | -12.8 | 35.7 |
| Advisor Technology T | FATEX | ST | 1,216 | 2,500 | 3.5 | 0 | Y | Y | N | Y | 89.4 | -36.7 | -26.9 | -39.0 | 56.7 |
| Real Estate Investment | FRESX | SRE | 2,496 | 2,500 | 0 | 0 | Y | Y | N | Y | -1.0 | 31.4 | 9.5 | 5.8 | 25.1 |

# FIDELITY

http://www.fidelity.com

| | SYMBOL | ASSET TYPE | MIL | MIN INV | LOAD IN | LOAD OUT | WITHDRAWAL OPTIONS P | W | C | I | ANNUAL RETURN 1999 | 2000 | 2001 | 2002 | (YTD) 2003 |
|---|---|---|---|---|---|---|---|---|---|---|---|---|---|---|---|
| Advisor Emerg Mkts Inc T | FAEMX | EMB | 145 | 2,500 | 3.5 | 0 | Y | Y | N | Y | 36.3 | 13.7 | 6.3 | 11.7 | 23.7 |
| Fidelity Worldwide | FFWFX | WS | 848 | 2,500 | 0 | 0 | Y | Y | N | Y | 30.8 | -8.0 | -6.2 | -18.8 | 28.8 |
| Fidelity Select Natural Gas | FSNGX | SNR | 177 | 2,500 | 0 | 0 | Y | Y | N | Y | 26.2 | 71.3 | -22.8 | -9.6 | 12.7 |
| Fidelity Select Energy | FSENX | SNR | 187 | 2,500 | 0 | 0 | Y | Y | N | Y | 34.3 | 31.8 | -12.0 | -11.5 | 8.3 |
| Fidelity Advisor Natural Res T | FAGNX | SNR | 265 | 2,500 | 3.5 | 0 | Y | Y | N | Y | 34.4 | 25.7 | -10.8 | -11.5 | 13.9 |
| Fidelity Select Technology | FSPTX | ST | 2,507 | 2,500 | 0 | 0 | Y | Y | N | Y | 131.7 | -32.5 | -31.7 | -37.8 | 58.2 |
| Fidelity Select Medical Delivery | FSHCX | SH | 100 | 2,500 | 0 | 0 | Y | Y | N | Y | -29.6 | 67.8 | -2.3 | -12.1 | 14.4 |
| Fidelity Select Energy Service | FSESX | SNR | 360 | 2,500 | 0 | 0 | Y | Y | N | Y | 72.2 | 50.3 | -21.0 | -0.7 | -2.2 |
| Select Electronics | FSLEX | ST | 3,768 | 2,500 | 0 | 0 | Y | Y | N | Y | 106.6 | -17.7 | -14.7 | -50.5 | 66.3 |
| Fidelity Contrafund | FCNTX | LB | 34,261 | 2,500 | 0 | 0 | Y | Y | N | Y | 25.0 | -6.8 | -12.6 | -9.6 | 22.4 |
| Select Developing Comm | FSDCX | SC | 669 | 2,500 | 0 | 0 | Y | Y | N | Y | 122.4 | -29.6 | -36.1 | -47.8 | 66.7 |
| Japan Smaller Companies | FJSCX | JS | 929 | 2,500 | 0 | 0 | Y | Y | N | Y | 237.4 | -50.2 | -20.1 | 0.9 | 60.7 |
| Spartan Interm Muni Income | FLTMX | MNI | 1,767 | 10,000 | 0 | 0 | Y | Y | Y** | Y | -1.1 | 9.3 | 5.5 | 9.0 | 3.7 |
| Select Telecommunications | FSTCX | SC | 346 | 2,500 | 0 | 0 | Y | Y | N | Y | 66.6 | -37.6 | -28.3 | -29.3 | 17.8 |
| Fidelity U.S. Bond Index | FBIDX | ITB | 4,712 | 100,000 | 0 | 0 | Y | Y | N | Y | -1.0 | 11.4 | 8.1 | 10.2 | 3.5 |
| Select Brokerage & Investmnt | FSLBX | SF | 410 | 2,500 | 0 | 0 | Y | Y | N | Y | 30.6 | 27.9 | -9.0 | -17.2 | 32.1 |
| Fidelity Select Insurance | FSPCX | SF | 105 | 2,500 | 0 | 0 | Y | Y | N | Y | -6.0 | 53.3 | -4.9 | -5.6 | 19.8 |
| Select Financial Services | FIDSX | SF | 508 | 2,500 | 0 | 0 | Y | Y | N | Y | 1.5 | 28.5 | -9.1 | -11.4 | 24.4 |
| Advisor Financial Svc T | FAFSX | SF | 540 | 2,500 | 3.5 | 0 | Y | Y | N | Y | 1.9 | 28.9 | -8.5 | -12.0 | 24.0 |
| Fidelity Select Gold | FSAGX | SPM | 769 | 2,500 | 0 | 0 | Y | Y | N | Y | 8.4 | -18.1 | 25.0 | 64.3 | 24.2 |
| Fidelity Select Health Care | FSPHX | SH | 1,864 | 2,500 | 0 | 0 | Y | Y | N | Y | -2.9 | 36.7 | -15.0 | -18.0 | 8.1 |
| Fidelity Select Biotechnology | FBIOX | SH | 1,870 | 2,500 | 0 | 0 | Y | Y | N | Y | 77.7 | 32.8 | -25.0 | -40.5 | 26.8 |
| Fidelity Spartan U.S. Equity Index | FUSEX | LB | 14,824 | 100,000 | 0 | 0 | Y | Y | N | Y | 20.7 | -9.2 | -12.1 | -22.2 | 21.1 |
| Fidelity Small Cap Stock | FSLCX | SG | 2,126 | 2,500 | 0 | 0 | Y | Y | N | Y | 42.7 | 11.8 | 6.4 | -15.7 | 33.5 |
| Select Medical Equip/Systems | FSMEX | SH | 330 | 2,500 | 0 | 0 | Y | Y | N | Y | 10.7 | 50.4 | 0.3 | -6.2 | 25.9 |
| Spartan Municipal Income | FHIGX | MNL | 4,703 | 10,000 | 0 | 0 | Y | Y | Y** | Y | -2.5 | 12.3 | 5.0 | 10.5 | 3.7 |
| Fidelity Small Cap Retirement | FSCRX | SG | 70 | 2,500 | 0 | 0 | Y | Y | N | Y | X | X | 23.3 | -21.0 | 26.6 |
| Fidelity Small Cap Independence | FDSCX | SG | 932 | 2,500 | 3.5 | 0 | Y | Y | N | Y | 14.1 | 5.8 | 6.3 | -20.8 | 26.8 |
| Fidelity Advisor Municipal Inc T | FAHIX | MNL | 644 | 2,500 | 0 | 0 | Y | Y | N | Y | -2.7 | 11.7 | 4.6 | 10.0 | 3.4 |
| Fidelity New Markets Income | FNMIX | EMB | 776 | 2,500 | 0 | 0 | Y | Y | N | Y | 36.7 | 14.4 | 6.6 | 12.6 | 24.3 |

* WITHDRAWAL OPTIONS

# FIDELITY
http://www.fidelity.com

| | SYMBOL | ASSET TYPE | MIL | MIN INV | LOAD IN | LOAD OUT | WITHDRAWAL OPTIONS P | W | C | I | 1999 | 2000 | 2001 | 2002 | (YTD) 2003 |
|---|---|---|---|---|---|---|---|---|---|---|---|---|---|---|---|
| Fidelity Select Banking | FSRBX | SF | 420 | 2,500 | 0 | 0 | Y | Y | Y | Y | -10.1 | 18.7 | 0.4 | -7.7 | 26.7 |
| Floating Rate High Income | FFRHX | BL | 1,444 | 2,500 | 0 | 0 | Y | Y | Y | Y | X | X | X | X | 5.7 |
| Advisor Diversified Intl T | FADIX | FLB | 1,386 | 2,500 | 3.5 | 0 | Y | Y | N | Y | 57.9 | -8.7 | -13.8 | -9.4 | 28.9 |
| Select Home Finance | FSLVX | SF | 399 | 2,500 | 0 | 0 | Y | Y | N | Y | -12.4 | 50.3 | -3.1 | -0.7 | 30.0 |
| Advisor Intl Capital App T | FIATX | FLG | 547 | 2,500 | 3.5 | 0 | Y | Y | N | Y | 90.0 | -29.2 | -9.5 | -12.7 | 32.7 |
| Advisor Value Strat T | FASPX | SB | 1,799 | 2,500 | 3.5 | 0 | Y | Y | N | Y | 18.8 | 11.2 | 12.1 | -26.3 | 54.6 |
| Advisor Float Rate Hi Inc C | FFRCX | BL | 1,444 | 2,500 | 0 | C | Y | Y | N | Y | X | X | 3.7 | 0.7 | 5.0 |
| nternational Small Cap | FISMX | FSMG | 332 | 2,500 | 0 | 0 | Y | Y | N | Y | X | X | X | X | 67.9 |
| International Growth & Inc | FIGRX | FLB | 12,241 | 2,500 | 0 | 0 | Y | Y | N | Y | 53.7 | -14.1 | -17.4 | -9.9 | 30.1 |
| Aggressive Intl | FIVFX | FLG | 554 | 2,500 | 0 | 0 | Y | Y | N | Y | 58.9 | -31.0 | -8.9 | -11.0 | 33.8 |
| Fidelity Overseas | FOSFX | FLB | 3,498 | 2,500 | 0 | 0 | Y | Y | N | Y | 42.9 | -18.3 | -20.2 | -19.5 | 32.7 |
| Advisor Overseas T | FAERX | FLB | 1,352 | 2,500 | 3.5 | 0 | Y | Y | N | Y | 42.0 | -18.5 | -20.3 | -20.3 | 32.5 |
| Fidelity Low-Priced Stock | FLPSX | SB | 23,529 | 2,500 | 0 | 0 | Y | Y | N | Y | 5.1 | 18.8 | 26.7 | -6.2 | 31.9 |
| Spartan International Index | FSIIX | FLB | 392 | 15,000 | 0 | 0 | Y | Y | N | Y | 29.1 | -14.9 | -21.9 | -16.0 | 25.7 |
| Diversified International | FDIVX | FLB | 11,489 | 2,500 | 0 | 0 | Y | Y | N | Y | 50.7 | -9.0 | -13.0 | -9.4 | 30.3 |
| Fidelity New Millennium | FMILX | MCG | 3,494 | 2,500 | 0 | C | Y | Y | N | Y | 108.8 | -6.0 | -18.2 | -19.9 | 33.1 |
| Fidelity Aggressive Growth | FDEGX | MCG | 5,119 | 2,500 | 0 | 0 | Y | Y | N | Y | 103.0 | -27.1 | -47.3 | -41.2 | 27.9 |
| Select Defense & Aerospace | FSDAX | MCB | 273 | 2,500 | 0 | 0 | Y | Y | N | Y | 11.8 | 18.9 | 1.2 | -6.8 | 25.6 |
| Fidelity Mid-Cap Stock | FMCSX | MCG | 7,552 | 2,500 | 0 | 0 | Y | Y | N | Y | 39.8 | 32.1 | -12.8 | -27.6 | 28.3 |
| Fidelity Japan | FJPNX | JS | 529 | 2,500 | 0 | 5 | Y | Y | N | Y | 146.1 | -36.5 | -33.8 | -7.4 | 32.6 |
| Fidelity Advisor Mid Cap B | FMCBX | MCG | 5,484 | 2,500 | 0 | 0 | Y | Y | N | Y | 37.5 | 30.5 | -13.7 | -19.2 | 32.3 |
| Fidelity Value | FDVLX | MCV | 6,324 | 2,500 | 0 | 0 | Y | Y | N | Y | 8.6 | 8.1 | 12.3 | -9.3 | 24.8 |
| Advisor Strategic Income T | FSIAX | MB | 1,362 | 2,500 | 3.5 | 0 | Y | Y | N | Y | 6.2 | 3.4 | 6.6 | 8.9 | 14.9 |
| Advisor High Inc Advant T | FAHYX | HYB | 2,744 | 2,500 | 3.5 | 0 | Y | Y | N | Y | 8.5 | -11.4 | -1.2 | -4.0 | 36.9 |
| Fidelity Strategic Income | FSICX | MB | 1,987 | 2,500 | 0 | 0 | Y | Y | N | Y | 6.4 | 4.1 | 6.5 | 8.9 | 14.5 |
| Structured Mid Cap Value | FSMVX | MCV | 48 | 2,500 | 0 | 0 | Y | Y | N | Y | X | X | X | -13.5 | 25.7 |
| Fidelity High-Income | SPHIX | HYB | 2,730 | 2,500 | 0 | 0 | Y | Y | N | Y | 8.9 | -14.2 | -4.8 | 1.5 | 22.9 |
| Advisor Leveraged Co Stk A | FLSAX | MCB | 76 | 10,000 | 5.75 | 0 | Y | Y | N | Y | X | X | 7.8 | -1.8 | 72.4 |
| Leveraged Company Stock | FLVCX | MCB | 904 | 10,000 | 0 | 0 | Y | Y | N | Y | X | X | 3.2 | -1.8 | 76.0 |
| Fidelity Southeast Asia | FSEAX | PAJ | 395 | 2,500 | 0 | 0 | Y | Y | N | Y | 91.5 | -30.4 | -3.7 | -11.4 | 42.1 |

* WITHDRAWAL OPTIONS

# FIDELITY
http://www.fidelity.com

| | SYMBOL | ASSET TYPE | MIL | MIN INV | LOAD IN | LOAD OUT | P | W | C | I | 1999 | 2000 | 2001 | 2002 | (YTD) 2003 |
|---|---|---|---|---|---|---|---|---|---|---|---|---|---|---|---|
| Fidelity Short-Term Bond | FSHBX | STB | 5,289 | 2,500 | 0 | 0 | Y | Y | Y*** | Y | 3.3 | 7.9 | 7.6 | 6.7 | 2.7 |
| Fidelity Capital & Income | FAGIX | HYB | 4,067 | 2,500 | 0 | 0 | Y | Y | N | Y | 13.3 | -9.4 | -4.7 | -0.4 | 33.8 |
| Fidelity OTC | FOCPX | LG | 7,713 | 2,500 | 0 | 0 | Y | Y | N | Y | 72.5 | -26.8 | -24.1 | -23.3 | 31.6 |
| Fidelity Growth Company | FDGRX | LG | 22,063 | 2,500 | 0 | 0 | Y | Y | N | Y | 79.5 | -6.3 | -25.3 | -33.5 | 38.7 |
| Fidelity China Region | FHKCX | PAJ | 231 | 2,500 | 0 | 0 | Y | Y | N | Y | 84.9 | -17.6 | -10.5 | -15.1 | 39.4 |
| Fidelity Pacific Basin | FPBFX | DPA | 419 | 2,500 | 0 | 0 | Y | Y | N | Y | 119.6 | -35.3 | -19.9 | -7.9 | 33.7 |
| Fidelity Focused Stock | FTQGX | LG | 34 | 2,500 | 0 | 0 | Y | Y | N | Y | 34.8 | -6.1 | -13.6 | -39.3 | 16.1 |
| Fidelity Total Bond | FTBFX | ITB | 89 | 2,500 | 0 | 0 | Y | Y | N | Y | X | X | X | X | 4.5 |
| Fidelity Intermediate Bond | FTHRX | ITB | 6,793 | 2,500 | 0 | 0 | Y | Y | Y*** | Y | 1.0 | 9.8 | 8.8 | 9.2 | 3.8 |
| Fidelity Capital Appreciation | FDCAX | LG | 3,933 | 2,500 | 0 | 0 | Y | Y | N | Y | 45.8 | -18.1 | -7.6 | -21.3 | 45.4 |
| Asset Manager: Aggressive | FAMRX | LG | 291 | 2,500 | 0 | 0 | Y | Y | N | Y | X | 15.4 | -15.7 | -35.0 | 43.2 |
| Fidelity Ultra-Short Bond | FUSFX | UB | 325 | 2,500 | 0 | 0 | Y | Y | N | Y | X | X | X | X | 1.5 |
| Fidelity Advisor Large Cap T | FALGX | LG | 583 | 2,500 | 3.5 | 0 | Y | Y | N | Y | 28.8 | -14.7 | -17.9 | -23.5 | 18.1 |
| Fidelity Investment Grade Bond | FBNDX | ITB | 5,422 | 2,500 | 0 | 0 | Y | Y | Y*** | Y | -1.0 | 10.8 | 8.5 | 9.4 | 3.4 |
| Fidelity Growth & Income | FGRIX | LB | 29,153 | 2,500 | 0 | 0 | Y | Y | N | Y | 10.4 | -2.0 | -9.4 | -18.1 | 13.0 |
| Fidelity Emerging Markets | FEMKX | DE | 431 | 2,500 | 0 | 0 | Y | Y | N | Y | 70.5 | -33.0 | -2.5 | -6.9 | 36.1 |
| Spartan Investment Gr Bond | FSIBX | ITB | 2,508 | 25,000 | 0 | 0 | Y | Y | Y** | Y | -0.7 | 11.0 | 8.8 | 9.6 | 3.6 |
| Spartan Total Market Index | FSTMX | LB | 1,765 | 15,000 | 0 | 0 | Y | Y | N | Y | 23.2 | -11.0 | -10.8 | -21.0 | 23.9 |
| Fidelity Magellan | FMAGX | LB | 65,008 | 2,500 | 0C | 0C | Y | Y | N | Y | 24.1 | -9.3 | -11.7 | -23.7 | 18.1 |
| Fidelity Tax-Managed Stock | FTXMX | LB | 55 | 10,000 | 0 | 0 | Y | Y | N | Y | 20.0 | -8.9 | -12.4 | -24.8 | 19.4 |
| Fidelity Disciplined Equity | FDEQX | LB | 3,719 | 2,500 | 0 | 0 | Y | Y | N | Y | 22.4 | -3.5 | -14.2 | -18.6 | 21.2 |
| Fidelity Stock Selector | FDSSX | LB | 790 | 2,500 | 0 | 0 | Y | Y | N | Y | 26.2 | -7.0 | -14.4 | -21.3 | 20.4 |
| Fidelity Dividend Growth | FDGFX | LB | 16,870 | 2,500 | 3.5 | 0 | Y | Y | N | Y | 8.8 | 12.3 | -3.8 | -20.4 | 15.7 |
| Advisor Dividend Growth T | FDGTX | LB | 3,965 | 2,500 | 0 | 0 | Y | Y | N | Y | 7.1 | 11.4 | -3.2 | -20.9 | 15.0 |
| Fidelity Mortgage Secs | FMSFX | IG | 1,300 | 2,500 | 0 | 0 | Y | Y | Y*** | Y | 1.9 | 11.3 | 7.6 | 9.1 | 2.5 |
| Structured Mid Cap Growth | FSMGX | MCG | 47 | 2,500 | 0 | 0 | Y | Y | N | Y | X | X | X | -30.5 | 35.2 |
| Structured Large Cap Growth | FSLGX | LG | 20 | 2,500 | 0 | 0 | Y | Y | N | Y | X | X | X | -29.1 | 20.4 |
| Advisor Asset Allocation T | FAATX | MA | 125 | 2,500 | 3.5 | 0 | Y | Y | N | Y | 16.2 | -2.9 | -9.6 | -14.9 | 17.4 |
| Fidelity Nordic | FNORX | ES | 81 | 2,500 | 0 | 0 | Y | Y | N | Y | 59.5 | -8.5 | -27.9 | -18.3 | 28.0 |
| Fidelity Select Leisure | FDLSX | LG | 174 | 2,500 | 0 | 0 | Y | Y | N | Y | 32.8 | -24.5 | 3.3 | -21.1 | 33.9 |

## FIDELITY
http://www.fidelity.com

| Name | SYMBOL | ASSET TYPE | MIL | MIN INV | LOAD IN | LOAD OUT | P | W | C | I | 1999 | 2000 | 2001 | 2002 | 2003 (YTD) |
|---|---|---|---|---|---|---|---|---|---|---|---|---|---|---|---|
| Spartan Extended Mkt Index | FSEMX | MCB | 799 | 15,000 | 0 | | Y | Y | N | Y | 33.1 | -16.0 | -8.8 | -18.1 | 35.2 |
| Select Food & Agriculture | FDFAX | LV | 93 | 2,500 | 0 | | Y | Y | N | Y | -20.5 | 29.9 | -0.5 | -6.7 | 8.9 |
| Select Retailing | FSRPX | LG | 94 | 2,500 | 0 | | Y | Y | N | Y | 5.3 | -10.9 | -2.4 | -18.9 | 29.8 |
| Fidelity Canada | FIDCDX | FLB | 166 | 2,500 | 0 | | Y | Y | N | Y | 40.6 | 12.3 | -9.6 | -4.3 | 38.7 |
| Select Wireless | FWRLX | SC | 53 | 2,500 | 0 | C | Y | Y | N | Y | X | X | -34.7 | -55.3 | 60.5 |
| Fidelity Value Strategies | FSLSX | SB | 21 | 2,500 | 0 | | Y | Y | N | Y | 19.4 | 11.9 | 12.8 | -25.8 | 55.5 |
| Fidelity Value Discovery | FVDFX | MCB | 40 | 2,500 | 0 | C | Y | Y | N | Y | X | X | X | X | 20.9 |
| Spartan Tax-Free Bond | FTABX | MNL | 216 | 25,000 | 0 | | Y | Y | N | Y | X | X | X | 10.7 | 3.8 |
| Spartan MN Municipal Income | FIMIX | MMI | 338 | 10,000 | 0 | | Y | Y | Y** | Y | -2.4 | 10.6 | 4.6 | 8.6 | 3.5 |
| Spartan MD Municipal Income | SMDMX | MSSI | 94 | 10,000 | 0 | | Y | Y | N | Y | -2.2 | 11.0 | 4.7 | 8.6 | 3.2 |
| Spartan AZ Municipal Income | FSAZX | MSSI | 72 | 10,000 | 0 | | Y | Y | N | Y | -1.8 | 11.0 | 4.8 | 9.9 | 3.2 |
| Select Transportation | FSRFX | MCV | 36 | 2,500 | 0 | | Y | Y | N | Y | 27.6 | 17.8 | 6.2 | -16.5 | 35.8 |
| Select Pharmaceuticals | FPHAX | SH | 59 | 2,500 | 0 | | Y | Y | N | Y | X | X | X | -23.4 | 12.5 |
| Select Paper & Forest Prod | FSPFX | SNR | 18 | 2,500 | 0 | | Y | Y | N | Y | 30.5 | 1.1 | 6.5 | -2.3 | 6.3 |
| Select Natural Resources | FNARX | SNR | 34 | 2,500 | 0 | | Y | Y | N | Y | 38.8 | 30.4 | -11.4 | -11.7 | 13.7 |
| Select Industrial Materials | FSDPX | SNR | 48 | 2,500 | 0 | | Y | Y | N | Y | 16.5 | -5.4 | 7.8 | 1.0 | 32.0 |
| Select Industrial Equipment | FSCGX | LB | 34 | 2,500 | 0 | | Y | Y | N | Y | 17.4 | -4.2 | -1.0 | -22.9 | 24.5 |
| Select Environmental | FSLEX | SG | 13 | 2,500 | 0 | | Y | Y | N | Y | -25.9 | 34.5 | -9.3 | -16.4 | 22.9 |
| Select Cyclical Industries | FCYIX | LV | 27 | 2,500 | 0 | | Y | Y | N | Y | 13.1 | 9.8 | 2.3 | -20.0 | 24.1 |
| Select Consumer Industries | FSCPX | LB | 35 | 2,500 | 0 | | Y | Y | N | Y | 10.1 | -9.4 | -3.2 | -17.1 | 20.1 |
| Select Construction&Housing | FSHOX | MCV | 62 | 2,500 | 0 | | Y | Y | N | Y | -12.6 | 8.9 | 20.0 | -8.5 | 37.9 |
| Select Chemicals | FSCHX | MCV | 35 | 2,500 | 0 | | Y | Y | N | Y | 19.2 | 2.9 | 12.4 | -9.6 | 18.5 |
| Select Business Serv&Outsrcg | FBSOX | MCG | 35 | 2,500 | 0 | | Y | Y | N | Y | 29.3 | -1.3 | 9.6 | -26.9 | 18.8 |
| Fidelity Select Automotive | FSAVX | MCV | 28 | 2,500 | 0 | | Y | Y | N | Y | -13.5 | -7.2 | 22.8 | -6.5 | 33.1 |
| Select Air Transportation | FSAIX | MCV | 49 | 2,500 | 0 | | Y | Y | N | Y | 34.6 | 39.8 | -15.1 | -26.2 | 37.8 |
| Fidelity Real Estate Income | FRIFX | SRE | 308 | 2,500 | 0 | | Y | Y | N | Y | X | X | X | X | X |
| Instl Short-Interm Govt | FFXSX | SG | 536 | 100,000 | 0 | | Y | Y | N | Y | 2.1 | 9.0 | 8.3 | 8.0 | 1.1 |
| Fidelity Congress Street | CNGRX | LV | 70 | *N/A | 0 | | Y | Y | N | Y | 11.1 | 2.8 | -9.0 | -16.2 | 14.6 |
| Advisor Telecomm&Util Gr T | FAUFX | SU | 213 | 2,500 | 3.5 | | Y | Y | N | Y | 43.4 | -27.8 | -15.9 | -30.0 | 22.9 |
| Advisor Tax Managed T | FTMSX | LB | 10 | 2,500 | 3.5 | | Y | Y | N | Y | X | X | X | -25.4 | 18.6 |

*WITHDRAWAL OPTIONS

# FIDELITY
http://www.fidelity.com

| | SYMBOL | ASSET TYPE | MIL | MIN INV | LOAD IN | LOAD OUT | P | W | C | I | 1999 | 2000 | 2001 | 2002 | (YTD) 2003 |
|---|---|---|---|---|---|---|---|---|---|---|---|---|---|---|---|
| Advisor Strat Gr T | FTQTX | LG | 24 | 2,500 | 3.5 | 0 | Y | Y | N | Y | 35.0 | -6.5 | -13.7 | -40.9 | 21.9 |
| Advisor Short Fixed-Inc T | FASFX | STB | 1,155 | 2,500 | 1.5 | 0 | Y | Y | N | Y | 3.2 | 7.7 | 7.0 | 6.3 | 2.4 |
| Advisor Real Estate T | FHETX | SRE | 39 | 2,500 | 3.5 | 5 | Y | Y | N | Y | X | X | X | X | 23.3 |
| Advisor NY Municipal Inc B | FNYBX | MNYL | 27 | 2,500 | 0 | 5 | Y | Y | N | Y | X | X | X | X | 2.6 |
| Advisor Mortgage Secs B | FMSBX | IG | 519 | 2,500 | 0 | 5 | Y | Y | N | Y | X | 10.3 | 6.6 | 8.0 | 1.6 |
| Advisor Latin America T | FLTTX | LAS | 5 | 2,500 | 3.5 | 0 | Y | Y | N | Y | 56.1 | -19.1 | -8.6 | -21.9 | 43.3 |
| Advisor Korea A | FAKAX | PAJ | 15 | 2,500 | 5.75 | 0 | Y | Y | N | Y | 134.5 | -58.8 | 32.1 | 3.0 | 23.1 |
| Advisor Japan B | FAJBX | JS | 48 | 2,500 | 0 | 5 | Y | Y | N | Y | 134.4 | -36.8 | -31.7 | -10.0 | 33.3 |
| Advisor Investment Gr Bd T | FGBTX | ITB | 36 | 2,500 | 3.5 | 0 | Y | Y | N | Y | X | X | X | X | 3.2 |
| Advisor Interm Bond Instl | EFIPX | ITB | 1,300 | 2,500 | 0 | 0 | Y | Y | N | Y | 0.7 | 9.7 | 8.1 | 10.3 | 3.6 |
| Advisor Inflat-Protect Bd B | FBIPX | IG | 101 | 2,500 | 0 | 5 | Y | Y | N | Y | X | X | X | X | 5.9 |
| Advisor High Income T | FHITX | HYB | 380 | 2,500 | 3.5 | 0 | Y | Y | N | Y | X | -5.8 | 9.3 | 1.4 | 19.6 |
| Advisor Health Care T | FACTX | SH | 811 | 2,500 | 3.5 | 0 | Y | Y | N | Y | 1.6 | 35.9 | -15.3 | -18.4 | 7.7 |
| Advisor Govt Investment T | FAGVX | IG | 727 | 2,500 | 3.5 | 0 | Y | Y | N | Y | -2.4 | 12.2 | 6.4 | 10.8 | 0.8 |
| Advisor Global Equity T | FGETX | WS | 30 | 2,500 | 3.5 | 0 | Y | Y | N | Y | 29.6 | -9.0 | -14.0 | -18.0 | 24.7 |
| Advisor Fifty T | FFYTX | LV | 70 | 2,500 | 3.5 | 0 | Y | Y | N | Y | X | X | -13.1 | -0.7 | 15.5 |
| Advisor Europe Cap Apprec T | FAECX | ES | 22 | 2,500 | 3.5 | 0 | Y | Y | N | Y | 20.6 | -8.1 | -15.9 | -16.2 | 23.8 |
| Advisor Equity Value T | FAVTX | LV | 61 | 2,500 | 3.5 | 0 | Y | Y | N | Y | X | X | X | -15.6 | 26.0 |
| Advisor Emerging Asia A | FEAAX | PAJ | 41 | 2,500 | 5.75 | 0 | Y | Y | N | Y | 77.3 | -37.0 | -5.7 | -12.4 | 33.7 |
| Advisor Electronics T | FELTX | ST | 59 | 2,500 | 3.5 | 0 | Y | Y | N | Y | X | X | -8.0 | -46.6 | 63.4 |
| Advisor Dynamic Cap App T | FRGTX | LB | 369 | 2,500 | 3.5 | 0 | Y | Y | N | Y | 65.2 | 1.4 | -27.6 | -13.3 | 21.0 |
| Advisor Developing Comm B | FDMBX | SC | 9 | 2,500 | 0 | 5 | Y | Y | N | Y | X | X | -22.1 | -46.5 | 66.0 |
| Advisor Cyclical Indst T | FCLTX | LV | 30 | 2,500 | 3.5 | 0 | Y | Y | N | Y | 12.5 | 6.8 | 3.2 | -19.2 | 24.7 |
| Advisor Consumer Indst T | FACPX | LB | 51 | 2,500 | 3.5 | 0 | Y | Y | N | Y | 9.9 | -9.2 | -3.3 | -15.8 | 20.5 |
| Advisor CA Municipal Inc C | FCMKX | MCL | 23 | 2,500 | 0 | 1 | Y | Y | N | Y | X | X | X | X | 2.1 |
| Advisor Biotechnology B | FBTBX | SH | 45 | 2,500 | 0 | 5 | Y | Y | N | Y | X | X | -25.4 | -40.6 | 26.8 |
| Advisor Aggressive Gr T | FGVTX | MCG | 33 | 2,500 | 3.5 | 0 | Y | Y | N | Y | X | X | -16.6 | -27.1 | 25.5 |

* WITHDRAWAL OPTIONS

**FIDELITY FUND REPRESENTATIVE: CINCINNATI, OH. 800.343.3548**

\*   Check writing is allowed on most Investment Grade, and Municipal Grade Bond Funds, as well as several Money-Market funds.

\*\*   Minimum check written on this account is $1,000.

\*\*\*   Minimum check written on this account is $500.

\*N/A This fund is only available for retirement accounts through 401k (or similar) retirement plans. Speak with representative about requirements.

Checkwriting can be attained on many of the above Fidelity Funds. First open a brokerage account and select a fund (not Select or Advisor funds) and link the account to a Core Account. You sell shares in the general Brokerage Account and write checks from the Core Account.

# FRANKLIN TEMPLETON

http://www.franklintempleton.com

| | SYMBOL | ASSET TYPE | MIL | MIN INV | LOAD IN | OUT | *WITHDRAWAL OPTIONS P | W | C | I | ANNUAL RETURN 1999 | 2000 | 2001 | 2002 | (YTD) 2003 |
|---|---|---|---|---|---|---|---|---|---|---|---|---|---|---|---|
| Franklin Equity Income A | FISEX | LV | 706 | 1,000 | 5.75 | 0 | Y | Y | N | N | Y | 0.8 | 18.6 | -1.3 | 15.3 | 15.4 |
| Templeton World A | TEMWX | WS | 7,003 | 1,000 | 5.75 | 0 | Y | Y | N | N | Y | 28.1 | -4.0 | -8.1 | -12.2 | 23.8 |
| Templeton Growth A | TEPLX | WS | 15,339 | 1,000 | 5.75 | 0 | Y | Y | N | N | Y | 30.4 | 1.7 | 0.5 | -9.5 | 21.7 |
| U.S. Government Secs A | FKUSX | IG | 8,976 | 1,000 | 4.25 | 0 | Y | Y | N | N | Y | 0.8 | 10.6 | 7.7 | 8.6 | 0.7 |
| AGE High Income A | AGEFX | HYB | 2,947 | 1,000 | 4.25 | 0 | Y | Y | N | N | Y | 0.5 | -7.4 | 2.9 | -3.4 | 29.8 |
| Franklin Income A | FKINX | CA | 16,714 | 1,000 | 4.25 | 0 | Y | Y | N | N | Y | -0.7 | 20.6 | 0.7 | -1.1 | 23.0 |
| MO Tax-Free Income A | FRMOX | MSSL | 534 | 1,000 | 4.25 | 0 | Y | Y | N | N | Y | -4.5 | 11.7 | 5.0 | 8.9 | 3.0 |
| OR Tax-Free Income A | FRORX | MSSL | 619 | 1,000 | 4.25 | 0 | Y | Y | N | N | Y | -3.9 | 11.1 | 4.2 | 8.2 | 3.3 |
| Double Tax-Free Income A | FPRTX | MSSL | 325 | 1,000 | 4.25 | 0 | Y | Y | N | N | Y | -2.4 | 10.3 | 4.2 | 9.3 | 2.0 |
| OH Insured Tax-Free Inc A | FTOIX | MO | 981 | 1,000 | 4.25 | 0 | Y | Y | N | N | Y | -3.1 | 11.4 | 4.7 | 8.4 | 2.9 |
| MI Insured Tax-Free Inc A | FTTMX | MSSL | 1,396 | 1,000 | 4.25 | 0 | Y | Y | N | N | Y | -2.3 | 11.1 | 4.8 | 9.1 | 3.1 |
| AZ Tax-Free Income A | FTAZX | MSSI | 934 | 1,000 | 4.25 | 0 | Y | Y | N | N | Y | -3.9 | 10.4 | 3.0 | 7.7 | 4.1 |
| PA Tax-Free Income A | FRPAX | MP | 843 | 1,000 | 4.25 | 0 | Y | Y | N | N | Y | -4.2 | 10.9 | 5.4 | 9.0 | 3.0 |
| NJ Tax-Free Income A | FRNJX | MNJ | 949 | 1,000 | 4.25 | 0 | Y | Y | N | N | Y | -3.5 | 11.6 | 4.7 | 8.7 | 2.6 |
| FL Tax-Free Income A | FRFLX | MF | 1,739 | 1,000 | 4.25 | 0 | Y | Y | N | N | Y | -3.4 | 11.0 | 5.3 | 8.8 | 3.4 |
| Utilities A | FKUTX | SU | 1,660 | 1,000 | 4.25 | 0 | Y | Y | N | N | Y | -15.0 | 41.6 | -8.1 | -10.5 | 12.3 |
| Global Communications A | FRGUX | SC | 75 | 1,000 | 5.75 | 0 | Y | Y | N | N | Y | 51.6 | -32.4 | -29.8 | -34.4 | 30.9 |
| CA Tax-Free Income A | FKTFX | MCL | 13,577 | 1,000 | 4.25 | 0 | Y | Y | N | N | Y | -4.4 | 12.6 | 5.4 | 6.8 | 2.2 |
| CA Insured Tax-Free Inc A | FRCIX | MCL | 2,034 | 1,000 | 4.25 | 0 | Y | Y | N | N | Y | -3.6 | 12.5 | 4.6 | 7.9 | 2.6 |
| Convertible Securities A | FISCX | CA | 401 | 1,000 | 5.75 | 0 | Y | Y | N | N | Y | 21.2 | 15.4 | 0.8 | -15.6 | 26.6 |
| Biotechnology Discovery A | FBDIX | SH | 603 | 1,000 | 5.75 | 0 | Y | Y | N | N | Y | 97.9 | 46.6 | -20.5 | -42.5 | 35.5 |
| Real Estate Securities A | FREEX | SRE | 747 | 1,000 | 5.75 | 0 | Y | Y | N | N | Y | -5.6 | 30.8 | 7.6 | 1.7 | 27.9 |
| NY Tax-Free Income A | FNYTX | MNYL | 5,123 | 1,000 | 4.25 | 0 | Y | Y | N | N | Y | -2.3 | 10.7 | 4.7 | 9.1 | 3.1 |
| Global Health Care A | FKGHX | SH | 112 | 1,000 | 5.75 | 0 | Y | Y | N | N | Y | -0.8 | 69.3 | -12.5 | -34.4 | 19.3 |
| Global Smaller Comp A | TEMGX | WS | 781 | 1,000 | 5.75 | 0 | Y | Y | N | N | Y | 10.1 | -8.4 | -1.7 | -8.8 | 42.8 |
| High Yield Tax-Free Inc A | FRHIX | HYM | 5,152 | 1,000 | 4.25 | 0 | Y | Y | N | N | Y | -3.2 | 5.9 | 5.9 | 5.2 | 5.5 |
| Global Bond A | TPINX | WB | 554 | 1,000 | 4.25 | 0 | Y | Y | N | N | Y | -4.8 | 2.8 | 4.2 | 20.0 | 13.6 |
| Insured Tax-Free Income A | FTFIX | MNL | 1,903 | 1,000 | 4.25 | 0 | Y | Y | N | N | Y | -3.5 | 12.1 | 4.6 | 8.7 | 3.5 |

## FRANKLIN TEMPLETON
http://www.franklintempleton.com

| | SYMBOL | ASSET TYPE | MIL | MIN INV | LOAD IN | LOAD OUT | *WITHDRAWAL OPTIONS P | W | C | I | 1999 | 2000 | 2001 | 2002 | (YTD) 2003 |
|---|---|---|---|---|---|---|---|---|---|---|---|---|---|---|---|
| Federal Tax-Free Income A | FKTIX | MNL | 7,329 | 1,000 | 4.25 | 0 | Y | Y | N | Y | -2.8 | 10.1 | 4.6 | 7.2 | 3.6 |
| Capital Accumulator | TECAX | WS | 499 | 1,000 | 3.33 | 0 | Y | Y | N | Y | 29.2 | 0.3 | -0.9 | -17.4 | 26.7 |
| Global Opportunities A | TEGOX | WS | 361 | 1,000 | 5.75 | 0 | Y | Y | N | Y | 27.9 | -3.2 | -0.9 | -21.8 | 24.5 |
| Gold and Precious Metals A | FKRCX | SPM | 561 | 1,000 | 5.75 | 0 | Y | Y | N | Y | 26.1 | -7.4 | 10.0 | 37.4 | 37.1 |
| Instl Foreign Equity | TFEQX | FLV | 4,163 | 5 MIL | 0 | 0 | Y | Y | N | Y | 27.3 | 5.9 | -12.1 | -14.8 | 30.2 |
| Instl Emerging Markets | TEEMX | DE | 1,836 | 5 MIL | 0 | 0 | Y | Y | N | * | 56.6 | -32.0 | -5.0 | 2.0 | 39.4 |
| Floating Rate | XFFLX | BL | 1,167 | 1,000 | 0 | 1 | * | * | N | * | 7.7 | 6.2 | -0.1 | -3.4 | 10.2 |
| Small Cap Value A | FRVLX | SV | 337 | 1,000 | 5.75 | 0 | Y | Y | N | Y | -0.8 | 22.2 | 15.1 | -9.6 | 22.4 |
| International (Ex EM) A | TEGEX | FLV | 56 | 1,000 | 5.75 | 0 | Y | Y | N | Y | 23.2 | -2.3 | -11.3 | -13.0 | -23.6 |
| Balance Sheet Investment A | FRBSX | SV | 3,299 | 1,000 | 0C | C | Y | Y | N | Y | -1.5 | 20.5 | 17.7 | -6.0 | 22.6 |
| Foreign Sm Companies A | FINEX | FSMV | 389 | 1,000 | 5.75 | 0 | Y | Y | N | Y | 25.3 | -3.3 | -6.7 | -3.6 | 37.0 |
| Strategic Income A | FRSTX | MB | 605 | 1,000 | 4.25 | 0 | Y | Y | N | Y | 2.3 | 2.6 | 5.4 | 4.7 | 17.0 |
| Foreign A | TEMFX | FLV | 12,554 | 1,000 | 5.75 | 0 | Y | Y | N | Y | 39.2 | -3.7 | -7.9 | -8.6 | 22.7 |
| Rising Dividends A | FRDPX | MCV | 1,447 | 1,000 | 5.75 | 0 | Y | Y | N | Y | -10.3 | 19.0 | 13.1 | -1.8 | 19.8 |
| Small-Mid Cap Growth A | FRSGX | MCG | 8,466 | 1,000 | 5.75 | 0 | Y | Y | N | Y | 97.1 | -9.8 | -20.5 | -29.6 | 30.7 |
| Flex Cap Growth A | FKCGX | MCG | 1,735 | 1,000 | 5.75 | 0 | Y | Y | N | Y | 95.2 | -7.0 | -23.2 | -24.9 | 33.6 |
| Capital Growth A | FKREX | LG | 1,429 | 1,000 | 5.75 | 0 | Y | Y | N | Y | 52.4 | 0.5 | -23.1 | -25.4 | 23.0 |
| DynaTech A | FKDNX | LG | 683 | 1,000 | 5.75 | 0 | Y | Y | N | Y | 37.2 | -12.2 | -13.1 | -19.9 | 32.0 |
| Developing Markets A | TEDMX | DE | 2,085 | 1,000 | 5.75 | 0 | Y | Y | N | Y | 51.6 | -31.9 | -5.8 | 1.7 | 38.7 |
| MicroCap Value A | FRMCX | SV | 311 | 1,000 | 5.75 | 0 | Y | Y | N | Y | -4.0 | 12.1 | 41.3 | 4.0 | 25.7 |
| Growth A | FKGRX | LB | 1,960 | 1,000 | 5.75 | 0 | Y | Y | N | Y | 12.2 | 7.5 | -9.5 | -24.2 | 19.6 |
| Short-Interm U.S. Govt A | FRGVX | SG | 355 | 1,000 | 2.25 | 0 | Y | Y | N | Y | 1.5 | 8.4 | 6.6 | 7.4 | 1.0 |
| U.S. Long-Short | FUSLX | MA | 135 | 1,000 | 5.75 | 0 | Y | Y | N | Y | X | 55.1 | -1.5 | -6.2 | -2.7 |
| Aggressive Growth A | FGRAX | MCG | 161 | 1,000 | 5.75 | 0 | Y | Y | N | Y | X | -25.8 | -22.6 | -35.7 | 36.9 |
| Franklin Blue Chip A | FKBCX | LB | 238 | 1,000 | 5.75 | 0 | Y | Y | N | Y | 34.6 | -4.4 | -13.1 | -22.5 | 20.8 |
| Global Long-Short A | TLSAX | MA | 139 | 10,000 | 5.75 | 0 | Y | Y | N | Y | X | X | X | -1.2 | 6.4 |
| VA Tax-Free Income A | FRVAX | MSSL | 467 | 1,000 | 4.25 | 0 | Y | Y | N | Y | -4.2 | 10.8 | 4.4 | 7.8 | 3.6 |
| Total Return Adv | FBDAX | ITB | 289 | 250,000 | 0 | 0 | Y | Y | N | Y | -0.7 | 10.8 | 7.1 | 8.5 | 5.8 |
| TN Municipal Bond | FRTIX | MSSL | 114 | 1,000 | 4.25 | 0 | Y | Y | N | Y | -6.5 | 13.2 | 4.4 | 9.3 | 3.6 |
| Moderate Target A | FMTIX | MA | 224 | 1,000 | 5.75 | 0 | Y | Y | N | Y | 26.9 | -3.0 | -2.2 | -6.8 | 16.5 |

## FRANKLIN TEMPLETON
http://www.franklintempleton.com

| | SYMBOL | ASSET TYPE | MIL | MIN INV | LOAD IN | LOAD OUT | * WITHDRAWAL OPTIONS P | W | C | I | 1999 | 2000 | 2001 | 2002 | (YTD) 2003 |
|---|---|---|---|---|---|---|---|---|---|---|---|---|---|---|---|
| Hard Currency A | ICPHX | WB | 153 | 1,000 | 2.25 | 0 | Y | Y | N | Y | -8.4 | -6.2 | -4.0 | 13.5 | 12.3 |
| Growth Target A | FGTIX | MA | 172 | 1,000 | 5.75 | 0 | Y | Y | N | Y | 40.4 | -5.1 | -11.2 | -13.3 | 22.2 |
| Conserv Target A | FTCIX | CA | 122 | 1,000 | 5.75 | 0 | Y | Y | N | Y | 20.0 | 2.1 | 0.1 | -3.3 | 12.8 |
| Franklin Technology A | FTCAX | ST | 63 | 1,000 | 5.75 | 0 | Y | Y | N | Y | X | X | -30.2 | -44.9 | 53.1 |
| Franklin Strategic Mortgage | FSMIX | IG | 416 | 1,000 | 4.25 | 0 | Y | Y | N | Y | 1.5 | 11.9 | 8.4 | 8.9 | 1.5 |
| Small Cap Growth II A | FSGRX | SG | 1,457 | 1,000 | 0 C | 0 C | Y | Y | N | Y | X | X | -3.3 | -27.3 | 41.8 |
| NY Intermediate T/F Income | FKNIX | MNYI | 216 | 1,000 | 3.35 | 0 | Y | Y | N | Y | -1.8 | 10.4 | 4.4 | 9.5 | 3.0 |
| NY Insured Tax-Free Inc A | FRNYX | MNYL | 335 | 1,000 | 4.25 | 0 | Y | Y | N | Y | -3.4 | 10.9 | 4.0 | 9.2 | 2.8 |
| Tax-Free Income A | FXNCX | MSSL | 481 | 1,000 | 4.25 | 0 | Y | Y | N | Y | -4.3 | 11.6 | 4.9 | 9.3 | 2.8 |
| Franklin Natural Resources | FRNRX | SNR | 44 | 1,000 | 5.75 | 0 | Y | Y | N | Y | 34.4 | 34.8 | -16.7 | -0.5 | 8.2 |
| MN Insured Tax-Free Inc A | FMINX | MMI | 576 | 1,000 | 4.25 | 0 | Y | Y | N | Y | -3.8 | 12.0 | 4.7 | 8.0 | 3.2 |
| MD Tax-Free Income A | FMDTX | MSSL | 378 | 1,000 | 4.25 | 0 | Y | Y | N | Y | -4.1 | 11.7 | 5.1 | 8.6 | 3.1 |
| MA Insured Tax-Free Inc A | FMISX | MMI | 470 | 1,000 | 4.25 | 0 | Y | Y | N | Y | -3.8 | 13.3 | 4.2 | 8.6 | 3.3 |
| Large Cap Value A | FLVAX | LV | 104 | 1,000 | 5.75 | 0 | Y | Y | N | Y | X | X | 7.7 | -15.5 | 18.6 |
| LA Tax-Free Income A | FKLAX | MSSL | 197 | 1,000 | 4.25 | 0 | Y | Y | N | Y | -3.9 | 11.8 | 4.9 | 8.3 | 3.2 |
| KY Tax-Free Income | FRKYX | MSSL | 114 | 1,000 | 4.25 | 0 | Y | Y | N | Y | -4.3 | 11.6 | 4.0 | 8.3 | 3.1 |
| GA Tax-Free Income A | FTGAX | MSSL | 201 | 1,000 | 4.25 | 0 | Y | Y | N | Y | -3.9 | 11.5 | 4.7 | 7.4 | 3.6 |
| Floating Rate Daily Access C | FCFRX | BL | 258 | 1,000 | 0 | 1 | Y | Y | N | Y | X | X | X | 1.7 | 5.4 |
| FL Insured Tax-Free Income | FFLTX | MF | 147 | 1,000 | 4.25 | 0 | Y | Y | N | Y | -4.6 | 13.2 | 4.4 | 8.7 | 2.7 |
| CT Tax-Free Income A | FXCTX | MSSL | 305 | 1,000 | 4.25 | 0 | Y | Y | N | Y | -4.9 | 9.9 | 5.6 | 8.8 | 1.6 |
| CO Tax-Free Income A | FRCOX | MSSL | 367 | 1,000 | 4.25 | 0 | Y | Y | N | Y | -4.5 | 11.6 | 5.0 | 8.1 | 3.0 |
| CA Interm-Term Tax-Fr Income | FKCIX | MCI | 2 | 1,000 | 2.25 | 0 | Y | Y | N | Y | -1.5 | 9.9 | 4.5 | 7.8 | 2.2 |
| CA High Yield Municipal A | FCAMX | MCL | 628 | 1,000 | 4.25 | 0 | Y | Y | N | Y | -6.8 | 11.2 | 5.4 | 6.8 | 3.3 |
| AL Tax-Free Income A | FRALX | MSSL | 260 | 1,000 | 4.25 | 0 | Y | Y | N | Y | -3.7 | 9.8 | 4.7 | 8.7 | 3.9 |
| Adjustable U.S. Govt Secs | FISAX | UB | 7 | 1,000 | 2.25 | 0 | Y | Y | N | Y | 4.4 | 6.7 | 6.4 | 3.1 | 0.8 |

**FRANKLIN TEMPLETON FUND REPRESENTATIVE: RANCHO CORDOVA, CALIFORNIA   800.632.2350**

Check-writing priveledges are associated with the Franklin Money Fund (FMFXX), FRANKLIN FEDERAL MONEY FUND (FMNXX), Tax Exempt Money

Fund (FTMXX), California Tax Exempt Money Fund (FCLXX), and New York Tax Exempt Money Fund (FRNXX)

The Franklin Flote Rate Fund (XFFLX) has a Quarterly withdrawal feature only speak with your representative to set up withdrawal options

# JANUS
http://www.janus.com

| Fund | SYMBOL | ASSET TYPE | MIL | MIN INV | LOAD IN | LOAD OUT | P | W | C | I | 1999 | 2000 | 2001 | 2002 | 2003 (YTD) |
|---|---|---|---|---|---|---|---|---|---|---|---|---|---|---|---|
| Janus High-Yield | JAHYX | HYB | 768 | 2,500 | O | O | Y | Y | N | Y | 5.5 | 2.5 | 4.6 | 2.6 | 12.8 |
| Janus Balanced | JABAX | CA | 3,939 | 2,500 | O | O | Y | Y | N | Y | 23.5 | -2.2 | -5.0 | -6.6 | 9.7 |
| Janus Aspen Balanced Instl | JABLX | CA | 3,642 | 5 MIL | O | O | Y | Y | N | Y | 26.8 | -2.3 | -4.7 | -6.4 | 9.9 |
| Janus Short-Term Bond | JASBX | STB | 366 | 2,500 | O | O | Y | Y | N | Y | 2.9 | 7.7 | 6.8 | 3.6 | 3.2 |
| Janus Flexible Income | JAFIX | MB | 1,533 | 2,500 | O | O | Y | Y | N | Y | 0.5 | 4.9 | 7.2 | 9.9 | 5.0 |
| Janus Overseas | JAOSX | FLG | 2,845 | 2,500 | O | O | Y | Y | N | Y | 86.1 | -18.6 | -23.1 | -23.9 | 27.5 |
| Janus Orion | JORNX | MCG | 514 | 2,500 | O | O | Y | Y | N | Y | X | X | -14.7 | -29.8 | 34.3 |
| Janus Global Technology | JAGTX | STB | 1,656 | 2,500 | O | O | Y | Y | N | Y | 209.6 | -33.7 | -40.0 | -40.9 | 45.6 |
| Janus Worldwide | JAWWX | WS | 11,396 | 2,500 | O | O | Y | Y | N | Y | 64.4 | -16.9 | -22.9 | -26.0 | 16.2 |
| Small Cap Value Instl | JSIVX | SV | 3,153 | 250,000 | O | O | Y | Y | N | Y | 14.7 | 27.2 | 20.4 | -15.3 | 26.3 |
| Mid Cap Value Investor | JMCVX | MCV | 1,781 | 2,500 | O | C | Y | Y | N | Y | 21.6 | 27.3 | 20.5 | -13.1 | 28.8 |
| Janus Global Value | JGVAX | WS | 143 | 2,500 | O | O | Y | Y | N | Y | X | X | X | -15.9 | 30.1 |
| Janus Special Equity | JSVAX | MCB | 2,501 | 2,500 | O | O | Y | Y | N | Y | X | X | -117.0 | -23.7 | 41.2 |
| Janus Mercury | JAMRX | LG | 5,288 | 2,500 | O | O | Y | Y | N | Y | 96.2 | -22.8 | -29.8 | -29.0 | 22.9 |
| Janus Growth & Income | JAGIX | LG | 6,011 | 2,500 | O | O | Y | Y | N | Y | 51.2 | -11.4 | -14.4 | -21.5 | 16.7 |
| Janus Enterprise | JAENX | MCG | 1,919 | 2,500 | O | O | Y | Y | N | Y | 121.9 | -30.5 | -39.9 | -28.3 | 30.8 |
| Janus Core Equity | JAEIX | LB | 710 | 2,500 | O | O | Y | Y | N | Y | 38.5 | -7.2 | -12.1 | -18.0 | 16.5 |
| Aspen Mid Cap Growth Instl | JAAGX | MCG | 1,830 | 5 MIL | O | O | Y | Y | N | Y | 125.4 | -31.8 | -39.5 | -27.9 | 30.1 |
| Adviser Mid Cap Growth I | JGRTX | MCG | 282 | 5 MIL | O | O | Y | Y | N | Y | 124.3 | -33.0 | -39.0 | -27.7 | 29.3 |
| Janus Olympus | JAOLX | LG | 2,771 | 2,500 | O | O | Y | Y | N | Y | 100.1 | -21.6 | -32.1 | -28.2 | 26.1 |
| Janus Global Life Sciences | JAGLX | SH | 1,266 | 2,500 | O | O | Y | Y | N | Y | 61.0 | 33.3 | -18.1 | -30.1 | 19.0 |
| Janus Aspen Growth Instl | JAGRX | LG | 1,859 | 5 MIL | O | O | Y | Y | N | Y | 44.0 | -14.6 | -24.7 | -26.5 | 26.4 |
| Adviser Capital Apprec I | JARTX | LG | 1,129 | 5 MIL | O | C | Y | Y | N | Y | 66.2 | -16.3 | -21.8 | -15.9 | 12.6 |
| Janus Twenty | JAVLX | LG | 9,837 | 2,500 | O | O | Y | Y | N | Y | 64.9 | -32.4 | -29.2 | -24.0 | 17.4 |
| Janus Venture | JAVTX | SG | 1,393 | 2,500 | O | O | Y | Y | N | Y | 140.7 | -45.8 | -11.9 | -27.2 | 49.3 |
| Aspen International Grth Instl | JAIGX | FLG | 1,080 | 500,000 | O | O | Y | Y | N | Y | 82.3 | -15.9 | -23.2 | -25.6 | 26.4 |
| Adviser Growth & Income I | JADGX | LG | 291 | 5 MIL | O | C | Y | Y | N | Y | 73.2 | -15.4 | -12.8 | -19.5 | 15.9 |
| Risk Managed Stock | JRMSX | LB | 89 | 2,500 | O | O | Y | Y | N | Y | X | X | X | X | X |
| Janus Federal Tax-Exempt | JATEX | MNL | 184 | 2,500 | O | O | Y | Y | N | Y | -4.4 | 8.9 | 3.1 | 9.4 | 2.2 |

## JANUS

http://www.janus.com

| | SYMBOL | ASSET TYPE | MIL | MIN INV | LOAD IN | LOAD OUT | *WITHDRAWAL OPTIONS P | W | C | I | ANNUAL RETURN 1999 | 2000 | 2001 | 2002 | (YTD) 2003 |
|---|---|---|---|---|---|---|---|---|---|---|---|---|---|---|---|
| Aspen Worldwide Growth Instl | JAWGX | WS | 3,970 | 5 MIL | 0 | 0 | Y | Y | N | Y | 64.2 | -15.7 | -22.4 | -25.5 | 16.1 |
| Aspen Mid Cap Value Svc | JAMVX | MCV | 5 | 5 MIL | 0 | 0 | Y | Y | N | Y | X | X | X | X | 25.5 |
| Aspen Growth & Income Instl | JGIIX | LG | 90 | 5 MIL | 0 | 0 | Y | Y | N | Y | 74.0 | -14.1 | -13.4 | -21.5 | 15.9 |
| Aspen Flexible Income Instl | JAFLX | MB | 621 | 5 MIL | 0 | 0 | Y | Y | N | Y | 1.6 | 7.6 | 7.7 | 10.5 | 5.1 |
| Aspen Core Equity Instl | JEIIX | LB | 11 | 5 MIL | 0 | 0 | Y | Y | N | Y | 41.6 | -8.1 | -11.8 | -18.3 | 16.4 |
| Aspen Capital Apprec Instl | JACAX | LG | 933 | 5 MIL | 0 | 0 | Y | Y | N | Y | 67.0 | -18.2 | -21.7 | -15.7 | 13.9 |
| Adviser Small Cap Value I | JISCX | SV | 14 | 2,500 | 0 | 0 | Y | Y | N | Y | X | X | X | X | 34.6 |
| Adviser Risk Mgd Lg Cp Gr I | JCGIX | LG | 44 | 100,000 | 0 | 0 | Y | Y | N | Y | X | X | X | X | 20.3 |
| Adviser Risk Mgd Lg Cp Cr I | JLCIX | LB | 11 | 100,000 | 0 | 0 | Y | Y | N | Y | X | X | X | X | 18.1 |
| Adviser Mid Cap Value I | JMVIX | MCV | 12 | 100,000 | 0 | 0 | Y | Y | N | Y | X | X | X | X | 25.2 |
| Adviser International Value I | JADVX | WS | 3 | 5 MIL | 0 | 0 | Y | Y | N | Y | X | X | X | -17.5 | 22.5 |
| Adviser International Growth I | JIGRX | FLG | 493 | 5 MIL | 0 | 0 | Y | Y | N | Y | 81.3 | -13.0 | -22.8 | -25.6 | 26.0 |
| Adviser Growth I | JGORX | LG | 434 | 5 MIL | 0 | 0 | Y | Y | N | Y | 44.1 | -13.1 | -23.2 | -26.5 | 25.2 |
| Adviser Flexible Income I | JADFX | MB | 113 | 5 MIL | 0 | 0 | Y | Y | N | Y | 0.9 | 6.1 | 7.2 | 9.7 | 4.6 |
| Adviser Core Equity I | JADEX | LB | 49 | 5 MIL | 0 | 0 | Y | Y | N | Y | 40.9 | -8.3 | -13.0 | -17.9 | 16.8 |
| Janus Adviser Balanced I | JABRX | CA | 1,029 | 5 MIL | 0 | 0 | Y | Y | N | Y | 26.1 | -2.1 | -4.9 | -6.6 | 9.8 |
| Adviser International Growth I | JIGRX | FLG | 493 | 5 MIL | 0 | 0 | Y | Y | N | Y | 81.3 | -13.0 | -22.8 | -25.6 | 26.0 |
| Janus Adviser Growth I | JGORX | LG | 434 | 5 MIL | 0 | 0 | Y | Y | N | Y | 44.1 | -13.1 | -23.2 | -26.5 | 25.2 |
| Adviser Flexible Income I | JADFX | MB | 113 | 5 MIL | 0 | 0 | Y | Y | N | Y | 0.9 | 6.1 | 7.2 | 9.7 | 4.6 |
| Janus Adviser Core Equity I | JADEX | LB | 49 | 5 MIL | 0 | 0 | Y | Y | N | Y | 40.9 | -8.3 | -13.0 | -17.9 | 16.8 |
| Janus Adviser Balanced I | JABRX | CA | 1,029 | 5 MIL | 0 | 0 | Y | Y | N | Y | 26.1 | -2.1 | -4.9 | -6.6 | 9.8 |

**JAUNS FUND REPRESENTATIVE: DENVER, COLORADO 800.525.0020**

Check-writing features are allowed with the Janus Money Market Fund (JAMXX), Government Money Market Fund (JAGXX), and

Tax-Exempt Money Market Fund (JATXX)

# PIMCO FUNDS

http://www.pimco.com

| | SYMBOL | ASSET TYPE | MIL | MIN INV | LOAD IN | LOAD OUT | WITHDRAWAL OPTIONS P | W | C | I | ANNUAL RETURN 1999 | 2000 | 2001 | 2002 | (YTD) 2003 |
|---|---|---|---|---|---|---|---|---|---|---|---|---|---|---|---|
| PIMCO Real Return Instl | PRRIX | IG | 8,303 | 5 MIL | 0 | 0 | Y | Y | N | Y | 5.7 | 13.5 | 8.7 | 17.1 | 7.2 |
| Real Return Asset Instl | PRAIX | LG | 254 | 5 MIL | 0 | 0 | Y | Y | N | Y | X | X | X | 23.4 | 9.7 |
| Long-Term U.S. Government Instl | PGOVX | LG | 772 | 5 MIL | 0 | 0 | Y | Y | N | Y | -8.0 | 20.4 | 5.5 | 18.9 | 2.0 |
| CCM Capital Appreciation Instl | PAPIX | LB | 832 | 250,000 | 0 | 0 | Y | Y | N | Y | 22.3 | 14.0 | -18.9 | -23.3 | 23.4 |
| PEA Value Instl | PDLIX | LV | 1,257 | 5 MIL | 0 | 1 | Y | Y | N | Y | 4.3 | 31.0 | 15.7 | -24.8 | 31.7 |
| PIMCO PEA Renaissance C | PQNCX | MCV | 4,388 | 2,500 | 0 | 0 | Y | Y | N | Y | 9.0 | 36.7 | 18.5 | -26.7 | 41.1 |
| NFJ Small Cap Value Instl | PSVIX | SV | 2,048 | 5 MIL | 0 | 0 | Y | Y | N | Y | -6.4 | 21.7 | 19.1 | 3.2 | 21.1 |
| CommodityRealRet Strat Instl | PCRIX | SNR | 736 | 5 MIL | 0 | 0 | Y | Y | N | Y | X | X | X | X | 20.8 |
| RCM Global Technology Instl | DRGTX | ST | 481 | 5 MIL | 0 | 0 | Y | Y | N | Y | 183.0 | -14.3 | -39.3 | -40.4 | 71.8 |
| RCM Global Health Care D | DGHCX | SH | 188 | 5,000 | 0 | 0 | Y | Y | N | Y | 28.7 | 73.4 | -13.8 | -26.6 | 22.3 |
| RCM Biotechnology D | DRBNX | SH | 335 | 2,500 | 0 | 1 | Y | Y | N | Y | 111.4 | 81.9 | -24.7 | -40.0 | 34.5 |
| PIMCO PEA Innovation C | PIVCX | ST | 1,185 | 2,500 | 0 | 0 | Y | Y | N | Y | 138.5 | -29.4 | -45.5 | -52.7 | 55.8 |
| PIMCO Municipal Bond Instl | PFMIX | MNI | 370 | 5 MIL | 0 | 0 | Y | Y | N | Y | -3.7 | 10.3 | 7.7 | 8.3 | 3.0 |
| Emerging Markets Bond Instl | PEBIX | EMB | 1053 | 5 MIL | 0 | 0 | Y | Y | N | Y | 26.6 | 14.6 | 28.2 | 12.8 | 26.4 |
| CCM Emerging Companies Instl | PMCIX | SG | 419 | 250,000 | 0 | 1 | Y | Y | N | Y | 5.4 | 17.8 | 10.0 | -15.8 | 48.0 |
| PEA Opportunity C | POPCX | SG | 339 | 2,500 | 0 | 0 | Y | Y | N | Y | 64.0 | -14.4 | -17.9 | -29.9 | 52.0 |
| PIMCO Global Bond Instl | PIGLX | WB | 576 | 5 MIL | 0 | 0 | Y | Y | N | Y | -4.3 | 0.4 | 2.5 | 21.3 | 10.4 |
| PIMCO Foreign Bond Instl | PFORX | WB | 1,548 | 5 MIL | 0 | 0 | Y | Y | N | Y | 1.6 | 9.9 | 9.0 | 7.7 | 2.5 |
| PIMCO CCM Mid Cap Instl | PMGIX | MCG | 696 | 250,000 | 0 | 0 | Y | Y | N | Y | 13.0 | 28.4 | -19.4 | -20.1 | 27.6 |
| PIMCO High Yield Instl | PHIYX | HYB | 7,636 | 5 MIL | 0 | 0 | Y | Y | N | Y | 2.8 | -0.4 | 5.0 | -0.9 | 19.3 |
| PIMCO PEA Target C | PTACX | MCG | 963 | 2,500 | 0 | 1 | Y | Y | N | Y | 65.1 | 9.4 | -29.2 | -33.2 | 38.0 |
| PIMCO Short-Term Instl | PTSHX | UB | 4,634 | 5 MIL | 0 | 0 | Y | Y | N | Y | 5.2 | 7.3 | 5.7 | 2.9 | 2.3 |
| PIMCO Low Duration Instl | PTLDX | STB | 14,279 | 5 MIL | 0 | 0 | Y | Y | N | Y | 3.0 | 7.7 | 8.0 | 7.7 | 2.3 |
| PIMCO Total Return Instl | PTTRX | ITB | 73,066 | 5 MIL | 0 | 0 | Y | Y | N | Y | -0.3 | 12.1 | 9.5 | 10.2 | 4.1 |
| RCM Tax-Managed Growth D | DRTNX | LG | 36 | 5,000 | 0 | 0 | Y | Y | N | Y | 52.0 | -8.1 | -12.6 | -18.8 | 14.2 |
| RCM Global Small-Cap Instl | DGSCX | WS | 30 | 5 MIL | 0 | 0 | Y | Y | N | Y | 104.6 | -13.9 | -25.1 | -17.4 | 50.9 |
| RCM Intl Growth Equity Instl | DRIEX | FLG | 81 | 250,000 | 0 | 0 | Y | Y | N | Y | 60.7 | -26.8 | -32.0 | -22.7 | 22.9 |
| PIMCO RCM Europe D | DRENX | ES | 25 | 5,000 | 0 | 0 | Y | Y | N | Y | 43.5 | -11.3 | -31.5 | -23.5 | 21.5 |
| PIMCO PEA Growth C | PGWCX | LG | 857 | 2,500 | 0 | 1 | Y | Y | N | Y | 39.8 | -14.9 | -29.6 | -29.7 | 19.5 |

* WITHDRAWAL OPTIONS

# PIMCO FUNDS
http://www.pimco.com

| | SYMBOL | ASSET TYPE | MIL | MIN INV | LOAD IN | LOAD OUT | WITHDRAWAL OPTIONS P | W | C | I | ANNUAL RETURN 1999 | 2000 | 2001 | 2002 | 2003 (YTD) |
|---|---|---|---|---|---|---|---|---|---|---|---|---|---|---|---|
| PIMCO StocksPlus Instl | PSTKX | LB | 1,304 | 5 MIL | 0 | 0 | Y | Y | Y | Y | 20.1 | -8.2 | -11.5 | -19.9 | 21.8 |
| Total Return Mortgage Instl | PTRIX | IG | 264 | 5 MIL | 0 | 0 | Y | Y | N | Y | 2.4 | 12.3 | 10.0 | 9.5 | 2.9 |
| PPA Tax-Eff Struc Emg Mkts Is | PEFIX | DE | 149 | 5 MIL | 0 | 0 | Y | Y | N | Y | 72.6 | -29.1 | -0.1 | 1.4 | 46.4 |
| PIMCO Total Return III Instl | PTSAX | ITB | 1,168 | 5 MIL | 0 | 0 | Y | Y | N | Y | -1.0 | 10.1 | 10.0 | 10.0 | 5.1 |
| PIMCO Total Return II Instl | PMBIX | ITB | 2,365 | 5 MIL | 0 | 0 | Y | Y | N | Y | -1.1 | 11.8 | 9.7 | 9.9 | 3.5 |
| Strategic Balanced Instl | PSIBX | MA | 31 | 5 MIL | 0 | 0 | Y | Y | N | Y | 11.6 | -1.7 | -2.8 | -8.4 | 14.7 |
| Short-Duration Muni Income Inst | PSDIX | MNS | 407 | 5 MIL | 0 | 0 | Y | Y | N | Y | X | 5.8 | 5.0 | 3.0 | 1.9 |
| PIMCO Real Return II Instl | PIRRX | IG | 48 | 5 MIL | 0 | 0 | Y | Y | N | Y | X | X | X | X | 6.9 |
| RCM Small-Cap Instl | DRSCX | SG | 9 | 10,000 | 0 | 0 | Y | Y | N | Y | 12.4 | -17.9 | -20.1 | -29.0 | 56.7 |
| RCM Mid-Cap Instl | DRMCX | MCG | 241 | 5 MIL | 0 | 0 | Y | Y | N | Y | 60.2 | 1.2 | -24.6 | -26.3 | 22.2 |
| RCM Large-Cap Growth Instl | DRLCX | LG | 505 | 5 MIL | 0 | 0 | Y | Y | N | Y | 44.8 | -8.4 | -22.0 | -22.9 | 13.8 |
| PIMCO PEA Target C | PTACX | MCG | 963 | 2,500 | 0 | 1 | Y | Y | N | Y | 65.1 | 9.4 | -29.2 | -33.2 | 38.0 |
| PIMCO Short-Term Instl | PTSHX | UB | 4,634 | 5 MIL | 0 | 0 | Y | Y | N | Y | 5.2 | 7.3 | 5.7 | 2.9 | 2.3 |
| PIMCO Low Duration Instl | PTLDX | STB | 14,279 | 5 MIL | 0 | 0 | Y | Y | N | Y | 3.0 | 7.7 | 8.0 | 7.7 | 2.3 |
| PIMCO Total Return Instl | PTTRX | ITB | 73,066 | 5 MIL | 0 | 0 | Y | Y | N | Y | -0.3 | 12.1 | 9.5 | 10.2 | 4.1 |
| RCM Tax-Managed Growth D | DRTNX | LG | 36 | 5,000 | 0 | 0 | Y | Y | N | Y | 52.0 | -8.1 | -21.6 | -18.8 | 14.2 |
| RCM Global Small-Cap Instl | DGSCX | WS | 30 | 5 MIL | 0 | 0 | Y | Y | N | Y | 104.6 | -13.9 | -25.1 | -17.4 | 50.9 |
| RCM Intl Growth Equity Instl | DRIEX | FLG | 81 | 250,000 | 0 | 0 | Y | Y | N | Y | 60.7 | -26.8 | -32.0 | -22.7 | 22.9 |
| PIMCO RCM Europe D | DRENX | ES | 25 | 5,000 | 0 | 0 | Y | Y | N | Y | 43.5 | -11.3 | -31.5 | -23.5 | 21.5 |
| PIMCO PEA Growth C | PGWX | LG | 857 | 2,500 | 0 | 1 | Y | Y | N | Y | 39.8 | -14.9 | -29.6 | -29.7 | 19.5 |
| PIMCO StocksPlus Instl | PSTKX | LB | 1,304 | 5 MIL | 0 | 0 | Y | Y | Y | Y | 20.1 | -8.2 | -11.5 | -19.9 | 21.8 |
| Total Return Mortgage Instl | PTRIX | IG | 264 | 5 MIL | 0 | 0 | Y | Y | N | Y | 2.4 | 12.3 | 10.0 | 9.5 | 2.9 |
| PPA Tax-Eff Struc Emg Mkts Is | PEFIX | DE | 149 | 5 MIL | 0 | 0 | Y | Y | N | Y | 72.6 | -29.1 | -0.1 | 1.4 | 46.4 |
| PIMCO Total Return III Instl | PTSAX | ITB | 1,168 | 5 MIL | 0 | 0 | Y | Y | N | Y | -1.0 | 10.1 | 10.0 | 10.0 | 5.1 |
| PIMCO Total Return II Instl | PMBIX | ITB | 2,365 | 5 MIL | 0 | 0 | Y | Y | N | Y | -1.1 | 11.8 | 9.7 | 9.9 | 3.5 |
| Strategic Balanced Instl | PSBIX | MA | 31 | 5 MIL | 0 | 0 | Y | Y | N | Y | 11.6 | -1.7 | -2.8 | -8.4 | 14.7 |
| Short-Duration Muni Income Inst | PSDIX | MNS | 407 | 5 MIL | 0 | 0 | Y | Y | N | Y | X | 5.8 | 5.0 | 3.0 | 1.9 |
| PIMCO Real Return II Instl | PIRRX | IG | 48 | 5 MIL | 0 | 0 | Y | Y | N | Y | X | X | X | X | 6.9 |
| PIMCO RCM Small-Cap Instl | DRSCX | SG | 9 | 10,000 | 0 | 0 | Y | Y | N | Y | 12.4 | -17.9 | -20.1 | -29.0 | 56.7 |
| PIMCO RCM Mid-Cap Instl | DRMCX | MCG | 241 | 5 MIL | 0 | 0 | Y | Y | N | Y | 60.2 | 1.2 | -24.6 | -26.3 | 22.2 |

* WITHDRAWAL OPTIONS

## PIMCO FUNDS

http://wwww.pimco.com

| | SYMBOL | ASSET TYPE | MIL | MIN INV | LOAD IN | LOAD OUT | * WITHDRAWAL OPTIONS P | W | C | I | ANNUAL RETURN 1999 | 2000 | 2001 | 2002 | (YTD) 2003 |
|---|---|---|---|---|---|---|---|---|---|---|---|---|---|---|---|
| RCM Large-Cap Growth Instl | DRLCX | LG | 505 | 5 MIL | 0 | 0 | Y | Y | N | Y | 44.8 | -8.4 | -22.0 | -22.9 | 13.8 |

**PIMCO FUND REPRESENTATIVE: STAMFORD, CONNECTICUT 800.426.0107**

Pimco does have money market accounts, but none have check-writing ability at this time

## PUTNAM FUNDS
http://www.putnam.com

| | SYMBOL | ASSET TYPE | MIL | MIN INV | LOAD IN | LOAD OUT | P | W | C | I | 1999 | 2000 | 2001 | 2002 | (YTD) 2003 |
|---|---|---|---|---|---|---|---|---|---|---|---|---|---|---|---|
| Convertible Income-Growth A | PCONX | C | 838 | 500 | 5.75 | 0 | Y | Y | N | Y | 17.5 | -8.4 | -8.1 | -5.5 | 23.4 |
| Putnam Classic Equity A | PXGIX | LV | 1,282 | 500 | 5.75 | 0 | Y | N | N | Y | -0.9 | 6.1 | -6.8 | -19.9 | 17.0 |
| Fund for Growth & Income A | PGRWX | LV | 20,576 | 500 | 5.75 | 0 | Y | N | N | Y | -1.3 | 7.9 | -6.4 | -19.1 | 18.4 |
| Putnam Equity Income A | PEYAX | LV | 3,231 | 500 | 5.75 | 0 | Y | N | N | Y | 1.1 | 13.2 | -1.6 | -12.9 | 17.5 |
| U.S. Government Income A | PGSIX | IG | 2,625 | 500 | 4.75 | 0 | Y | N | N | Y | 0.1 | 10.4 | 6.9 | 7.7 | 0.9 |
| American Government Income A | PAGVX | IG | 1,384 | 500 | 4.75 | 0 | Y | N | N | Y | -2.6 | 12.0 | 6.0 | 8.4 | 0.6 |
| Putnam New Value A | PANVX | LV | 1,318 | 500 | 5.75 | 0 | Y | N | N | Y | -0.1 | 22.0 | 3.3 | -15.7 | 22.1 |
| International New Opport A | PINOX | FLG | 927 | 500 | 5.75 | 0 | Y | N | N | Y | 105.0 | -37.7 | -28.6 | -14.1 | 23.8 |
| International Growth & Inc A | PNGAX | FLV | 675 | 500 | 5.75 | 0 | Y | N | N | Y | 25.7 | 1.0 | -21.6 | -14.3 | 24.2 |
| International Capital Opp A | PNVAX | FSMG | 1,397 | 500 | 5.75 | 0 | Y | N | N | Y | 93.3 | -12.1 | -27.3 | -14.0 | 31.3 |
| Putnam Global Equity A | PEQUX | WS | 3,192 | 500 | 5.75 | 0 | Y | N | N | Y | 59.7 | -10.3 | -22.0 | -18.8 | 21.8 |
| Putnam Europe Equity A | PEUGX | ES | 725 | 500 | 5.75 | 0 | Y | N | N | Y | 23.2 | -5.5 | -22.9 | -19.6 | 17.9 |
| Capital Opportunities A | PCOAX | SB | 1,197 | 500 | 5.75 | 0 | Y | N | N | Y | 27.0 | 21.9 | -2.1 | -24.8 | 27.3 |
| Asset Allocation: Growth A | PAEAX | MA | 1,459 | 500 | 5.75 | 0 | Y | N | N | Y | 24.7 | -9.4 | -10.0 | -14.8 | 22.5 |
| Asset Allocation: Balanced A | PABAX | MA | 2,185 | 500 | 5.75 | 0 | Y | N | N | Y | 18.3 | -2.6 | -6.4 | -12.3 | 16.1 |
| International Equity A | POVSX | FLB | 12,451 | 500 | 5.75 | 0 | Y | N | N | Y | 60.8 | -9.0 | -19.8 | -17.0 | 17.6 |
| MA Tax Exempt Income A | PXMAX | MM | 433 | 500 | 4.75 | 0 | Y | N | N | Y | -3.6 | 11.4 | 4.4 | 8.6 | 3.2 |
| NY Tax Exempt Income A | PTEIX | MNYL | 1,396 | 500 | 4.75 | 0 | Y | N | N | Y | -3.5 | 12.4 | 3.6 | 9.3 | 2.5 |
| CA Tax Exempt Income A | PCTEX | MCL | 2,866 | 500 | 4.75 | 0 | Y | N | N | Y | -4.4 | 12.6 | 4.0 | 7.7 | 2.1 |
| Utilities Growth & Income A | PUGIX | SU | 601 | 500 | 5.75 | 0 | Y | N | N | Y | -1.0 | 17.3 | -22.5 | -23.9 | 16.0 |
| Global Natural Resources A | EBERX | SNR | 282 | 500 | 5.75 | 0 | Y | N | N | Y | 24.3 | 20.1 | -10.4 | -5.3 | 10.7 |
| Health Sciences A | PHSTX | SH | 3,685 | 500 | 5.75 | 0 | Y | N | N | Y | -4.4 | 40.0 | -19.8 | -20.4 | 10.8 |
| Tax-Free High Yield B | PTHYX | HYM | 1,222 | 500 | 0 | 5 | Y | N | N | Y | -3.5 | 4.5 | 3.4 | 2.4 | 3.4 |
| Municipal Income A | PTFHX | MNL | 992 | 500 | 4.75 | 0 | Y | N | N | Y | -4.0 | 9.1 | 4.0 | 5.4 | 2.7 |
| Tax Exempt Income A | PTAEX | MNL | 1,688 | 500 | 4.75 | 0 | Y | N | N | Y | -3.7 | 10.4 | 4.4 | 7.1 | 3.7 |
| Global Income A | PGGIX | WB | 203 | 500 | 4.75 | 0 | Y | N | N | Y | -3.3 | 8.3 | 0.3 | 16.2 | 9.7 |
| Small Cap Value A | PSLAX | SV | 903 | 500 | 5.75 | CO C | Y | Y | N | Y | X | 24.4 | 19.0 | -18.7 | 36.9 |
| Putnam Vista A | PVISX | MCG | 4,009 | 500 | 5.75 | 0 | Y | N | N | Y | 53.2 | -4.0 | -33.6 | -30.7 | 31.9 |
| Discovery Growth A | PVIIX | MCG | 1,719 | 500 | 5.75 | 0 | Y | N | N | Y | 79.9 | -32.2 | -30.6 | -29.2 | 31.5 |

\* WITHDRAWAL OPTIONS; ANNUAL RETURN

# PUTNAM FUNDS
http://www.putnam.com

| | SYMBOL | ASSET TYPE | MIL | MIN INV | LOAD IN | LOAD OUT | *WITHDRAWAL OPTIONS P | W | C | I | ANNUAL RETURN 1999 | 2000 | 2001 | 2002 | (YTD) 2003 |
|---|---|---|---|---|---|---|---|---|---|---|---|---|---|---|---|
| OTC Emerging Growth A | POEGX | MCG | 2,225 | 500 | 5.75 | 0 | Y | Y | N | Y | 126.9 | -51.3 | -46.1 | -32.8 | 34.9 |
| Diversified Income A | PDINX | MB | 5,692 | 500 | 4.75 | 0 | Y | Y | N | Y | 2.9 | -0.2 | 3.7 | 7.0 | 15.1 |
| Putnam High Yield A | PHIGX | HYB | 3,575 | 500 | 4.75 | 0 | Y | Y | N | Y | 6.5 | -9.1 | 3.4 | -0.1 | 21.7 |
| Putnam Income A | PINCX | ITB | 3,454 | 500 | 4.75 | 0 | Y | Y | N | Y | -2.0 | 7.7 | 7.8 | 8.4 | 3.2 |
| New Opportunities A | PNOPX | LG | 9,952 | 500 | 5.75 | 0 | Y | Y | N | Y | 69.7 | -26.2 | -30.1 | -30.6 | 29.7 |
| Putnam Voyager A | PVOYX | LG | 18,751 | 500 | 5.75 | 0 | Y | Y | N | Y | 56.1 | -16.8 | -22.5 | -26.5 | 21.4 |
| Growth Opportunities A | POGAX | LG | 1,969 | 500 | 5.75 | 0 | Y | Y | N | Y | 51.4 | -26.6 | -32.2 | -30.1 | 20.1 |
| Tax Smart Equity A | PATSX | LB | 347 | 500 | 5.75 | 0 | Y | Y | N | Y | X | 4.3 | -19.9 | -19.1 | 21.8 |
| Putnam Research A | PNRAX | LB | 1,844 | 500 | 5.75 | 0 | Y | Y | N | Y | 27.6 | -2.1 | -18.9 | -22.2 | 18.6 |
| Putnam Investors A | PINVX | LB | 5,503 | 500 | 5.75 | 0 | Y | Y | N | Y | 30.1 | -18.5 | -24.8 | -23.8 | 20.9 |
| Capital Appreciation A | PCAPX | LB | 947 | 500 | 5.75 | 0 | Y | Y | N | Y | 17.9 | -6.1 | -15.5 | -23.8 | 22.1 |
| Mid Cap Value A | PMVAX | MCV | 723 | 50 | 5.75 | 0 | Y | Y | N | Y | X | 28.1 | 16.3 | -16.1 | 23.7 |
| Tax-Free Insured B | PTFIX | MNL | 523 | 500 | 0 | 5 | Y | Y | N | Y | -4.5 | 12.3 | 3.2 | 9.0 | 2.0 |
| Small Cap Growth A | PNSAX | SG | 193 | 500 | 5.75 | 0 | Y | Y | N | Y | 155.7 | -16.5 | -0.8 | -32.2 | 44.5 |
| PA Tax Exempt Income A | PTEPX | MP | 248 | 500 | 4.75 | 0 | Y | Y | N | Y | -4.3 | 9.8 | 5.6 | 8.5 | 2.8 |
| OH Tax Exempt Income A | PXOHX | MO | 219 | 500 | 4.75 | 0 | Y | Y | N | Y | -3.4 | 10.3 | 4.8 | 8.4 | 3.4 |
| NY Tax Exempt Opportunities A | PTNHX | MNYL | 197 | 500 | 4.75 | 0 | Y | Y | N | Y | -4.1 | 11.0 | 5.1 | 8.3 | 3.3 |
| NJ Tax Exempt Income A | PTNJX | MNJ | 299 | 500 | 4.75 | 0 | Y | Y | N | Y | -3.5 | 10.3 | 4.0 | 8.1 | 3.0 |
| MN Tax Exempt Income A | PXMNX | MMI | 156 | 500 | 4.75 | 0 | Y | Y | N | Y | -4.1 | 10.3 | 4.6 | 8.0 | 3.6 |
| MI Tax Exempt Income A | PXMIX | MSSI | 181 | 500 | 4.75 | 0 | Y | Y | N | Y | -4.5 | 10.1 | 5.1 | 7.7 | 3.0 |
| Intermediate U.S. Govt Inc A | PBLGX | SG | 1,051 | 500 | 3.25 | 0 | Y | Y | N | Y | 0.2 | 9.2 | 7.3 | 7.8 | 0.4 |
| High Yield Advantage A | PHVIX | HYB | 1,575 | 500 | 4.75 | 0 | Y | Y | N | Y | 6.8 | -9.0 | 2.5 | -0.6 | 22.7 |
| FL Tax Exempt Income A | PTFLX | MF | 255 | 500 | 4.75 | 0 | Y | Y | N | Y | -3.6 | 11.4 | 4.4 | 8.8 | 1.8 |
| AZ Tax Exempt Income A | PTAZX | MSSL | 134 | 500 | 4.75 | 0 | Y | Y | N | Y | -3.2 | 10.2 | 4.4 | 8.1 | 3.2 |
| Asset Allocation: Conserv A | PACAX | MB | 1,042 | 500 | 5.75 | 0 | Y | Y | N | Y | 9.5 | -0.3 | -0.2 | -3.4 | 12.8 |

**PUTNAM FUND REPRESENTATIVE: PROVIDENCE, RI 800.225.1581**

Putnam has check-writing priveledges for the following money-market mutual-funds: Putnam American Government Income Fund (PAVX), Intermediate US Government Fund (PBLGX), Putnam M. M. Fund (PDDXX), Putnam Tax-Exempt M. M. Fund (PTXXX), and Putnam US Government Income Trust (PGSIX)

## T.ROWE PRICE
http://www.troweprice.com

| | SYMBOL | ASSET TYPE | MIL | MIN INV | LOAD IN | LOAD OUT | * WITHDRAWAL OPTIONS P | W | C | I | ANNUAL RETURN 1999 | 2000 | 2001 | 2002 | (YTD) 2003 |
|---|---|---|---|---|---|---|---|---|---|---|---|---|---|---|---|
| Latin America | PRLAX | LAS | 148 | 2,500 | 0 | 0 | Y | Y | N | Y | 59.4 | -11.2 | -0.2 | -18.1 | 37.4 |
| Value | TRVLX | LV | 1,343 | 2,500 | 0 | 0 | Y | Y | N | Y | 9.2 | 15.8 | 1.6 | -16.6 | 20.6 |
| Dividend Growth | PRDGX | LV | 610 | 2,500 | 0 | 0 | Y | Y | N | Y | -2.8 | 10.1 | -3.6 | -18.5 | 17.9 |
| European Stock | PRESX | ES | 751 | 2,500 | 0 | 0 | Y | Y | N | Y | 19.7 | -6.7 | -20.7 | -18.7 | 21.4 |
| T. Rowe Price Equity Index 500 | PREIX | LB | 3,302 | 2,500 | 0 | 0 | Y | Y | Y | Y | 20.6 | -9.3 | -12.2 | -22.2 | 20.9 |
| U.S. Treasury Long-Term | PRULX | LG | 262 | 2,500 | 0 | 0 | Y | Y | N | Y | -8.8 | 19.1 | 3.4 | 15.1 | 0.6 |
| Equity-Income | PRFDX | LV | 11,606 | 2,500 | 0 | 0 | Y | Y | N | Y | 3.8 | 13.1 | 1.6 | -13.0 | 17.1 |
| Growth & Income | PRGIX | IV | 1,809 | 2,500 | 0 | 0 | Y | Y | N | Y | 3.8 | 9.0 | -2.2 | -23.9 | 19.6 |
| T. Rowe Price GNMA | PRGMX | IG | 1,388 | 2,500 | 0 | 0 | Y | Y | N | Y | 0.2 | 10.9 | 7.7 | 9.0 | 1.3 |
| Personal Strat Balanced | TRPBX | MA | 726 | 2,500 | 0 | 0 | Y | Y | N | Y | 8.0 | 5.6 | -2.5 | -7.7 | 17.6 |
| Balanced | RPBAX | MA | 1,823 | 2,500 | 0 | 0 | Y | Y | Y | Y | 10.3 | 2.1 | -4.0 | -8.5 | 15.6 |
| VA Tax-Free Bond | PRVAX | MSSL | 398 | 2,500 | 0 | 0 | Y | Y | Y | Y | -3.4 | 12.0 | 4.9 | 9.7 | 3.1 |
| MD Tax-Free Bond | MDXBX | MSSL | 1,301 | 2,500 | 0 | 0 | Y | Y | N | Y | -3.2 | 11.4 | 5.0 | 9.5 | 3.0 |
| Tax-Free Short-Interm | PRFSX | MNS | 586 | 2,500 | 0 | 0 | Y | Y | N | Y | 1.0 | 6.8 | 5.8 | 6.2 | 1.9 |
| Capital Appreciation | PRWCX | MA | 2,282 | 2,500 | 0 | 0 | Y | Y | N | Y | 7.1 | 22.2 | 10.3 | 0.5 | 17.3 |
| Science & Tech | PRSCX | ST | 4,245 | 2,500 | 0 | 0 | Y | Y | N | Y | 101.0 | -34.2 | -41.2 | -40.6 | 44.0 |
| Developing Tech | PRDTX | ST | 30 | 2,500 | 0 | 0 | Y | Y | N | Y | X | X | -30.6 | -48.7 | 53.5 |
| T. Rowe Price Real Estate | TRREX | SRE | 207 | 2,500 | 0 | 0 | Y | Y | N | Y | -1.2 | 31.9 | 8.9 | 5.4 | 25.3 |
| Global Technology | PRGTX | ST | 68 | 2,500 | 0 | 0 | Y | Y | N | Y | X | X | -36.1 | -29.9 | 42.9 |
| NY Tax-Free Bond | PRNYX | MNYL | 223 | 2,500 | 0 | 0 | Y | Y | N | Y | -4.8 | 12.8 | 4.1 | 9.7 | 3.1 |
| CA Tax-Free Bond | PRXCX | MCL | 261 | 2,500 | 0 | 0 | Y | Y | N | Y | -3.3 | 12.8 | 3.9 | 8.5 | 2.7 |
| Growth Stock | PRGFX | LG | 4,686 | 2,500 | 0 | 0 | Y | Y | N | Y | 22.2 | 0.3 | -9.8 | -23.0 | 23.2 |
| Blue Chip Growth | TRBCX | LG | 6,163 | 2,500 | 0 | 0 | Y | Y | N | Y | 20.0 | -2.5 | -14.4 | -24.2 | 22.6 |
| Media & Telecom | PRMTX | SC | 538 | 2,500 | 0 | 0 | Y | Y | N | Y | 93.1 | -25.1 | -6.9 | -28.4 | 43.6 |
| Global Stock | PRGSX | WS | 71 | 2,500 | 0 | 0 | Y | Y | N | Y | 28.8 | -8.0 | -15.4 | -20.8 | 20.0 |
| T. Rowe Price New Era | PRNEX | SNR | 1,016 | 2,500 | 0 | 0 | Y | Y | N | Y | 21.2 | 20.4 | -4.4 | -6.3 | 17.4 |
| Health Sciences | PRHSX | SH | 957 | 2,500 | 0 | 0 | Y | Y | N | Y | 8.0 | 52.2 | -6.0 | -27.7 | 27.7 |
| Emerging Markets Bond | PREMX | EMB | 237 | 2,500 | 0 | 0 | Y | Y | N | Y | 23.0 | 15.2 | 9.3 | 9.5 | 21.1 |
| Pice New Horizons | PRNHX | SG | 4,289 | 2,500 | 0 | 0 | Y | Y | N | Y | 32.5 | -1.9 | -2.8 | -26.6 | 42.3 |
| Tax-Free Income | PRATX | MNL | 1,506 | 2,500 | 0 | 0 | Y | Y | Y | Y | -3.9 | 12.3 | 4.4 | 9.2 | 3.2 |

# T.ROWE PRICE
http://www.troweprice.com

| | SYMBOL | ASSET TYPE | MIL | MIN INV | LOAD IN | LOAD OUT | P | W | C | I | 1999 | 2000 | 2001 | 2002 | (YTD) 2003 |
|---|---|---|---|---|---|---|---|---|---|---|---|---|---|---|---|
| Tax-Free High-Yield | PRFHX | HYM | 1,105 | 2,500 | O | O | Y | Y | Y | Y | -5.1 | 8.1 | 4.7 | 6.4 | 5.0 |
| Price Financial Services | PRISX | SF | 322 | 2,500 | O | O | Y | Y | Y | Y | 1.7 | 36.8 | -3.1 | -10.1 | 29.4 |
| Small-Cap Stock | OTCFX | SB | 4,691 | 2,500 | O | O | Y | Y | N | Y | 14.7 | 16.5 | 6.8 | -14.2 | 24.3 |
| International Discovery | PRIDX | FSMG | 483 | 2,500 | O | C | Y | Y | N | Y | 155.0 | -15.6 | -24.6 | -16.3 | 57.0 |
| Small-Cap Value | PRSVX | SV | 3,000 | 2,500 | O C | O C | Y | Y | N | Y | 1.2 | 19.8 | 21.9 | -1.8 | 28.1 |
| International Bond | RPIBX | WB | 1,178 | 2,500 | O | O | Y | Y | N | Y | -7.9 | -3.1 | -3.4 | 21.8 | 11.2 |
| International Stock | PRITX | FLG | 4,597 | 2,500 | O | O | Y | Y | N | Y | 34.6 | -17.1 | -22.0 | -18.2 | 20.1 |
| Spectrum Income | RPSIX | MB | 3,155 | 2,500 | O | O | Y | Y | N | Y | 0.3 | 7.4 | 4.5 | 7.0 | 10.7 |
| Mid-Cap Growth | RPMGX | MCG | 8,135 | 2,500 | O | O | Y | Y | N | Y | 23.8 | 7.4 | -1.0 | -21.2 | 32.5 |
| Mid-Cap Value | TRMCX | MCV | 1,286 | 2,500 | O | O | Y | Y | N | Y | 3.5 | 22.8 | 14.4 | -7.4 | 27.9 |
| Em Eur & Mediterranean | TREMX | DE | 34 | 2,500 | O | O | Y | Y | N | Y | X | X | -7.7 | 3.7 | 49.3 |
| New Income | PRICX | ITB | 2,192 | 2,500 | O | O | Y | Y | N | Y | -1.6 | 11.1 | 8.2 | 7.5 | 4.2 |
| Price High-Yield | PRHYX | HYB | 3,228 | 2,500 | O | O | Y | Y | N | Y | 4.2 | -3.3 | 6.1 | 3.1 | 18.0 |
| New America Growth | PRWAX | LG | 885 | 2,500 | O | O | Y | Y | N | Y | 12.8 | -10.5 | -11.9 | -28.5 | 27.6 |
| Price New Asia | PRASX | PAJ | 662 | 2,500 | O | O | Y | Y | N | Y | 99.9 | -30.8 | -10.0 | -9.4 | 45.6 |
| Japan | PRJPX | JS | 120 | 2,500 | O | O | Y | Y | N | Y | 112.7 | -37.2 | -32.3 | -16.9 | 41.6 |
| Emerging Markets Stock | PRMSX | DE | 227 | 2,500 | O | O | Y | Y | N | Y | 87.4 | -26.4 | -5.7 | -4.9 | 39.9 |
| Short-Term Bond | PRWBX | STB | 1,129 | 2,500 | O | O | Y | Y | N | Y | 2.3 | 8.5 | 8.5 | 5.3 | 3.2 |
| Spectrum Growth | PRSGX | LB | 1,961 | 2,500 | O | O | Y | Y | N | Y | 21.2 | -0.1 | -7.8 | -19.7 | 25.0 |
| Capital Opportunity | PRCOX | LB | 67 | 2,500 | O | O | Y | Y | N | Y | 11.5 | -6.3 | -10.1 | -22.3 | 23.7 |
| Corporate Income | PRPIX | LTB | 101 | 2,500 | O | O | Y | Y | N | Y | -0.8 | 8.0 | 9.8 | 4.2 | 10.3 |
| Tax-Efficient Balanced | PRTEX | CA | 44 | 2,500 | O | O | Y | Y | N | Y | 10.7 | 5.2 | -6.4 | -6.9 | 11.1 |
| U.S. Treasury Interm | PRTIX | IG | 392 | 2,500 | O | O | Y | Y | N | Y | -3.2 | 12.2 | 7.5 | 12.0 | 1.1 |
| Personal Strat Growth | TRSGX | LB | 437 | 2,500 | O | O | Y | Y | N | Y | 11.2 | 4.7 | -6.0 | -12.4 | 20.9 |
| Tax-Efficient Growth | PTEGX | LG | 71 | 2,500 | O | O | Y | Y | N | Y | X | -0.8 | -15.5 | -22.2 | 23.1 |
| Diversified Sm Cap Grth | PRDSX | SG | 64 | 2,500 | O | O | Y | Y | N | Y | 27.7 | -8.3 | -9.8 | -27.5 | 35.7 |
| U.S. Bond Index | PBDIX | ITB | 85 | 2,500 | O | O | Y | Y | N | Y | X | X | 7.4 | 9.4 | 2.9 |
| Total Equity Market Idx | POMIX | LB | 244 | 2,500 | O | O | Y | Y | N | Y | 23.3 | -10.3 | -11.2 | -21.2 | 23.7 |

* WITHDRAWAL OPTIONS

ANNUAL RETURN

## T.ROWE PRICE

http://www.troweprice.com

| | SYMBOL | ASSET TYPE | MIL | MIN INV | LOAD IN | LOAD OUT | P | W | C | I | 1999 | 2000 | 2001 | 2002 | (YTD) 2003 |
|---|---|---|---|---|---|---|---|---|---|---|---|---|---|---|---|
| Tax-Free Interm Bond | PTIBX | MNI | 165 | 2,500 | 0 | 0 | Y | Y | N | Y | -2.6 | 8.9 | 5.2 | 8.7 | 2.3 |
| Tax-Efficient Multi Gr | PREFX | MCG | 21 | 2,500 | 0 | 0 | Y | Y | N | Y | X | X | -9.7 | -23.5 | 32.4 |
| Summit Municipal Interm | PRSMX | MNI | 112 | 25,000 | 0 | 0 | Y | Y | N | Y | -1.2 | 8.8 | 5.7 | 8.7 | 2.8 |
| Summit Municipal Income | PRINX | MNL | 92 | 25,000 | 0 | 0 | Y | Y | N | Y | -4.0 | 11.9 | 5.2 | 9.2 | 4.0 |
| Summit GNMA | PRSUX | IG | 100 | 25,000 | 0 | 0 | Y | Y | N | Y | -0.3 | 11.3 | 7.7 | 9.0 | 1.4 |
| Spectrum International | PSILX | FLB | 61 | 2,500 | 0 | 0 | Y | Y | N | Y | 39.5 | -14.7 | -19.7 | -16.6 | 25.9 |
| Retirement Income | TRRIX | CA | 29 | 2,500 | 0 | 0 | Y | Y | N | Y | X | X | X | X | 12.3 |
| Retirement 2040 | TRRDX | LB | 17 | 2,500 | 0 | 0 | Y | Y | N | Y | X | X | X | X | 21.8 |
| Retirement 2030 | TRRCX | LB | 51 | 2,500 | 0 | 0 | Y | Y | N | Y | X | X | X | X | 21.7 |
| Retirement 2020 | TRRBX | LB | 75 | 2,500 | 0 | 0 | Y | Y | N | Y | X | X | X | X | 20.1 |
| Retirement 2010 | TRRAX | MA | 59 | 2,500 | 0 | 0 | Y | Y | N | Y | X | X | X | X | 17.7 |
| Personal Strat Income | PRSIX | CA | 303 | 2,500 | 0 | 0 | Y | Y | N | Y | 5.2 | 6.6 | 1.0 | -3.4 | 13.5 |
| NJ Tax-Free Bond | NJTFX | MNJ | 149 | 2,500 | 0 | 0 | Y | Y | N | Y | -4.1 | 11.4 | 4.8 | 9.7 | 3.2 |
| MD Short-Term Tax-Free | PRMDX | MSSI | 243 | 2,500 | 0 | 0 | Y | Y | Y | Y | 1.5 | 5.5 | 5.7 | 4.1 | 1.4 |
| Intl Gr & Inc | TRIGX | FLV | 35 | 2,500 | 0 | 0 | Y | Y | N | Y | 19.6 | -4.3 | -17.6 | -11.7 | 27.0 |
| International Eq Index | PIEQX | FLB | 16 | 2,500 | 0 | 0 | Y | Y | N | Y | X | X | -21.4 | -15.4 | 25.8 |
| Instl Mid-Cap Equity Gr | PMEGX | MCG | 320 | 1 MIL | 0 | 0 | Y | Y | N | Y | 25.1 | 7.9 | -1.2 | -21.6 | 34.2 |
| Instl Large Cap Value | TILCX | LV | 8 | 1 MIL | 0 | 0 | Y | Y | N | Y | X | X | 4.4 | -14.6 | 20.7 |
| Instl Large Cap Growth | TRLGX | LG | 9 | 1 MIL | 0 | 0 | Y | Y | N | Y | X | X | X | -24.9 | 30.3 |
| Instl High Yield | TRHYX | HYB | 631 | 1 MIL | 0 | 0 | Y | Y | Y | Y | X | X | X | X | 16.5 |
| Instl Emerging Mkts Eq | IEMFX | DE | 8 | 1 MIL | 0 | 0 | Y | Y | N | Y | X | X | X | X | 39.4 |
| Inflation Protected Bd | PRIPX | IG | 25 | 2,500 | 0 | 0 | Y | Y | N | Y | X | X | X | X | 6.2 |
| GA Tax-Free Bond | GTFBX | MSSL | 85 | 2,500 | 0 | 0 | Y | Y | N | Y | -3.7 | 11.6 | 4.8 | 8.9 | 3.2 |
| Foreign Equity | PRFEX | FLG | 1,190 | 1 MIL | 0 | 0 | Y | Y | Y | Y | 34.7 | -16.7 | -21.7 | -17.7 | 20.5 |
| FL Interm Tax Free | FLTFX | MF | 109 | 2,500 | 0 | 0 | Y | Y | Y | Y | -1.1 | 8.6 | 4.7 | 8.8 | 2.3 |
| Extended Eq Mrkt Index | PEXMX | MCB | 93 | 2,500 | 0 | 0 | Y | Y | N | Y | 33.7 | -15.6 | -9.6 | -18.1 | 35.1 |

(Columns under * WITHDRAWAL OPTIONS: P W C I; ANNUAL RETURN: 1999 2000 2001 2002 (YTD) 2003)

**T ROWE PRICE CUSTOMER REPRESENTITIVE: BALTIMORE, MD. 800.225.5132**

Check-writing is allowed in most all of their money-market funds.

## VANGUARD
http://www.vanguard.com

| | SYMBOL | ASSET TYPE | MIL | MIN INV | LOAD IN | LOAD OUT | P | W | C | I | 1999 | 2000 | 2001 | 2002 | (YTD) 2003 |
|---|---|---|---|---|---|---|---|---|---|---|---|---|---|---|---|
| Vanguard Windsor II | VWNFX | LV | 23,059 | 3,000 | 0 | 0 | Y | Y | N | Y | -5.8 | 16.9 | -3.4 | -16.9 | 19.6 |
| Vanguard Windsor | VWNDX | LV | 15,904 | 3,000 | 0 | 0 | Y | Y | N | Y | 11.6 | 15.9 | 5.7 | -22.3 | 27.7 |
| Capital Value | VCVLX | LV | 292 | 3,000 | 0 | 0 | Y | Y | N | Y | X | X | X | -28.1 | 30.8 |
| Dividend Growth | VDIGX | LV | 659 | 3,000 | 0 | 0 | Y | Y | N | Y | -3.0 | 18.8 | -19.5 | -23.2 | 19.6 |
| International Explorer | VINEX | FSMG | 284 | 10,000 | 0 | 0 | Y | Y | Y | Y | 90.3 | -2.7 | -22.5 | -13.9 | 45.2 |
| Inflation-Protected Secs | VIPSX | IG | 4,101 | 3,000 | 0 | 0 | Y | Y | N | Y | X | X | 7.7 | 16.6 | 7.0 |
| Equity-Income | VEIPX | LV | 2,637 | 3,000 | 0 | 0 | Y | Y | N | Y | -0.2 | 13.6 | -2.3 | -15.7 | 15.3 |
| Vanguard GNMA | VFIIX | IG | 25,499 | 3,000 | 0 | 0 | Y | Y | N | Y | 0.8 | 11.2 | 8.0 | 9.7 | 1.4 |
| Vanguard Value Index | VIVAX | LV | 3,567 | 3,000 | 0 | 0 | Y | Y | N | Y | 12.6 | 6.1 | -11.9 | -20.9 | 22.1 |
| Total Intl Stock Index | VGTSX | FLB | 4,136 | 3,000 | 0 | 0 | Y | Y | N | Y | 29.9 | -15.6 | -20.2 | -15.1 | 27.5 |
| Vanguard U.S. Value | VUVLX | LV | 474 | 3,000 | 0 | 0 | Y | Y | Y | Y | X | X | 2.9 | -15.3 | 20.6 |
| LifeStrategy Growth | VASGX | LB | 4,124 | 3,000 | 0 | 0 | Y | Y | N | Y | 17.3 | -5.4 | -8.9 | -15.8 | 21.4 |
| Developed Markets Index | VDMIX | FLB | 536 | 3,000 | 0 | 0 | Y | Y | N | Y | X | X | -22.1 | -15.7 | 25.8 |
| European Stock Index | VEURX | ES | 5,943 | 3,000 | 0 | 0 | Y | Y | N | Y | 16.7 | -8.2 | -20.3 | -18.0 | 23.0 |
| Emerging Mkts Stock Idx | VEIEX | DE | 1,513 | 3,000 | 0 | 0 | Y | Y | Y | Y | 61.6 | -27.6 | -2.9 | -7.4 | 44.7 |
| Long-Term U.S. Treasury | VUSTX | LG | 2,072 | 3,000 | 0 | 0 | Y | Y | Y | Y | -8.7 | 19.7 | 4.3 | 16.7 | 1.1 |
| nterm-Term U.S. Treas | VFITX | IG | 4,226 | 3,000 | 0 | 0 | Y | Y | Y | Y | -3.5 | 14.0 | 7.6 | 14.2 | 1.5 |
| Balanced Index | VBINX | MA | 5,224 | 3,000 | 0 | 0 | Y | Y | N | Y | 13.6 | -2.0 | -3.0 | -9.5 | 15.2 |
| Tax-Managed Balanced | VTMFX | CA | 463 | 10,000 | 0 | 0 | Y | Y | N | Y | 15.5 | -0.5 | -3.5 | -7.1 | 13.1 |
| Vanguard Wellington | VWELX | MA | 25,516 | 3,000 | 0 | 0 | Y | Y | N | Y | 4.4 | 10.4 | 4.2 | -6.9 | 13.9 |
| Wellesley Income | VWINX | CA | 9,445 | 3,000 | 0 | 0 | Y | Y | N | Y | -4.1 | 16.2 | 7.4 | 4.6 | 5.4 |
| Total Stock Mkt Idx | VTSMX | LB | 33,732 | 3,000 | 0 | 0 | Y | Y | N | Y | 23.8 | -10.6 | -11.0 | -21.0 | 24.0 |
| Short-Term Tax-Ex | VWSTX | MNS | 4,482 | 3,000 | 0 | 0 | Y | Y | Y | Y | 2.6 | 4.9 | 4.8 | 3.5 | 1.5 |
| Ltd-Term Tax-Ex | VMLTX | MNS | 6,308 | 3,000 | 0 | 0 | Y | Y | Y | Y | 1.5 | 6.4 | 5.6 | 6.3 | 2.4 |
| Institutional Index | VINIX | LB | 35,564 | 10 MIL | 0 | 0 | Y | Y | N | Y | 21.1 | -8.9 | -11.9 | -22.0 | -21.2 |
| Capital Opportunity | VHCOX | MCB | 5,292 | 25,000 | 0 | 0 | Y | Y | N | Y | 97.8 | 18.0 | -9.7 | -27.9 | 42.8 |
| Vanguard STAR | VGSTX | MA | 8,323 | 1,000 | 0 | 0 | Y | Y | N | Y | 7.1 | 11.0 | 0.5 | -9.9 | 17.3 |
| FL Long-Term Tax-Exempt Inv | VFLTX | MF | 1,181 | 3,000 | 0 | 0 | Y | Y | Y | N | -2.8 | 13.2 | 4.6 | 10.8 | 3.3 |
| OH Long-Term Tax-Exempt | VOHIX | MO | 497 | 3,000 | 0 | 0 | Y | Y | Y | N | -3.0 | 12.9 | 4.6 | 10.8 | 3.2 |
| LifeStrategy Moderate Growth | VSMGX | MA | 4,911 | 3,000 | 0 | 0 | Y | Y | N | Y | 12.0 | -0.9 | -4.5 | -10.3 | 16.9 |
| Vanguard 500 Index | VFINX | LB | 82,216 | 3,000 | 0 | 0 | Y | Y | N | Y | 21.1 | -9.1 | -12.0 | -22.2 | 21.1 |

* WITHDRAWAL OPTIONS
ANNUAL RETURN

## VANGUARD
http://www.vanguard.com

| | SYMBOL | ASSET TYPE | MIL | MIN INV | LOAD IN | LOAD OUT | P | W | C | I | 1999 | 2000 | 2001 | 2002 | (YTD) 2003 |
|---|---|---|---|---|---|---|---|---|---|---|---|---|---|---|---|
| Vanguard LifeStrategy Income | VASIX | CA | 1,276 | 3,000 | O | | Y | Y | N | Y | 2.8 | 8.1 | 4.1 | 0.1 | 8.3 |
| LifeStrategy Conserv Growth | VSCGX | CA | 2,682 | 3,000 | O | | Y | Y | N | Y | 7.9 | 3.1 | -0.1 | -5.4 | 12.6 |
| Vanguard Asset Allocation | VAAPX | MA | 8,160 | 3,000 | O | | Y | Y | N | Y | 5.2 | 4.9 | -5.3 | -15.4 | 20.1 |
| NJ Long-Term Tax-Exempt Inv | VNJTX | MNJ | 1,531 | 3,000 | O | | Y | Y | Y | Y | -2.4 | 12.5 | 4.6 | 9.9 | 3.0 |
| PA Long-Term Tax-Exempt Inv | VPAIX | MP | 2,380 | 3,000 | O | | Y | Y | Y | Y | -2.7 | 12.8 | 4.8 | 10.1 | 3.7 |
| Vanguard REIT Index | VGSIX | SRE | 3,170 | 3,000 | O | | Y | Y | N | Y | -4.0 | 26.4 | 12.4 | 3.8 | 26.2 |
| Convertible Securities | VCVSX | CA | 686 | 3,000 | O | | Y | Y | Y | Y | 30.4 | 4.2 | -3.1 | -9.4 | 25.3 |
| NY Long-Term Tax-Exempt Inv | VNYTX | MNYI | 2,100 | 3,000 | O | | Y | Y | Y | Y | -3.4 | 13.8 | 4.1 | 10.8 | 3.1 |
| CA Long-Term Tax-Exempt Inv | VCITX | MCL | 1,992 | 3,000 | O | | Y | Y | Y | Y | -3.1 | 15.2 | 3.4 | 9.5 | 3.1 |
| CA Interm-Trm Tax-Exempt Inv | VCAIX | MCI | 2,438 | 3,000 | O | | Y | Y | Y | Y | -0.6 | 10.9 | 4.4 | 9.2 | 2.7 |
| Health Care | VGHCX | SH | 17,783 | 25,000 | O | | Y | Y | N | Y | 7.0 | 60.6 | -6.9 | -11.4 | 15.9 |
| Vanguard Global Equity | VHGEX | WS | 559 | 3,000 | O | | Y | Y | N | Y | 26.0 | -0.2 | -3.7 | -5.6 | 33.5 |
| Vanguard Energy | VGENX | SNR | 1,918 | 3,000 | O | | Y | Y | N | Y | 21.0 | 36.4 | -2.6 | -0.6 | 17.2 |
| Interm-Term Corp Bd | VFICX | ITB | 3,891 | 3,000 | O | | Y | Y | Y | Y | -1.5 | 10.7 | 9.4 | 10.3 | 4.9 |
| Interm-Term Tax-Ex | VWITX | MNI | 11,732 | 3,000 | O | | Y | Y | Y | Y | -0.5 | 9.2 | 5.1 | 7.9 | 2.9 |
| Precious Metals | VGPMX | SPM | 570 | 3,000 | O | | Y | Y | N | Y | 22.8 | -7.3 | 18.3 | 33.4 | 42.4 |
| Small Cap Growth Index | VISGX | SG | 704 | 3,000 | O | | Y | Y | N | Y | 19.8 | 1.6 | -0.8 | -15.4 | 37.3 |
| Insured Long-Trm T/E Inv | VILPX | MNL | 2,925 | 3,000 | O | | Y | Y | Y | Y | -2.9 | 13.6 | 4.2 | 10.0 | 3.6 |
| High-Yield Tax-Exempt | UWAHX | MNL | 4,052 | 3,000 | O | | Y | Y | Y | Y | -3.4 | 10.7 | 5.3 | 7.3 | 4.3 |
| Vanguard Explorer | VEXPX | SG | 5,629 | 3,000 | O | | Y | Y | N | Y | 37.3 | 9.2 | 0.6 | -24.6 | 38.9 |
| Long-Term Tax-Exempt | VWLTX | MNL | 1,956 | 3,000 | O | | Y | Y | Y | Y | -3.5 | 13.3 | 4.5 | 10.1 | 3.1 |
| International Growth | VWIGX | FLB | 6,605 | 3,000 | O | | Y | Y | Y | Y | 26.3 | -8.6 | -18.9 | -17.8 | 23.9 |
| Tax-Managed Intl | VTMGX | FLB | 484 | 10,000 | O | | Y | Y | Y | Y | X | -14.3 | -21.9 | -15.6 | 25.8 |
| Small Cap Value Index | VISVX | SV | 1,480 | 3,000 | O | | Y | Y | Y | Y | 3.4 | 21.9 | 13.7 | -14.2 | 26.4 |
| Long-Term Bond Index | VBLTX | LTB | 914 | 3,000 | O | | Y | Y | Y | Y | -7.9 | 16.6 | 8.2 | 14.4 | 3.4 |
| Tax-Managed Small Cap Ret | VTMSX | SB | 798 | 10,000 | O | | Y | Y | N | Y | X | 13.4 | 5.4 | -14.4 | 31.1 |
| Vanguard Small Cap Index | NAESX | SB | 5,746 | 3,000 | O | | Y | Y | N | Y | 23.1 | -2.7 | 3.1 | -20.0 | 37.0 |
| International Value | VTRIX | FLB | 1,363 | 3,000 | O C | C | Y | Y | Y | Y | 21.8 | -7.4 | -14.1 | -13.4 | 30.3 |
| High-Yield Corporate | VWEHX | HYB | 9,210 | 3,000 | O C | C | Y | Y | Y | Y | 2.5 | -0.9 | 2.9 | 1.7 | 13.6 |
| Vanguard Mid Cap Growth | VMGRX | MCG | 169 | 2,000 | O | | Y | Y | N | Y | 83.3 | 13.0 | -25.4 | -28.5 | 40.9 |

* WITHDRAWAL OPTIONS / ANNUAL RETURN

# VANGUARD

http://www.vanguard.com

| | SYMBOL | ASSET TYPE | MIL | MIN INV | LOAD IN | LOAD OUT | P | W | C | I | 1999 | 2000 | 2001 | 2002 | (YTD) 2003 |
|---|---|---|---|---|---|---|---|---|---|---|---|---|---|---|---|
| Short-Term Bond Index | VBISX | STB | 4,027 | 3,000 | 0 | 0 | Y | Y | Y | Y | 2.1 | 9.0 | 8.8 | 6.1 | 2.6 |
| Vanguard Selected Value | VASVX | MCV | 1,200 | 25,000 | 0 | 0 | Y | Y | N | Y | -2.7 | 17.4 | 15.1 | -9.8 | 23.0 |
| Interm-Term Bond Index | VBIIX | ITB | 3,393 | 3,000 | 0 | 0 | Y | Y | Y | Y | -3.0 | 12.8 | 9.3 | 10.9 | 4.2 |
| Total Bond Market Index | VBMFX | ITB | 25,000 | 3,000 | 0 | 0 | Y | Y | Y | Y | -0.8 | 11.4 | 8.4 | 8.3 | 2.8 |
| Mid Capitalization Index | VIMSX | MCB | 4,487 | 3,000 | 0 | 0 | Y | Y | N | Y | 15.4 | 18.2 | -0.5 | -14.6 | 27.0 |
| Vanguard Strategic Equity | VSEQX | MCB | 1,503 | 3,000 | 0 | 0 | Y | Y | N | Y | 19.3 | 7.5 | 5.4 | -13.1 | 36.3 |
| Vanguard Short-Term Corp | VFSTX | STB | 14,697 | 3,000 | 0 | 0 | Y | Y | Y | Y | 3.3 | 8.2 | 8.1 | 5.2 | 3.5 |
| Vanguard Extended Market Idx | VEXMX | MCB | 5,593 | 3,000 | 0 | 0 | Y | Y | N | Y | 36.2 | -15.5 | -9.2 | -18.1 | 35.8 |
| Vanguard Morgan Growth | VMRGX | LG | 3,720 | 3,000 | 0 | 0 | Y | Y | N | Y | 34.1 | -12.5 | -13.6 | -23.5 | 28.5 |
| Tax-Managed Capital App | VMCAX | LG | 2,370 | 10,000 | 0 | 0 | Y | Y | N | Y | 33.6 | -10.1 | -15.3 | -23.5 | 24.6 |
| Vanguard Growth Index | VIGRX | LG | 8,582 | 3,000 | 0 | 0 | Y | Y | N | Y | 28.8 | -22.2 | -12.9 | -23.7 | 21.2 |
| Vanguard Growth Equity | VGEQX | LG | 724 | 10,000 | 0 | 0 | Y | Y | N | Y | 53.6 | -23.1 | -27.4 | -30.9 | 33.1 |
| Short-Term Treasury | VFISX | SG | 4,003 | 3,000 | 0 | 0 | Y | Y | Y | Y | 1.9 | 8.8 | 7.8 | 8.0 | 1.9 |
| Vanguard Short-Term Federal | VSGBX | SG | 3,512 | 3,000 | 0 | 0 | Y | Y | Y | Y | 2.1 | 9.2 | 8.6 | 7.6 | 1.5 |
| Vanguard Pacific Stock Index | VPACX | JS | 2,577 | 3,000 | 0 | 0 | Y | Y | Y | Y | 57.1 | -25.7 | -26.3 | -9.3 | 32.7 |
| Vanguard Calvert Social Index | VCSIX | LG | 156 | 3,000 | 0 | 0 | Y | Y | N | Y | X | X | -14.1 | -24.2 | 24.4 |
| Vanguard Growth & Income | VQNPX | LB | 5,932 | 3,000 | 0 | 0 | Y | Y | N | Y | 26.0 | -9.0 | -11.1 | -21.9 | 22.7 |
| Vanguard U.S. Growth | VWUSX | LG | 6,819 | 3,000 | 0 | 0 | Y | Y | N | Y | 22.3 | -20.2 | -31.7 | -35.8 | 21.2 |
| Tax-Managed Grth & Inc | VTGIX | LB | 2,045 | 10,000 | 0 | 0 | Y | Y | N | Y | 21.2 | -9.0 | -11.9 | -22.0 | 21.1 |
| Long-Term Corporate Bond | VWESX | LTB | 4,567 | 3,000 | 0 | 0 | Y | Y | Y | Y | -6.2 | 11.8 | 9.6 | 13.2 | 4.3 |
| Vanguard Primecap | VPMCX | LB | 18,741 | 25,000 | 0 | 0 | Y | Y | N | Y | 41.3 | 4.5 | -13.4 | -24.6 | 32.5 |
| Vanguard MA Tax-Exempt | VMATX | MM | 408 | 3,000 | 0 | 0 | Y | Y | N | Y | -4.2 | 13.8 | 4.3 | 9.1 | 3.2 |
| Inst Total Bond Market Index | VITBX | ITB | 1,012 | 100 MIL | 0 | 0 | Y | Y | N | Y | X | X | X | X | 2.8 |
| Inst Developed Markets Index | VIDMX | FLB | 531 | 10 MIL | 0 | 0 | Y | Y | Y | Y | X | X | -22.1 | -15.5 | 25.8 |

*WITHDRAWAL OPTIONS — ANNUAL RETURN

VANGUARD FUND REPRESENTITIVE: VALLEY FORGE, PA 877.662.7447
Check-writing is allowed in Vanguard money-market funds such as the Vanguard Admiral Treasury Money Market Fund (VUSXX), Vanguard Cali Tax-Exempt M.M. Fund (VCTXX), Vanguard Federal M.M. Fund (VMFXX), New Jersey Tax-Exempt M.M. Fund (VNJXX), Vanguard New York Tax-Exempt M.M. Fund(VYFXX), Ohio T.E.M.M. Fund (VOHXX), Penn. T.E.M.M. Fund (VPTXX), Prime M.M. Fund (VMMXX), T.E.M.M. Fund (VMSXX), Treasury M.M. Fund (VMPXX).

# About Dr. Richard

Richard M. Krawczyk, Ph.D. is *America's Financial Fitness Trainer*™ and is one of the nation's leading expert on personal finance and consumer credit. As a television and radio personality, author, public speaker and consultant, Dr. Richard has traveled the world educating individuals and businesses on financial fitness, wealth building, entrepreneurship, and marketing.

As the television host of *Consumer Credit in the 80's*, he began his quest in showing individuals how to get their credit in shape. Over the course of several decades, Dr. Richard developed a proven system for personal finance education, which he calls *Financial Aerobics*™.

A former investment banker, Dr. Richard participated in over $700 million in real estate transactions - all before the age of thirty. In 1996, he was featured on the television show *Living the American Dream - Today's Success Stories*.

In realizing that many people think finance is about as exciting as watching paint dry or a fly crawl up the wall, he begin the **$200,000 Financial Fitness Challenge**™ as a way of keeping people motivated on their way to financial fitness. His techniques are starting a **finance revolution**!

He has earned the designations of Registered Financial Analyst® and Master Financial Professional®.

Dr. Richard is married and resides in Southern California and Las Vegas.

> **Dr. Richard is available for speaking engagements, and business/personal finance and marketing consulting. You can call our offices at 310.348.1100 or visit our website for more information.**

If you're one of the millions of individuals that are living their lives paycheck-to-paycheck and are seeking to live a better lifestyle... I have an important question for you:

# "What's It Going To Take For You To Let Me Help You Get Your Finances In Shape In Only 30 Days?"

## What if I offered you a strong incentive?

## Would $100,000 motivate you?

This **amazing breakthrough wealth building** system almost magically helps you get your finances in shape in only 30 days - **Guaranteed!**

## Financial Fitness For The Price Of Lunch At A Fast Food Restaurant

Think if you didn't spend that $6 a day at one of those fast food restaurants for one month. Your financial and physical waistline will thank you.

## Let Me Make One Prediction...

**These techniques will change your life**! You may discover, as many individuals already have, that other changes will appear in your life. A recent study has shown that money matters are the number one cause of stress in relationships. And I'm sure you are aware that 50% of all marriages end in divorce. Once you gain control of your finances, a lot of stress will disappear from your life. With a reduction of stress, you may end up quitting smoking, losing weight, or maybe even save a failing relationship.

## It's Time To Take Control Of Your Finances...NOW!

And don't forget the chance at winning the **$100,000 Grand Prize** in the *Financial Fitness Challenge*™.

**Go for it!**

For complete details, go to:
## www.FinancialAerobics.com

**How much easier would it be if you could have access to talk to a financial expert for an <u>unlimited</u> amount every month?**

**Would you see yourself succeeding even FASTER?**

Dr. Richard introduces...

# Financial Fitness Monthly

As a subscriber to Financial Fitness Monthly, you will receive one of the top newsletters in the country regarding personal finances. **Unlimited** telephone conversations with some of Dr. Richard's *Financial Fitness Trainers™* are one of the most popular features of this unique service.

We can answer your questions on:
- Personal Finances
- Starting Your Own Business
- Taxes
- Real Estate
- Insurance
- Investments

## FREE TAX INSTITUTE MEMBERSHIP

Your subscription will also include a free membership in Dr. Richard's *Tax Institute.*
- **FREE** Tax Preparation of Form 1040. Other schedules are available at a discounted price.
- **FREE** Tax Audit. We will audit your last two tax returns. Any money which we saved you will go directly into your pocket.

## NO MORE EXCUSES!

With a pay-as-you-go subscription to *Financial Fitness Monthly*, there is no reason for you to **get your finances into shape even faster than you can even imagine**!

For complete details, go to:

www.FinancialFitnessMonthly.com

# ENTER THE 2004

# $200,000

## FINANCIAL
## FITNESS
## CHALLENGE

---

## Grand Prize Winner
## $100,000

## 10 Finalists
## $10,000 Each

For complete details, go to:
www.FinancialFitnessChallenge.com